Between Democracy and Law

This volume purports to explore the legal and political issues triggered by the new wave of secessionism. More specifically, those issues concern the interplay between notions of democracy (and democratic ends and means) and law (and the rule of law and constitutionalism). Against this background, the editors use amorality in order to escape the terrain of the justification of secession by making a distinction between the democratic theory of secession and the theory of democratic secession. In the first section, the theoretical nexus democracy-secession has been approached both from a legal and political theory perspective. The second section of the book examines the instruments that the theory of democratic secession invokes in order to justify secession and presents both legal and political science contributions. The third section focuses on social movements and political actors. The fourth section focuses on two case studies due to the awareness of the importance of the difference between secession in a democratic occidental context (which call into play the discussion of the democratic theories) and separations in a non-democratic context (where the nexus between secession and democracy is not really central).

Carlos Closa, Spanish National Research Council (CSIC), Madrid and European University Institute (EUI), Florence. Professor Closa has been Jean Monnet Fellow at the European University Institute (EUI), Florence, Visiting Fellow at the Centre for European Studies, Harvard University, Visiting Professor at the College of Europe, Bruges, Emile Nöel Fellow at the Jean Monnet Centre, NYU and Visiting Professor at the University of Groningen, The Netherlands. He is Member of the Scientific Board of the Real Instituto Elcano de Estudios Internacionales y Estratégicos (RIE). He has published widely in various languages on EU citizenship, the EU constitutional structure and the relationship with the Member States.

Costanza Margiotta is Associate Professor of Philosophy and Theory of Law, University of Padua, Italy. She holds a PhD in Legal Theory from the European University Institute, Florence. Her research focuses on secession in international law, European citizenship and on slavery, race and law. She has published widely on these and related areas.

Giuseppe Martinico is Associate Professor of Comparative Public Law at the Scuola Superiore Sant'Anna, Pisa and Centre for Studies on Federalism, Turin, Italy. Prior to joining the Sant'Anna School of Advanced Studies he was García Pelayo Fellow at the Centro de Estudios Políticos y Constitucionales (CEPC), Madrid, and Max Weber Fellow at the European University Institute, Florence. He is also affiliated to several international research centres where he has been carrying out international projects related to comparative federalism and sub-national constitutionalism, and to the constitutional dimensions of EU law and international human rights law, especially the European Convention on Human Rights. He has published widely on these and related areas.

Between Democracy and Law

The Amorality of Secession

Edited by Carlos Closa, Costanza Margiotta and Giuseppe Martinico

Routledge
Taylor & Francis Group
LONDON AND NEW YORK

First published 2020
by Routledge
2 Park Square, Milton Park, Abingdon, Oxon OX14 4RN

and by Routledge
605 Third Avenue, New York, NY 10017

First issued in paperback 2020

Routledge is an imprint of the Taylor & Francis Group, an informa business

British Library Cataloguing-in-Publication Data
A catalogue record for this book is available from the British Library

Library of Congress Cataloging-in-Publication Data
Names: Closa, Carlos, editor. | Margiotta, Costantino, 1972- editor. | Martinico, Giuseppe, editor. | Routledge (Firm)
Title: Between democracy and law: the amorality of secession/edited by Carlos Closa, Costanza Margiotta, and Giuseppe Martinico.
Other titles: Amorality of secession
Description: New York: Routledge, 2019. | Includes index.
Identifiers: LCCN 2019032584 (print) | ISBN 9780367145804 (Hardback) | ISBN 9780429032400 (eBook)
Subjects: LCSH: Secession. | Separatist movements–Case studies. | Constitutional law.
Classification: LCC JC327 .B565 2019 (print) | LCC JC327 (ebook) | DDC 320.1/5–dc23
LC record available at https://lccn.loc.gov/2019032584
LC ebook record available at https://lccn.loc.gov/2019032585

Typeset in Galliard
by Deanta Global Publishing Services, Chennai, India.

ISBN 13: 978-0-367-72672-0 (pbk)
ISBN 13: 978-0-367-14580-4 (hbk)

Contents

Contributors

Stéphane Beaulac is a full professor at the Université de Montréal; he began his academic career at Dalhousie Law School in 1998. He holds a PhD in international public law from the University of Cambridge, where he also earned an LL.M. (first class honour). His background is bijural: civil law at Ottawa (summa cum laude) and common law at Dalhousie (first in the national programme); he clerked at the Supreme Court of Canada. He was a Max Weber Fellow at the European University Institute in Florence, a Neil MacCormick Fellow at the University of Edinburgh School of Law, and a visiting professor in Amsterdam, Ulster and Trento. He co-edited with E. Mendes the fifth edition of the collective book Canadian Charter of Rights and Freedoms; he is also responsible, with J.-F. Gaudreault-DesBiens, for the public law series for JurisClasseur Québec. His writings have won awards and, indeed, were cited by the International Court of Justice in The Hague. A lawyer with the Ontario Bar, Stéphane Beaulac has been invited to testify before parliamentary committees in Ottawa; he is also a public intellectual, regularly contributing to current debates in the media multilingualism and European integration and the theory of state and nation.

Joxerramon Bengoetxea (PhD, Edinburgh) is Professor of Jurisprudence and Sociology of Law at the University of the Basque Country (UPV/EHU). Courses taught include "Philosophy and Sociology of Law", European Law (free movements and cohesion policy) and "Comparing Legal Cultures" at the International Master in Sociology of Law at the Oñati Institute, which he coordinates together with the Doctorate in Sociology of Law. He is a member of the Academic Board of the "Renato Treves" International PhD in Law and Society. While at Stanford, Professor Bengoetxea will be teaching the course "Cultural, Legal and Constitutional Pluralism in Europe" at the School of Law. This course raises interesting political, legal, socio-legal, comparative and jurisprudential questions from phenomena like Muslim law, national minorities, the Roma and other sources of diversity in Europe, and their challenges to supranational outlooks adopted at the two major European Courts. In addition, he has edited several books and published over 140 articles or book chapters in law reviews, journals, collective editions and readers dealing with issues of legal reasoning and legal theory, EU law and institutions, regionalism in the EC, comparative law, political philosophy (theory of nationalism and of European integration).

Mattia Casula is currently a Post-Doctoral Research Fellow in Political Science at Ca' Foscari University of Venice. He had visiting positions at the European University Institute, University of Strathclyde and at the University of Edinburgh. His research and publications focus on comparative public policy and administration, with an emphasis on the sub-national/local level. Within these topics, he wrote several articles that have been published in international peer-reviewed journals.

Carlos Closa (Spanish National Research Council (CSIC), Madrid and European University Institute (EUI), Florence) directed the research area European, Transnational and Global Governance within the EUI Global Governance Programme until December 2015. He has been Deputy Director at the Centre for Political and Constitutional Studies (CEPC), Madrid and member of the Venice Commission for Democracy through Law of the Council of Europe. He has served formerly as Senior Lecturer in Political Science at the University of Zaragoza (Spain) and Lecturer at the Universidad Complutense de Madrid. He holds a PhD in Politics, and an MA in European Integration and Cooperation by the University of Hull (UK). He has been Jean Monnet Fellow at the European University Institute (EUI), Florence, Visiting Fellow at the Centre for European Studies (Harvard University), Visiting Professor at the College of Europe (Bruges) and Emile Nöel Fellow at the Jean Monnet Centre, NYU and Visiting Professor at the University of Groningen (The Netherlands), the University of Maastricht (the Netherlands) and the University of Passau (Germany). He is Member of the Scientific Board of the Real Instituto Elcano de Estudios Internacionales y Estratégicos (RIE). He has published a large number of articles (in Spanish, English and Italian) on EU citizenship, the EU constitutional structure and the relationship with the Member States in journals such as *Common Market Law Review*, *Journal of European Integration*, *Law and Philosophy*, *Comparative European Politics or the Revista de Estudios Políticos* (in Spanish). As consultant, he has collaborated with the European Commission (DG Justice, Freedom and Security), the UN Programme for Development (UNDP) in Iraq (UNAMI) and the Friedrich Neumann Foundation on advising on constitution-making in Iraq and territorial de-centralization in Thailand; he has also participated in a Council of Europe programme for capacity building involving national parliamentarians in Serbia and Montenegro and with the Spanish Cooperation Agency (AECID) in formation and training on regional integration in Latin America, decentralization processes in the Andean area and formation of parliamentarians. He also collaborated with the EU Commission and the Council of Europe in a project on the implementation of the Constitution of Bolivia. He collaborates usually with the Real Instituto Elcano de Estudios Internacionales y Estratégicos and the Fundación Alternativas, where he has published several policy papers, with the Foundation Notre Europe, the EU Committee of Regions and with the Bureau of Policy Advisers (BEPA) of the President of the European Commission.

Luigi Crema is Assistant of International Law at the Law School of the University degli Studi of Milan. He graduated summa cum laude in law at the University degli Studi of Milan (2005), and holds a PhD in Public International Law from the universities of Geneva and Milan (joint degree). He has been invited as visiting scholar by the faculties of law at the universities of Neuchatel and Geneva (Switzerland) and Notre Dame (USA). His research has been primarily dedicated to international investment law, transitional justice in Latin America and treaty interpretation.

Donatella della Porta is Professor of Political Science, Dean of the Institute for Humanities and the Social Sciences and Director of the PD program in Political Science and Sociology at the Scuola Normale Superiore in Florence, where she also leads the Center on Social Movement Studies (Cosmos). Among the main topics of her research: social movements, political violence, terrorism, corruption, the police and protest policing. She has directed a major ERC project Mobilizing for Democracy, on civil society participation in democratization processes in Europe, the Middle East, Asia and Latin America. In 2011, she was the recipient of the Mattei Dogan Prize for distinguished achievements in the field of political sociology. She is Honorary Doctor of the universities of Lausanne, Bucharest and Goteborg. She is the author of 85 books, 130 journal articles and 127 contributions in edited volumes.

Ander Errasti obtained a BA in Philosophy at University of Barcelona (UB) in 2010. In 2011, he pursued Philosophy studies with an MA in Political Philosophy at the Pompeu Fabra University (UPF), with a final thesis on the concept of self-determination in W. Kymlicka and M. Seymour: an analytical approach supervised by Dr Requejo. In 2013, he gained a Business Administration Diploma at UB. He started a PhD in Humanities – Ethics and Political Philosophy – at UPF in 2011. He is supervised by Dr Sonia Arribas and Dr Daniel Innerarity. His research is focused on a normative analysis of Ulrich Becks' Cosmopolitanism. In 2014, he obtained the Advanced LLM in Legal Sciences at the UPF with a thesis on the articulation of diversity and universality at the European Court of Human Rights, supervised by Dr González-Pascual.

Mattia Guidi is Assistant Professor of Political Science at the Department of Social, Political and Cognitive Studies of the University of Siena. His research focuses on delegation and institutions, independent regulatory agencies, EU competition policy and EU macroeconomic governance. He has published articles on several international journals, including *JCMS: Journal of Common Market Studies*, *Regulation & Governance*, *European Union Politics*, *European*

Political Science Review, *Acta Politica*, *Comparative European Politics* and several book chapters. His monograph *Competition Policy Enforcement in EU Member States* (2016) is published under the European Administrative Governance series.

Daniel Innerarity is part-time Professor at the School of Transnational Governance (STG). He is Professor of Political and Social Philosophy at the University of the Basque Country and the Ikerbasque Foundation for Science, Spain. He is also director of the Instituto de Gobernanza Democrática. Previously, he was a Robert Schuman Visiting Professor at the European University Institute (EUI), Fellow of the Alexander von Humboldt Foundation at the University of Munich and visiting professor at the University of Paris 1-Sorbonne. He has been awarded the Miguel de Unamuno Essay Prize, the 2003 National Literature Prize in the Essay category, the Espasa Essay Prize and the Euskadi Essay Prize. He has also received the Prize for Humanities, Culture, Arts and Social Sciences from the Basque Studies Society/Eusko Ikaskuntza in 2008 and the Príncipe de Viana Culture Prize 2013.

Costanza Margiotta is Associate Professor in Philosophy and Theory of Law, University of Padova. Attached to the Department of Political Science, Legal Science and International Studies. She holds a PhD in Legal Theory from the European University Institute (Florence). Her research has been focusing on Secession in international law, European Citizenship and on Slavery, race and law. Among her books are: *L'ultimo diritto. Profili storici e teorici della secessione* (*The Ultimate Right. Theoretical and Historical Profiles of Secession*, 2005) (Awarded the Essays International Prize "Salvatore Valitutti", XIII Edition, in 2006); *Cittadinanza europea. Istruzioni per l'uso* (*European Citizenship. Instructions for use*, 2014) and La recezione di Kelsen nel dibattito italiano sulla democrazia costituzionale (1950–1980), (Kelsen's Legacy in the Italian Debate on Constitutional Democracy (1950–1980), Firenze, Le Lettere, 2005.

Giuseppe Martinico (Scuola Superiore Sant'Anna, Pisa and Centre for Studies on Federalism, Turin) is an Associate Professor of Comparative Public law at the Sant'Anna School of Advanced Studies, Pisa. Prior to joining the Sant'Anna School of Advanced Studies he was García Pelayo Fellow at the Centro de Estudios Políticos y Constitucionales (CEPC), Madrid, and Max Weber Fellow at the European University Institute, Florence. He is also affiliated to several international research centres (among others, the Centre for Judicial Cooperation of the European University Institute, Florence, and the Centre for Studies on Federalism, Turin-Moncalieri). There he has been carrying out international projects related to comparative federalism and subnational constitutionalism and to the constitutional dimensions of EU law and international human rights law (especially the European Convention on Human Rights).

His research interests cover both comparative and European law, fields in which he published extensively, including two monographs in English (one with Elgar and one with Routledge) he has published extensively in international peer-reviewed journals in three languages (English, Italian and Spanish). His volumes have been reviewed in top-class reviews. As evidence of the impact of his research, his first monograph, *L'Integrazione Silente* (2009), was quoted in the Opinion given by Advocate General Dámaso Ruiz-Jarabo Colomer in the Umweltanwalt von Kärnten and Alpe Adria Energia SpA case decided by the Court of Justice of the European Union (C 205/08). More recently he was also cited by Advocate General Cruz Villalon in his Opinion on the Gauweiler (OMT) case and by. Advocate General Tanchev in his Opinion (ft 45) on Case C-541/16 European Commission v Kingdom of Denmark.

Francis O'Connor is Postdoctoral Researcher at PRIF (Peace Research Institute Frankfurt). Previously he was Postdoctoral Researcher in the Research Project "PRIME – Predicting, Interdicting and Mitigating Extremism" at the University of Aarhus (Denmark) and Research Fellow at the Centre on Social Movement Studies (COSMOS) at Scuola Normale Superiore in Florence (Italy). He obtained a PhD in Political and Social Sciences from the European University Institute in Florence (Italy).

Martín Portos is a Postdoctoral Fellow at the Centre on Social Movements (COSMOS), Scuola Normale Superiore (Florence). He completed a PhD in Political and Social Sciences at the European University Institute in February 2017, with a thesis focused on anti-austerity protests in Southern Europe. His research interests include political participation, social movements, democratic attitudes, institutions and nationalism. Martín holds a BA (Hons) in Political Science from the University of Santiago de Compostela (Regional and National Award for Excellence in Academic Performance, 2011), an MSc Politics Research from the University of Oxford and an MRes from the EUI.

Matt Qvortrup is Professor of Applied Political Science and International Relations at Coventry University. An expert on comparative constitutional engineering and European Politics, Professor Qvortrup's book *Angela Merkel: Europe's Most Influential Leader* was described by Kirkus Reviews as "necessary reading for anyone who wants to broaden his or her perspective on the world today" (www.kirkusreviews.com/search/?q=Qvortrup&t=all). Awarded the PSA Prize in 2013 for his research on "Terrorism and Political Science," he served as a Specialist Advisor to the House of Commons Public Administration and Constitutional Affairs Committee. He has previously worked as a member of President Obama's Special Envoy Team in Africa (2009–2010). Before his career as an academic, Dr Qvortrup served as Head of the Gun Crime Section in the British Home Office (2002–2004) and before that as a Special Advisor to the Home Secretary (Minister for the Interior). Professor Qvortrup earned his doctorate in Politics at Brasenose College, University of Oxford in 2000. Also a qualified lawyer, he holds a Diploma from the College of Law, London.

Nikos Skoutaris received his PhD in Law from the European University Institute (Florence, Italy) in 2009. Since then, he has worked as a Post-doctoral Fellow at the University of Tilburg, as an Assistant Professor at Maastricht University (The Netherlands) and as a Senior Research Fellow at the European Institute, LSE. Since October 2013, he is a Lecturer in EU Law at the UEA Law School.

His research lies in the interface between EU law, comparative constitutional law and conflict resolution theory. His first monograph (*The Cyprus Issue: The Four Freedoms in a Member State under Siege*, 2011) has been characterized as "an indispensable piece of literature for anybody interested" in the interrelationship between the EU and an age-old international conflict. His second monograph *Territorial Pluralism in Europe: Vertical Separation of Powers in the EU and its Member States* (2019) is the end result of his participation in a project funded by the European Research Council. He has also edited a volume (2014) and a special issue (*European Journal of Human Rights*, 2013) on the EU Accession to the ECHR.

Apart from the two monographs, Nikos is the author of numerous articles in leading peer-reviewed journals such as the *Cambridge Yearbook of European Legal Studies*, the *German Yearbook of International Law*, the *European Law Review* and the *Common Market Law Review*.

His most recent research project focuses on the idea of a differentiated Brexit that would accommodate the different demands of the UK constituent nations. It has been widely discussed in media such as the BBC, The National and The Scotsman. It has also provided the basis for a number of pieces of written evidence he has submitted to the House of Commons and the Scottish Parliament. Its main conclusions were presented before the European Parliament. The GUE/NGL parliamentary group of the European Parliament has entrusted him with writing a policy brief on a special designated status for Northern Ireland post-Brexit.

His ability to produce research that has a wider social impact was the reason he received the 2017 UEA Engagement Award for outstanding contribution to Public and Community.

You can find more information on his website "On Secessions, Constitutions and EU law" (www.skoutaris.eu/).

1 Introduction

The "amorality of secession" is not a thought-provoking title. It refers to the approach chosen for this collective volume. According to the Collins online dictionary, "amoral is often wrongly used where immoral is meant. Immoral is properly used to talk about the breaking of moral rules, amoral about people who have no moral code or about places or situations where moral considerations do not apply".[1] Building upon the second meaning of amoral, which refers to a situation (a secessionist process) in which moral considerations do not apply, this book avoids entering the terrain of the moral foundations of secession. This interdisciplinary volume does not deal with the subject of the immorality or morality of secession, but tries to go beyond the traditional approach that has characterized this field.[2]

Our idea implies that an account of the morality of secession is interesting for sure, yet not necessary in order to take secession seriously from a legal and political point of view. This does not imply confining morality to a sort of pre-legal and pre-political sphere or considering moral claims irrelevant, however. Simply, we try to go beyond this debate about the moral justification of secession and in this sense we assume that there might be a margin for an amoral (i.e. non-moral) approach to the relationship between democracy and law. In other words, we do not put the motivations behind secession into question and do not deny that the reasons provided by secessionist movements might be well grounded. However, this volume purports to explore the legal and political issues triggered by the new wave of secessionism (the one within EU member states). More specifically, those issues concern the interplay between notions of democracy (and democratic ends and means) and law (and the rule of law and constitutionalism).

Against this background, we use amorality in order to escape the terrain of the justification of secession. This book is very far from suggesting that there must be a univocal approach to this matter; on the contrary, the contributions gathered in this volume respond to a variety of positions. Despite the different

1 https://www.collinsdictionary.com/dictionary/english/amoral

2 A. Buchanan, *Secession: The Morality of Political Divorce from Fort Sumter to Lithuania and Quebec*, Westview Press, 1991.

approaches taken by the contributors, the connecting thread linking the chapters of the book lies in the *critical* distinction between the "democratic theory of secession" and the "theory of democratic secession". This distinction is key to understanding the new wave of secessionism. Indeed, the rebirth of secessionism in fully democratic contexts is a problem that has been emerging over recent decades in some plurinational states (Canada, UK, Spain). Unsurprisingly, secessionist claims have received growing attention in established democracies. In these contexts, the rise of populism adds another level of complexity. Although from a conceptual point of view populism differs widely from secessionism, populist movements have applied secessionist and identity claims sometimes by relying on a questionable concept of democracy. Questionability derives from the severance of the link between democracy and rule of law (and/or constitutionalism) and the concomitant reduction of democracy to simple majority rule (Carlos Closa Montero, Chapter 4). Against this background, both secessionists and unionists have appealed to democracy to question the claims of the respective interlocutor. We are of course aware of the fact that there are different definitions of and competing views of democracy. Making a critical distinction between the democratic theory of secession and the theory of democratic secession is needed, not to enter the huge debate about what democracy is or ought to be, but to stress the strategic choice of the new secessionist movements to emphasize democratic axes over traditional nationalist and identity components (Donatella della Porta, Francis O'Connor and Martín Portos, Chapter 9).

In this respect, the *democratic theory of secession* argues the existence of a fundamental value which ultimately justifies secessionist claims, in a sort of "teleological justification" (Carlos Closa Montero, Chapter 4), while the *theory of democratic secession* legitimates relying on procedures, that is the instruments used to achieve secession. In this second context, the mere application of certain requirements (i.e. majority) legitimates secession.

The first theory is one of the classic normative theories of secession (along with the just-cause theory of secession and the national self-determination theory of secession), while the second approach cannot be traced back to the classic theories of secession because it does not look for an ultimate justification for secession but only assumes that democratic means justifies any end. Endorsing a non-legal concept of democracy, these approaches tend to reduce democracy to the majoritarian principle only. Here, the clash with prevalent conceptions of law, rule of law and constitutionalism, but also international law, may emerge.

The situation is different from the perspective of a moral justification of secession in democratic terms. Here, the fundamental value of individual autonomy ultimately justifies secessionist claims. Supporters of choice theory argue that consensus is necessary to political obligation and from this they infer the existence of a right to secede, but it does not seem that consent can provide valid reasons *for* or *against* secession (Costanza Margiotta, Chapter 2).

These two theories are *critically* used to divide the book into different parts. In the first, the theoretical nexus democracy secession has been approached both from a legal and political theory perspective. In Chapter 2 Costanza Margiotta, from a legal–philosophical perspective, starts from the contradictory nature of secession which at the same time presents both a revolutionary and conservative character explaining many of the problematic interactions between democracy and secession and between law and secession. To avoid simply admitting that law cannot deal with secessionist crises, she poses the question of the peculiar legality of secession, which results in residing on the border between international and domestic legal spheres. Finally, she also critically explores the principal statements of the democratic theories of secession since the respect for democratic principles is necessary for the international community to accommodate the secessionist process.

In Chapter 3, Joxerramon Bengoetxea frames secession from the viewpoint of jurisprudence and gives conceptual and axiological priority to the norm-user perspective, as opposed to the norm-giver perspective. He finds it necessary to analyze the normative weight of positions both defending and opposing secession, in a sort of dialogue engaged in an ideal discourse situation. Therefore, he analyzes the responses that a constitutional democracy can design when addressing secessions not falling into the trap of stressing only the democratic will of the people as the main argument for secession: in some way he inverts the "burden of proof".

Dealing with the "secessionism of a new type', Chapters 4 and 5 critically assess both "the right to decide" (Carlos Closa Montero, Chapter 4) and the "will to decide" (Daniel Innerarity and Ander Errasti, Chapter 5). In Chapter 4, Carlos Closa Montero questions the theories of democratic secession, i.e. those theories arguing that a democratic process makes secession legitimate on the basis of a democratic procedure and the existence of the will of a majority. His criticism targets the fundamentals of this theory: the confusion between democracy and majoritarianism, the weakness of its theoretical construction of the demos and the associated lack of response to the issues of symmetric divisibility, externalities and reversibility. First of all, these theories of democratic secession rely on the assumption that democracy may legitimately achieve any end whatsoever. Second, this approach does not resolve the central problem of the issue of the delimitation of the demos. Because of this, democratic secession creates what Closa Montero calls a "symmetry problem", since any group within the seceding territory must also be able to secede. Finally, a last critique regards the fact that the democratic theory does not resolve the reversibility issue.

In Chapter 5, Daniel Innerarity and Ander Errasti try to rethink the way we frame the "will to decide" claims, avoiding addressing them in terms of pure conflict. Going back to reflection on the democratic theories of secession, the authors admit that "there is no democracy when the status quo cannot be changed, but neither is there democracy if change is merely subjected to the popular will": "it would be hard to hold that a regime is democratic if people do not have the final words (substantive requirement), but it is equally true that this decision cannot plainly ignore the legal framework (procedural requirement)". In this way, they argue why the debate should move from the unique focus on the "how" and the "who" to the fundamental inquiry about the "what" and "why" of the decision, increasing the possibilities of achieving a rational decision-making process.

Indeed, a more complex approach to the disputes around "will to decide" claims could achieve two main goals: it could foster the co-decision dynamics required in European democracy, on the one hand, and diminish the incentives for secession on the other.

The second part of the book examines the instruments that the theory of democratic secession invokes in order to justify secession and presents both legal and political science contributions. Dealing with the issue of the means adopted to pursue secession, the part focuses on the use of referendums for secession purposes. What can the role of referendum be in this scenario? Referendum has been considered by comparative lawyers as a useful instrument with which to "proceduralize" secession. Indeed, comparative lawyers have analyzed the provisions concerning the possibility of secession, and legal and political theorists have dealt with the issue of how to justify the option of secession (even in legal systems whose constitutions say nothing about that, including the Canadian one).

In Chapter 6, Giuseppe Martinico looks at the populist use of the secessionist arguments in divided societies and aims to explore the relationship between constitutional democracy and referendum in contexts characterized by new waves of populism. In so doing, the author looks at the legacy of the seminal Reference Re Secession of Quebec of the Canadian Supreme Court, in order to show the anti-populist potential of that decision which employed a substantive and complex notion of democracy.

Stéphane Beaulac (Chapter 7) deals with the problematic concept of "clear majority" in referendum processes employed by the Canadian Supreme Court in its Reference Re Secession of Quebec. What do we mean by "majority"? What is the reference group to calculate the majority? Does it mean the majority of the actual votes cast? Can it be the majority of the registered voters (the electorate)? Who are the registered voters and what is the voting age? What is the role of the rate of participation in the referendum? Should a minimum turnout be a requirement for clear majority support? These are some of the questions that will be addressed in this chapter.

Chapter 8 by Matt Qvortrup analyzes the relevant factors conducive to recognizing independence referendums and to winning these votes and argues that independence referendums are most likely to be implemented when this is in the interest of the three Western Powers on the UN Security Council. The explanation of the recognition of the results of independence referendums would all come down to power politics and would relegate law outside the frame of the politics of secession.

The third part focuses on social movements and political actors and opens with the chapter by Donatella della Porta, Francis O'Connor and Martín Portos (Chapter 9). Building upon their previous research on referendums "from below," they explore the Catalan and Scottish scenarios to have a further look at frames for mobilization in light of more recent developments. The key argument they develop throughout their chapter is that the implementation of austerity policies, along with a crisis of political legitimacy (and self-government), has facilitated the emergence of democratic-emancipatory and social justice frames for mobilization. In so doing, they look at the Great Recession that hit Europe, dated 2008, as a critical juncture, which has triggered not only socioeconomic but also political transformations.

In Chapter 10, Mattia Guidi and Mattia Casula study the ambivalent use of the European argument by the Catalan government which has indeed relied on the internationalization of the crisis. In so doing, the authors analyze the confrontation between the Catalan and the Spanish governments as a "war of attrition" game, in which each actor's strategy consists of both signalling its willingness to resist and making the counterpart's resistance as costly as possible.

The choice to have a fourth part on two case studies is due to the awareness of the importance of the difference between secession in a democratic occidental context (which call into play the discussion of the democratic theories) and separations in a non-democratic context (where the nexus between secession and democracy is not really central). The secessionist movements in advanced democracy are analyzed by Nikos Skoutaris, who, in his chapter (Chapter 11) explores the interrelationship between Brexit and secession. He first compares Article 50 TEU with constitutional provisions governing secession in comparative law. Second, he focuses on the constitutional framework concerning the possible secession of Scotland and Northern Ireland. Finally, focusing on the "Irish border" conundrum, the author offers some pragmatic solutions that could overcome the current impasse.

The second case study, chosen as an example of secession in a non-democratic context, is Crimea. Luigi Crema in Chapter 12 deals with the Crimean issue between Ukraine and Russia and, in particular, on the contradictory elements it entails. In so doing, he wonders what we can make of manifestations of political will in a context where the use of force is in play.

This book originates from a workshop organized by the editors at the European University Institute, Florence. It was an event made possible thanks to the financial support of the Robert Schuman Centre for Advanced Studies, the DIRPOLIS (Law, Politics and Development) Institute of the Scuola Superiore Sant'Anna, Pisa. This volume is also part of the Jean Monnet Module "Eur. Publ. IUS" (European Public Law), generously funded by the European Union. Special thanks to Prof. Deidre Curtin who helped us in organizing the workshop and to the other participants, especially Rainer Bauböck, Giacomo Delledonne, Bruno de Witte, Cristina Fasone and Robert Schütze.

We have decided to gather different voices and perspectives on this issue and do hope that this volume will trigger a fruitful debate even beyond the academic circles. We hope to have delivered a very pluralistic collection of chapters. When dealing with a very divisive topic like secession, pluralism is definitely an added value and will not, we are sure, negatively affect the quality of the final product.

Part I

The theoretical nexus democracy – secession

2 An update on secession as the "ultimate right"

For a liminal legality

Costanza Margiotta[1]

1. Introduction: the conservative and revolutionary character of secession

Secessionist movements within the European Union (EU) have attracted a lot of scholarly attention in recent years, particularly during the referendum on Scottish independence in 2014 and, more recently, the referendum on Catalan independence that was held in October 2017.

Secessionist movements have gained momentum within the EU in recent years. Old scholars, silent for a long period, and new scholars of secession have reopened the debate on one of the most contested issues for political and legal studies. The approaches used to address secession vary between normative disciplines including morality-ethics, politics and law.

I will approach secession from the perspective of legal theory. From a legal–philosophical perspective, the concept of secession has both a *conservative* and a *revolutionary* character,[2] which explains many of the problematic interactions between law and secession and between democracy and secession and the difficulties in identifying which of the existing legal orders (constitutional, international or European) should govern secession.

From the point of view of internal sovereignty, secession appears a conservative concept, rather than a revolutionary one, since it does not challenge the very notions of statehood and sovereignty: the creation of states is still the goal

1 Associate Professor of Legal Philosophy at the University of Padua, Department of Political Science, Law, and International Studies. An early version of this chapter was presented at the EUI Robert Schuman Centre, at the ARENA Centre for European Studies (Oslo) and the Inaugural conference of the Italian Chapter of the ICON Society in 2018. I would like to thank the organizers and participants for their comments, especially Agustín José Menéndez, John Erik Fossum and Antonello Tancredi. I am particularly grateful to Carlos Closa and Giuseppe Martinico for their helpful comments on an earlier version of this chapter. All websites accessed on 21 January 2019.

2 I first explored this contradictory nature of secession in 2005 when I published my book on secession: Costanza Margiotta, 2005, *The Ultimate Right. Theoretical and Historical Profiles of Secession*), at 9 et seq. This idea has been thereafter proposed again by many authors, for instance by Susanna Mancini (2012, at 481) who argued that secession is, simultaneously, "the most revolutionary and the most institutionally conservative of political constructs."

of secessionist movements. While its revolutionary character lies in its ultimate challenge to world stability, from the international perspective, secession presents itself as a challenge to the conservative side of international society, including the defence of intangible borders. This ambivalence explains why secession has found legal recognition neither in the overwhelming majority of state constitutions nor in international legal order. Nonetheless, to put the question of legality or illegality of secession it is necessary to avoid simply admitting that law cannot deal with secessionist crises and that it all comes down to power politics.

It is not by chance that secession is still frightening: the possible recursive nature of secession could be the explanation of this fear. In this chapter, I shall try to decode and explain the fear of secession opening interesting questions for scholars: most particularly the chapter aims to deal with the following issues: (1) the fear of secession in two different contexts, the exit of a member state from the EU and the secession of a territorially concentrated group from a European country; (2) the tricky relationship between secession and law from the international perspective and the question of its peculiar *legality*; and (3) the problematic interactions between democracy and secession, outlining the principal statements of the democratic theories of secession. Finally, in the conclusion (4), I shall turn again to the relationship between secession and law and ask whether the issue of legality when referring to secession can be discussed in terms of *liminal legality*, residing on the border between internal and international legal order, and what its implications are for the current secessionist phenomena.

2. European Union and secession

This first part of the chapter will briefly explore secession in two different contexts: the exit of a member state from the EU and the secession of a territorially concentrated group from a member state of the EU. Brexit and Catalonia can be viewed as two different examples of the reaction of European institutions to the issue of separation and can help to theoretically explain which case of secession is more frightening from a European perspective, as well as why secession is still frightening.

I am convinced that secession[3] is frightening because we have not been able to think about politics beyond the state. In fact, if carried through to its extreme consequences, secession may result in the end of the state: secession if applied *ad infinitum* may dissolve the system of states. When secession aspires to become a right, it turns into an uncertain and destructive right that can only be perceived as the "ultimate right," the ultimate position in the system to be covered before the system dissolves.[4]

3 Among the most recent books on the issue, Norman, 2006; Pavković and Radan, 2007, 2011; Cabestan and Pavković (eds), 2013; Walter, Ungern-Sternberg and Abushov, 2014; Sterio, 2018.

4 I am aware of the paradox, since few secessions would, instead, confirm the state system, confirming the conservative character of secession, but those frightened by secession most probably perceive the revolutionary dimension of secession.

The EU context can help decode and explain the fear of secession. The EU is not neutral on issues of secession: in fact, the term "withdrawal" was preferred when referring to the exit of a member state from the Union,[5] while the term "secession" was used to refer to separationist movements in Scotland and Catalonia[6]. Brexit has not been discussed in terms of secession probably in order to avoid scaring the European public opinion, as secession is indeed a term that carries a negative connotation. The choice of wording has not just been a terminological problem, but also a value choice. The attitudes of the European institutions in relation to the exit of the United Kingdom and the secession of Catalonia has confirmed that my theory of secession as the "ultimate right" (Margiotta 2005) is still valid more than ten years after I first envisioned it.

The European public opinion has not been anxious about Brexit and certainly not as much as for the secession of a member state. For example, the risks of contagion for other member states of secession within a European country was taken more seriously than the contagious risk of Brexit for other countries of Europe.

It seems to me that the leading European commentators have not clearly understood how conservative (from a conceptual point of view) the *laissez-faire* approach of the European institutions has been towards the exit of Britain. There is nothing revolutionary in the approach of disagreement that EU institutions have taken towards secession of a member state, a disagreement simultaneously revealed by the "non-immediate entry" attitude towards Scotland and the not-so-veiled opposition toward Catalonia. Both attitudes (*laissez-faire* and disagreement) are, in my opinion, the result of the same feeling: the fear of secession.

Essentially, with Brexit, there is no fear because the possible dissolution of the EU would do nothing more than bring politics back *within* the state, while secession of a member state is frightening precisely because we have not been able to think about politics *beyond* the state.

Looking at the approach taken by European institutions and, more generally, by European public opinion, it seems that the British exit did not really scare the political institutions of EU. Of course, the political reaction to Brexit can be considered absolutely in line with a legal order, such as Article 50 of the Lisbon Treaty, which explicitly regulates the separation of a member state from the EU after having introduced a clause to govern exit from the Union.[7] But this is also a paradox, as Brexit could have been the beginning of the end. Brexit can trigger

5 This preference was based on the assumption that withdrawal operates on the basis of existing sovereignty, while secession aims to create a new sovereignty: but, looking back to J.C. Calhoun and his theory of secession, this difference dissolves in front of secession in federal systems.

6 To make a bibliographical example: Closa (ed.), 2017b.

7 In other words, the European legal order "legalizes" secession, authorizing the member states to leave the Union unilaterally and unconditionally, although not immediately (obligation to negotiate in the next two years from the declaration of exit). Closa, 2017a.

a domino effect in Europe[8] and has sown the seeds for the potential destruction of the EU.

The paradox is this: from a strictly European perspective, Brexit should have been perceived as riskier than the secession of a territorial concentrated group from a member state. It is evident that the European institutions have not fully understood how non-revolutionary (again from a *conceptual* point of view) it would be to establish a new state (particularly within the same legal, political and economic landscape of the state from which it has withdrawn) and how the British secession could expose the EU to the risk of dissolution, opening the possibility for the state to remain the unique form of political organisation conceived from modernity for dealing with territorial space. To expose Europe to dissolution may also signify the destruction of the only political and legal experiment that differs from the state: the EU.

The EU has been given the chance to attempt a different form of relationship between politics, law and territorial space compared to the modern state. The EU has been an attempt at a different way of dealing with territorial space, both politically and legally, compared to modern statehood. Destruction of the EU would be a destruction of the only experiment different from the state that we have allowed the opportunity to succeed.

Brexit should have been perceived as more frightening than secession within a member state, since it could represent the beginning of the dissolution of the EU. While the Catalan case presented itself as a *pro*-European secession, with the Catalan government wanting immediate entry into the EU as a new member state,[9] Brexit is itself *anti*-European and has the potential to destroy the EU. Brexit is against the EU while secession of territorial concentrated groups is made on the basis of retaining membership (Walker, 2017), although European institutions, while repeating that Catalonia is a Spanish rather than European issue, clearly support Spain and its territorial integrity.

It is secession *within* Europe and not *from* Europe that is still considered more frightening. In my opinion, the (unwritten) veto on secession subconsciously hides the fear that the formation of new states following secession, beyond a certain number, may put the survival of the state system at risk. Secession, if brought to its extreme consequences, can result in the end of the state itself. In fact, an endless competition for statehood may lead to a proliferation of states, provoking a crisis of the state system. Accepting secession implies accepting its recursive nature: at the moment when secession of a territorially concentrated group is accepted, we must consequently accept the secession of another territorially concentrated group from the new state, and so on. Secession is frightening precisely because it is always possible, through its exercise, to bring the right of secession to its extreme consequence. It is not by chance that secession has not

8 Italexit is just one example. It is the new born word in the Italian public opinion between the so-called parties of Populist Sovereignism. I am aware that the domino effects will depend on the kind of UK exit: negotiated or no deal.

9 See Guidi and Casula, Chapter 10, this volume.

found legal recognition in domestic legal orders[10] nor in the international legal order, though, as we have seen, the *exit* is legal in the atypical and unusual form of political organisation that is the EU, whose dissolution would bring politics firmly back *within* the state.

The possible recursive nature of secession opens the most interesting question for scholars: which is the group legitimized to secede? A question that remains open, as no univocal answer could be located from a field of scholars, lawyers, sociologists, philosophers, anthropologists and historians. When is it possible to stop to recognize the right to secession of a territorially concentrated group within a state previously granted to another territorially concentrated group?

This problem arises from the difficult, if not impossible, correspondence between state and nation. It is always in the space of non-correspondence between state and nation, and between the nation and the people, that new requests for secession are made. Secession always questions the full account of the reciprocal identity between the state and the nation-people, and of the unique identity of the nation-state. In fact, the attempt to break the unity of the nation-people, which is inherent in the secession process, highlights what has always been taken for granted: identification within a specific territory of nation, people and state.

It is secession that causes the crisis of what is assumed and established by the law, which is the stability, unity and homogeneity of the subject (the people) in a state-territory. Secession thus reveals the biggest mistake made by those who consider state and people to be a single entity, bringing the issue of unity of the people to centre-stage.

3. The international perspective

The difficult relationship between law and secession is explained by the contradictory character of secession, which, as said, is both *conservative* and *revolutionary*. In fact, from the viewpoint of internal sovereignty or of sovereign states, secession appears to be a conservative rather than a revolutionary concept, as it does not force us to re-think the traditional opinions concerning the nature and structure of the state as political space, around which modernity has developed. In other words, secession is still politics *within* the state, and not *beyond* it. Secession does not entail a change in the concepts of state and border. The creation of states is still the goal of secessionist movements. Such forces do not envision any new or atypical forms of political organisation, they are not against the idea of the state, they just want to create a *new* one. Secessionist claims are demands to draw new borders, proving that borders are still relevant on a global scale.

From the international perspective, secession, on the contrary, is a revolutionary rather than a conservative concept, as it presents itself as a challenge to the conservative side of international society, including the defence of intangible borders. From the point of view of external sovereignty, the cornerstone of the

10 Only few exceptions. See Martinico, 2017; Mancini, 2014; Haljan, 2014; Weinstock, 2001.

international order, secession shows destabilizing potential and represents the most dangerous threat to the stability and preservation on which the international community is based, namely that secessions are not desirable, and they jeopardize world stability. Secession highlights the most conservative aspect of the community of states, the strenuous defence of the prerogatives of external sovereignty, which requires the absence of a right of secession in the international legal system. Secession weakens the status of territorial integrity as an absolute principle. Secession forces us to reconsider the idea that borders are necessarily fixed. It makes territorial choice an issue that can be discussed and attracts attention to the issue of borders, to the fixation of borders that impedes the rise of new legal instruments capable of overcoming that fixation (Irti, 2001). Secession has an inherently dynamic element that allows borders of a territorial unity to be changed through specific procedures, independently from the geopolitical original unity and against the principle of safeguarding territorial integrity.

Frightened by the erosion of external sovereignty, the international community of states has mostly adopted a critical stance against state proliferation and the shifting of borders.[11] Though if international law explicitly aspires to critically determine the very *raison d'être* of states promoting and sanctioning their own disintegration through recognition of the right to secede, it could turn law into a revolutionary instrument, different from and contrary to what tends to be expected from law, namely stability and conservation.

The *revolutionary* character of secession – which paradoxically would legitimize its *conservative* dimension (the state building within the context of a new sovereign entity) – emerges in the international context. The international community deplores secession, as the exercise of such a right would threaten the territorial integrity of the states that are part of the international community as well as international law. Secession can put the systemic structure of international law at risk.

Rather than an arbitrary interpretation of *exit*, secession is a complex problem inherent in the relationship between legal and political systems and has its roots in the very nature of the right of secession, being both uncertain and largely destructive. Among contemporary rights, this right seems external to the legal system, though it claims to be conceivable by that same system, if not really to be part of it, and to be a legal title in the international framework. Its function is both external and internal to the dynamics of the system of states: secession closes the curtain on an old equilibrium and opens on a new perspective.

If secession aspires to present itself as a "right," it can be conceived, in systemic terms, only as the "ultimate right," the ultimate advantage that can be taken from a system that has been left behind and is at risk. When secession aspires to become

11 On secession and international law, see Sterio, 2018; Kohen (ed.), 2006; Walter, von Ungern-Sternberg and Abushov (eds), 2014; Dahlitz, 2003; Copp, 1998; Tancredi, 2001. It is no coincidence that the international lawyers themselves have many difficulties in proposing a law that legitimizes secession, except recently Sterio (2018) has found it necessary to develop a new normative framework on secession.

a real right, it turns into an uncertain and destructive right, a legal source of instability.[12] Secession stands against the traditional notion of perpetuity of state constitutions (as the constituent power) and of indivisibility of sovereignty.[13]

From an international perspective, the close connection between secession and borders – the former necessarily entails a claim to the latter – constitutes one of the main differences between secession and self-determination, which are often incorrectly associated.[14] Self-determination, as a concept and as a principle of international law, as well as a right, has always been in line with the idea of territorial integrity and has never meant territorial choice.[15] Generally, its exercise has not entailed new borders.

The right of self-determination, already recognized by the UN Charter, has been accompanied by the rules of border intangibility and territorial integrity. In the decolonisation process, people who are recognized as having the right to self-determination have the corresponding duty not to modify borders as they stood after colonialism ended.[16] Groups that are entitled to the right of self-determination are identified and limited by borders and territory, with peoples being defined by international law on the basis of geographic location. Self-determination concerns the content of political action rather than its "container," with political action developing within existing borders without concerning these borders. Unlike secession, the object of self-determination is not to draw new borders, but to choose by whom to be governed and not to have an alien government in a given territory. "People" refers to the people located within the borders established by colonial powers, as it was the territory set by colonial forces that identified the people who are now entitled to the right of self-determination. People are therefore identified with the entire population that settled in a pre-existing geopolitical unity, with the people's destiny being decided by territory rather than the territory being decided by the people. Not surprisingly, the territory that was mapped by colonial powers was not subject to relevant changes when colonized people exercised their right for self-determination, allowing the international community to absorb, in accordance with international law, the crisis caused by anti-colonial forces. Self-determination, as a legal foundation of the decolonisation process, was therefore able to reduce disorder in the international

12 It is no coincidence that the majority of the states with a constitutional provision on secession have ended in dissolution, on this issue see Margiotta, 2005, 2017a,b.

13 Calhoun, *15–16 February 1833* (1992), at 433–434: "The sovereignty is in the several States, and that our system is a union of twenty-four sovereign powers, under a constitutional compact, and not of a divided sovereignty between the States severally and the United States. In spite of all that has been said, I maintain that sovereignty is in its nature indivisible. It is the supreme power in a State, and we might just as well speak of half a square, or half of a triangle, as of half a sovereignty" (1851; 1853); on this see Margiotta, 2007, at VII.

14 Even recently this incorrect association was reaffirmed, for example by Klabbers, 2006.

15 On this Margiotta (2005) ch. VI; Hannum, 1993; Knop, 2002; Guarino, 1984.

16 This is why I do not think it is possible to think self-determination in a post-colonial age. On the contrary, Torbisco Casal (2017) thinks it is possible.

community, even though self-determination had political consequences inside the colonial system.

a. Liminal legality[17]

In the post-colonial era, the people's right to self-determination has always been used as an easy legitimation (a legal coverage) at the international level for secession, by placing the former as legal foundation for the latter, but the principle of self-determination has always been applied in a way that does not include secession. It is incorrect to speak of secessionist movements as possible holders of the right to self-determination, because they are not considered so by law and by the international community. In the event that the international community decides to recognize a right to secede, there should be no reference to self-determination, as the latter has never provided the delineation of borders.

Only by separating the two concepts is it possible to ask about the right of secession in the international order and to understand why the international community is so reluctant to recognize this right. Secession has no legal protection in international law. Concerning the question of legality, even though there are no absolute truths, there is certainly no right to secession by a sovereign state that is expressly recognized by international law (let alone by European law), nor is there yet a custom to constitutionalize secession in domestic legal orders. But looking at the question of legality or illegality of secession it is necessary to avoid simply admitting that law cannot deal with secessionist crises[18] and that it all comes down to power politics.[19]

Consequently, if one can talk of such a thing as legality when referring to secession, this can only be discussed in terms of *liminal legality*, a legality that resides on the border between internal and international legal order.

The problematic dimension of legality in the secessionist process has to be found in the border between constitutional law and international law. One of the main errors in the recent debate on secession in the European context is to have relegated the international legal order to a peripheral area and put the constitutional legal order at the centre. It has rightly been stated that it is inappropriate to evaluate the lawfulness of a unilateral secession according to the legal order against which it is directed,[20] as long as "an act of secession consists precisely of

17 I borrow, using it in a different way, the expression from Kilpatrick (2017), who uses the expression to define the legal status of the EU sovereign debt programmes.

18 In this sense, we should admit that law, accepting social facts, is following them and not coming first.

19 Qvortrup, 2014, 2013, Chapter 8, this volume. One of the reasons why the Canadian Reference on Quebec has to be considered an important message of hope is because it recognizes a fundamental role of the law in cases of secession: Giuseppe Martinico, Chapter 6, this volume.

20 Weller, 2017 and International Court of Justice, *Accordance with International Law of the Unilateral Declaration of Independence in Respect of Kosovo*, Advisory Opinion, I.C.J. Reports 2010, 403 para. 121.

the removal of a population and territory from an existing legal order and the consecration of a new, independent legal order."[21] The issue of legality raises the question of which legal order has governance over an act of secession. From a strictly legal point of view and except in the (very rare) case where secession is constitutionalized, if EU law has nothing to say about internal secession (secession of a territorial group from a member state) and if the national legal order is not the correct one to turn to when considering the question of legality, the question remains, which is the correct status of secession within the international legal order?

Before referring to the international legal system, it should be recalled that secession, from the point of view of constitutional legal order, has been viewed as a taboo and, until recently, constitutions have tried to avoid mentioning it, considering such a phenomenon an extra-legal fact, "a fact characterized by an exquisitely political nature, not regulated by legal instruments because inherently implying the break of the established order" (Martinico, 2017, at 22). In Western constitutional systems, since the end of the civil war, which divided the young United States in the mid-nineteenth century, secession has been demonized and has suffered the same repugnance (doctrinal and legal) as other extra-legal phenomena belonging to the realm of exception, such as constituent power and revolution.

Today, a broad debate has opened on the opportunity to constitutionalize the right to secede (Weinstock, 2001), arising from the question of whether the lack of constitutionalisation would demonize secession (Norman, 2003). If secession "is constructed as one among the many rights and options offered to a state's subnational groups, chances are that it will lose much of its appeal."[22] In my opinion, the history of modern states, and recently Brexit, has proven how the constitutionalisation of secession (the attempt to neutralize a possible conflict), can end, at a given moment, encouraging it,[23] while the lack of constitutionalisation, which would make the process much more complex, even after a possible declaration of independence, may discourage secession or at least discourage the separatists' enthusiasm when a referendum is called (consider the results of the referendums in Québec and Scotland). It is for these reasons that the right to secede has not found an easy place in constitutional orders.

From the point of view of the international legal system, secession, despite being a situation of fact (the recognition *a posteriori* of new states born from

21 Weller, 2017. Following this direction, it has no sense to question the constitutionality or unconstitutionality of the act of seceding.

22 Mancini, 2012, at 482. Against the constitutional recognition of secession, as it is well known, Cass Sunstein has argued that constitutional recognition of a right to secede is incompatible with the principles of constitutionalism (or at least democratic constitutionalism): Sunstein, 1991.

23 I have recently observed, in a post on the CJEU judgment in Wightman, that Brexit also demonstrates that even when "constitutionalised," as through art. 50 TEU, separation is never easy, Margiotta, 2019a.

secessionist processes does not imply the existence of a rule to be invoked *a priori*), is a normative fact that produces law and specific effects in the international legal order. I am inclined to think that if it is not possible to give proper legal relevance to secession, it is possible to give that relevance to its result, even though I do agree that legal philosophers should be as realistic as possible[24] (not necessarily positivistic in the strong sense, looking only at "black letter"), meaning that I know how political the acceptance of a new state's independence can be.[25] Following the secessionist act, in fact, all of the relevant regulatory ideals of international law come back into play.

The fact always remains the condition for the application of rules but it is not its source. The fact is essential for the activation of law but does not prevail upon it. The peculiarity of the secessionist insurrection is having a temporary nature. The position of the insurgents changes according to the result of the insurrection itself: they disappear, having been defeated by the "legitimate" government, or they become a state, a new autonomous subject of international law, which necessitates recognition (declarative and not constitutive of statehood) to shape the viability of the new entity at the international level.[26] International recognition conventionally arrives only after the new state is born and has been recognized by the state from which it has withdrawn.[27]

Illegal secessions, on the contrary, do not give rise to a right of secession *a posteriori*. Before the International Court of Justice (ICJ) opinion on Kosovo, "illegal" was used to identify all of the secessions that are recognized as illegal by the state from which the territorial group secedes. Unilateral independence cannot lawfully occur, as it would breach the rule of territorial integrity in international law (*ex iniuria ius non oritur*). The only way to remedy this defect would be to

24 In my book of 2005 (Margiotta, 2005) I analyzed the existing international practice and I affirmed that there is no such thing as a right of secession in the international legal order; that the independence of new states was always recognized only after the original state had recognized the seceding state. I also acknowledged that holding a referendum on independence and ensuring that the result of that referendum is implemented were two very different things. Two very different things are also declaring independence and making independence real, which means that the new state is recognized by the international community and takes up a seat in the UN (to understand the difference it is sufficient to look at the International Court of Justice in the Kosovo Opinion). The only exception was, at that time (2005), the Republic of Ex-Yugoslavia, but the "trick" of the Badinter Commission was to consider Yugoslavia in dissolution instead of considering it a process of recursive secessions from Yugoslavia (more on that Margiotta, 2005, ch. VII).

25 Qvortrup, Chapter 8, this volume.

26 Weller, 2017. It is of course clear that recognition remains crucial, if not for statehood as such, then for the ability of an emerging state to actualize its statehood through international intercourse and membership in international relations. As Somaliland has found for over two decades, statehood in the absence of significant recognition remains precarious. And as Kosovo still finds, despite having assembled some 115 recognitions, independence without membership in key international institutions can be uncomfortable.

27 There is an existing rule of customary international law that establishes that the new states cannot be recognized without the previous recognition of the state from which it wants to secede. (Margiotta, 2005, ch. VI, para. 3).

obtain consent for independence from the parent state.[28] In a kind of synergy between international legal order and internal legal order, the legality of secession is, in some way, *liminal*, and should be identified in a border area between the two systems.

In the international legal order, no rules pretend to govern secessionist aspirations. There is no rule that prohibits secession, but at the same time, the criteria of international law, which marks the path followed by the international community to absorb secessionist crises, favours territorial integrity. The international legal order, in fact, does neither legitimize nor prohibit secession.

The international legal system is neutral on the issue of secession, except in cases where rules of *ius cogens* have been violated. The prohibition of a unilateral declaration of independence, according to the opinion of the ICJ on Kosovo, would no longer be implicit in the principle of territorial integrity, except in cases where another state violates the territorial integrity. In the Kosovo opinion, the court declared, "the principle of territorial integrity is confined to the sphere of relations between states."[29] In other words, the principle excludes the violation of territorial integrity by a foreign state, but does not apply this principle within the state, in relation to populations pursuing secession. It is clear that there is a strong preference for maintaining territorial unity, which has been reflected in pronouncements by the UN Security Council. However, as a matter of law, the international system, from the point of "black letters" and legal positivism, is still neutral on the question of secession.[30]

From the international perspective, the option conceived in October 2017 by Catalan President Puigdemont, to make the Catalan parliament declare independence and then to freeze the declaration, cannot be considered illegal in international law as interpreted both by the ICJ in the Kosovo case and by the Canadian Court in the Québec case. In fact, the combined reading of the opinions of the two courts permits us to assume that,

a) unlike the claim made by the Canadian Court, for the ICJ the declaration of independence of a secessionist group is admissible from a legal point of view. Therefore, the group is no longer forbidden to declare independence before the end of the (mandatory) negotiations and the acceptance of the independence by the central state;

   and

b) "freezing" the declaration complies with the opinions of both the ICJ and the Canadian Court. The ICJ did not take into account the legal and political

28 An overwhelming international acceptance of statehood could, in exceptional circumstances, substitute the recognition of the parent state.

29 International Court of Justice, *Accordance with International Law of the Unilateral Declaration of Independence in Respect of Kosovo*, Advisory Opinion, I.C.J. Reports 2010, 403 para. 80

30 Canadian Supreme Court, Reference Re Secession of Quebec [1998] 2 S.C.R. 217, para. 140.

consequences of the declaration itself, while the Canadian Court required that these consequences be negotiated to have the precondition for international recognition of the new state entity, which can only take place after the separation process has succeeded in imposing itself on the parent state.

This does not mean that international law confers any entity within a state with the right to declare its independence unilaterally. The legal and political consequences of the declaration itself, including recognition by the international community, depend on the way in which the new state was born. Certainly, recent practice seems to reveal that respect for the democratic principle is necessary, but not sufficient, for the international community to absorb the secessionist process.

The request for the legitimacy of the process by which secession is pursued or has been pursued confirms that it is desirable for the secessionist community to obtain, through negotiations, the recognition of the parent state as this allows for easier recognition as an autonomous entity by the international community. The elements that determine the success of a secessionist process cannot be found in the remedial right of secession (as some philosophers[31] and international lawyers[32] believe), but following the democratic rules provides more opportunities for the secessionist movement to enter into a negotiation process with the central state and to have the support of the international community. According to the Canadian Supreme Court, "a failure of the duty to undertake negotiations and pursue them according to constitutional principles may undermine that government's claim to legitimacy which is generally a precondition for recognition by the international community."[33] In the opinion of the court, on the one hand, after a referendum of independence is successful the secessionist movement cannot declare unilateral secession, on the other a state cannot "remain indifferent to the clear expression of a clear majority of Quebecers that they no longer wish to remain in Canada" and "the rights of other provinces and the federal government cannot deny the right of the government of Québec to pursue secession, should a clear majority of the people of Québec chose that goal, so long as in doing so, Québec respects the rights of others."[34]

In this sort of "border legality" between legal systems, the relevant element for the international test of the internal lawfulness of secession seems to be the fulfilment of the obligation by the central state to negotiate secession, following a vote showing a clear majority in favour of secession. In other words, alongside the traditional elements of statehood (people, territory, government) there is also the legitimacy of the process of state formation. The legitimacy of the process of state formation must counterbalance that of effectiveness, by virtue of which an act of secession, even unilateral and unconstitutional, should be recognized by the international system, if successful.

31 The so-called "Just cause theories of secession": Allen Buchanan and Lea Brilmayer.
32 Tomuschat, 2006; Oeter, 2012.
33 Canadian Supreme Court, Reference Re Secession of Quebec [1998] 2 S.C.R. 217, para. 103.
34 Canadian Supreme Court, Reference Re Secession of Quebec [1998] 2 S.C.R. 217, para. 87.

4. Secession and democracy

What remains to be discussed is the question of which democratic rules are useful for the *international* system to prove the *internal* lawfulness of secession (even in the absence, like with the Scottish case, of a constitutional right of secession). Here arises the problem of the (difficult) relationship between secession and democracy and of the value of the majority rule (Closa in this volume) and of the referendum in the secessionist process.[35] When referring to the definition of new external borders, majority rule and referendum can be considered respectful of the accepted democratic principles.[36] As it is well known, majority is an artificial rather than a neutral concept (Martinico in this volume), and can be constructed through political and legal decisions, by including or excluding people or groups from the right to vote.

It seems impossible to me to justify secession *exclusively* in democratic terms, since democratic theories always find it necessary to refer to the pre-democratic definition of the criteria for belonging to secessionist groups. Secession cannot be justified entirely on the basis of democracy because it is always reinforced by other pre-democratic elements. Groups that are traditionally settled in a specific territory and that express a will to secede are, in the overwhelming majority of cases, national (ethnic or cultural) minorities. In this respect, *choice theories of secession*[37] reproduce,[38] at least in part, the weaknesses of *national self-determination theories.*

In order to secede democratically, a group must express its will in a referendum or plebiscite. Accordingly, in order to democratically address a secessionist dispute, the first step would be to determine who would be given the right to vote. Although theorists of democratic secession tend to argue that the expression of a desire to secede by a territorial group through a referendum or plebiscite is sufficient to legitimize it, it is clear that they need to determine in advance which group can claim a given territory. Appeal to historical tradition, which would link the group to the territory, and a common attachment to the territory itself, appears to precede any democratic consensus. Territory and voters must, in some way, be determined before deciding anything. In practice, the right to secede is granted primarily on the basis of nationality, as is demonstrated by the fact that *choice theories of secession* affirm that the right to secede should not be granted to groups that are not in a position to give birth to viable states and do not satisfy certain conditions (Wellman, 2005). As a consequence, from the

35 Beaulac, Chapter 7, this volume; Beaulac and Bérard, 2017; Ziegler, Shaw and Bauböck (eds), 2014.

36 Democracy means more than simple majority rule, as specified by the Canadian Supreme Court, Reference Re Secession of Quebec [1998] 2 S.C.R. 217. On this, Martinico, Chapter 6, this volume.

37 Joxerramon Bengoetxea, Chapter 3, this volume: "When it comes to the normative, practical philosophical debate, claim of sovereign right and the democratic will of the people is the most recurrent argument for secession." The most important justification for secession relies on the democratic principle, especially when based on a general consensus.

38 See Beran, 1998; Wellman, 1995, 2005; Philpott, 1995; McGee, 1992.

democratic point of view, the overall practicability of secession prevents many territorially concentrated groups from enjoying the democratic right to secede. But, as I have previously stated, from a purely democratic point of view, if one accepts the secession of a territorial group from a state, one must also accept the secession of another territorial group within the seceding state, and so on, accepting the recursive nature of secession.[39]

Moreover in democratic terms, as long as it is unlikely that all individuals within a territorially concentrated group would actually agree to secede, and if consensus remains the ultimate criterion of democratic legitimacy, the borders of the new state may be just as undemocratic as the old borders. For the *choice theories of secession*, individual autonomy is the fundamental value that justifies secessionist claims, as it constitutes the ground in which the right to associate is rooted, and that is the basis of any legitimate government. But if, for these theories, consensus is a prerequisite for the legitimacy of political authority, and if the individuals who form part of a group within a state no longer consent to the state's authority, they must be granted the right to secede and should bring the theory of individual autonomy to its extreme consequence, recognizing the right of every territorial group (even the most exiguous groups) to secede and also foreseeing the possibility that to secede could be the same individual (McGee, 1992, at 33 ff.). If the fundamental value of autonomy should be increased by the exercise of the right to secede, this right should be granted to all. Otherwise it is unclear what the *democratic theory of secession* would add to the *national self-determination theories* of secession, for which the collective autonomy of the group justifies the right to secessionist self-determination. It does not seem that consent can provide valid reasons *for* or *against* secession. This new type of secessionism, whose purpose is to correct the form of the existing state through democratic means, risks reflecting itself in the old nationalistic secessionism.

In any case, as a general rule, the creation of a state cannot be in contrast with the aspirations of the people and the consensus of the population involved. Internal consent is a necessary condition if the movement for independence wants to self-legitimize in front of the international community, but, contrary to the assumptions of choice theories of secession, it is not sufficient to give someone else a moral obligation to recognize independence.

This explains why it seems politically correct to seek help from the *democratic theories* for claiming secession, rather than call on nationalist sentiment. Democratic theories are more suitable for understanding the current age of secessionist phenomenon as recent practice indicates that respect for democratic principles is necessary for the international community to accommodate the secessionist process. The respect for majority rule, in the final analysis, does not affect the final outcome of the secessionist attempt, but it does guarantee that the factual situation, if it manages to produce the requirements of statehood, will

39 Margiotta, 2005, ch. VIII para. 3 and Baubock, 2019.

not encounter obstacles in the international realm concerning the extension of all sovereign prerogatives and duties to the new subjects. What I call a "secessionism of a new type," like the ones attempted by Catalonia and Scotland,[40] refers to the *democratic theories of secession* rather than turning to *self-determination theories of secession*.

In current public debates, secessionist movements no longer use the *honourable* language of the principle of self-determination and have begun to use the *demonized* concept of secession. The recent rejection of the language of self-determination by secessionist leaders in Europe shows that when there is a question of breaking the territorial integrity of existing states, the exact terms to use are those of secession and not of self-determination, even though there is no international legal coverage to legitimize the separation. More importantly, the democratic appeal for this "secessionism of a new type" is strategic, because the consequences of declaring independence, including recognition by the international community, depend on the way in which the new state was born. The democratic framework seems to be the most attractive for these new movements, particularly against the anti-liberal stigma that was often attributed to separatist movements, their leaders, and scholars of ethnic nationalism. The new leaders tend to value the right to vote and freedom of the members of a territorially concentrated group.

As a scholar of the right to secede and of the history of secession, I think it is important not to abandon the democratic framework. If denying the right to secede can result in an "unconditional act of faith" towards national unity (defending the mythical identification, within a given territory, of a nation, people and state), recognizing it can have two very different consequences. The *first* consequence, also from a democratic theory perspective, is that accepting the nation as a whole has an inherent moral value or, at least, that the justification for recognizing the right of secession must be found in the importance of national identity and of national belonging for the individuals. Despite the efforts of democratic theories to disengage separatism from nationalist sentiments, it seems impossible to justify secession entirely in terms of democracy, as it is always necessary to refer to the pre-democratic determination of criteria for belonging to the secessionist group.

If we do not recognize an intrinsic moral value of nations, the *second* consequence is the necessary recognition of the right for all groups, if not all individuals, to secede, bringing the "ultimate right" to its extreme consequence and obliging us to rethink the only form of political organisation invented since modernity.

40 Kraus and Vergès Gifra, 2017, at 20: "The most characteristic feature of this new secessionism is the goal of 'correcting' the shape of a given state unit by democratic means. In this respect, Catalonia has obvious commonalities with Quebec and Scotland. We do not argue that [ethno-nationalist] motives are completely absent in Catalonia today, but we want to highlight that they clearly play a secondary role in comparison with the *civic* demands to find a democratic solution to the Catalan question."

5. Final remarks: liminal legality applied

If the right to secede is not to be taken to its extreme consequences, where its legal recognition is always destructive, *legality* in this context certainly remains a *peculiar* type of legality. Following the well-known reference of the Canadian Supreme Court,[41] it is now necessary to admit that the expression of popular will through a referendum (free and open to all) in favour of secession cannot leave the central state indifferent. Rather, after a vote in favour of secession by part of the state, the central state is obligated to enter into negotiations with the group that intends to separate, negotiations that do not necessarily have to result in secession. The court, while not recognizing an obligation for the state to accept a unilateral declaration of independence, does not deny that a state should allow separation in cases where a clear majority in a given region supports that request. Based on the reference of the Canadian Court, we can deduce that when there is an obligation for the central state to diligently search for a political solution to the crisis, the secessionist group must not declare independence before the end of negotiations.

In my view, *if and only if* the process through which the separatist movement arrived at a referendum was legitimate and agreed to by all parties,[42] then *liminal legality* would allow something different from what was recommended by the Canadian Court. *Liminal legality* would allow for: a) the inevitability of secession following a referendum in favour of independence, no matter how the negotiations are going or have gone; and b) the possibility for the secessionist group, after a vote with a clear majority in favour of secession, to declare independence immediately, even before the end of negotiations and the possibility for the international community to recognize the new state before the recognition by the parent state.

The test of *liminal legality* between an internal legal system and the international order, neither of which recognize secession, could occur when the process through which secession is pursued, or was pursued, is legitimate and respects the democratic principle. To some extent, two illegalities may make a liminal legality.[43]

Realistically, it is necessary to understand if and how it is possible to democratically determine the external borders of a new state, which instruments would be appropriate for that and to oblige the central state to tolerate a possible secession.

41 See Delledonne and Martinico (eds.), 2019.

42 Joxerramon Bengoetxea, Chapter 2, this volume: "The conditions regulating the process of self-determination or the right to decide need to be agreed to by the relevant actors involved for the process to have any relevant consequences."

43 To change the epistemic perspective on law, in this context, means not to use the classic monist or dualist system-based paradigm, which would require the identification of the legitimacy source for the legality of secession in one of the legal order (international or constitutional), and to admit that legalities or illegalities are today hardly arbitrated by hierarchy. In this direction goes the current work of Gianluigi Palombella (2018) on interlegality; see also de Sousa Santos (1990).

In this sense, the Scottish case, despite its failure and even in the absence of explicit legal clauses, shows how it is possible to attempt to govern this phenomenon. The Scottish case can be considered an excellent example of the secession process through the accomplishment of a consensual (democratic?) referendum.[44] In my opinion, the test of *liminal legality* between the internal legal system (which did not recognize secession) and the international legal system (which does not yet recognize secession as such) would have certainly been possible in the case of the success of Scottish independence.

If the main question is of the *clear* and *free* manifestation of a desire to separate, this question remains unanswered in the Catalonian case. The referendum for independence cannot be considered a real act of *free* will of the population because it was not agreed upon by both parties. Moreover, there were too many threats by the Spanish government against the Catalan population who wanted to vote and the Spanish authorities cannot invoke the non-credibility of the referendum on the basis of non-participation. In the Catalan situation, determining the terms of *liminal legality* is, at the moment, almost impossible. In the border area between legal systems (domestic and international), a shadow cone still remains, represented by the way in which the Catalan referendum was held.

If "it seems not too exaggerated to predict that secession will continue to be one of the major political themes of the 21st century" (Kraus, Vergès Gifra, 2017, at 21), then the effort to defend the mythical congruency, within a given territory, of state, people and nation and the sacredness of borders in the name of the nation-state, even by unconstitutional means or in violation of internationally recognized fundamental human rights, against the possibility of a referendum for a new nation-state, means risking the imposition of the defence of secessionist groups by those who do not feel particular sympathy towards the desire for statehood proper to the secessionist phenomenon.[45]

Secession, while bringing the issue of unity of the people to centre-stage, does not challenge the very notion of statehood. The potentiality of secession to look at the limits of the idea of state and nation as whole identities goes along with the awareness of the close connection between secession and state and between secession and borders.

Decoding and explaining, in the previous sections of this chapter, the fear of secession, does not mean denying at all costs any discourse on the legality of secession. Underlying the problematic interactions between democracy and

44 The franchise for the election, for example, did not include Scottish citizens overseas or those living in the rest of the United Kingdom. For many the exclusion of these voters was not justified, and violated established democratic principles. On the contrary, 16- and 17-year-olds were able to vote. Palermo (2019, at 274), argues that "The outcome of the referendums on Scottish independence in 2014 and on Brexit in 2016 were largely determined by the definition of the eligible voters."

45 I would agree here with what is stated by Joxerramon Bengoetxea in this volume: "I do not ... see myself as a prima facie supporter of secession, understood as separation from one state in order to create another."

secession and between law and secession, while proposing the possibility of a peculiar legality of secession, means taking secession seriously.

But, in the end, to take secession seriously it is important to demonstrate that the fear of secession will last until contemporary humanity is divided into states, which, as Kelsen (1920) teaches, are only temporary, "by no means forever."

References

Rainer Bauböck, 'A Multilevel Theory of Democratic Secession' (2019) 3 *Ethnopolitics* 227.

Stéphane Beaulac in this volume.

Stéphane Beaulac and Frédéric Bérard, *The Law of Independence: Quebec, Montenegro, Kosovo, Scotland, Catalonia* (Lexisnexis, 2017).

Joxerramon Bengoetxea in this volume.

Harry Beran, A Democratic Theory of Political Self-Determination for a New World Order in Percy B. Lehning (ed.), *Theories of Secession* (Routledge, 1998) 32.

J.P. Cabestan and A. Pavković (eds.), *Secessionism and Separatism in Europe and Asia: To Have a State of One's Own* (Routledge, 2013).

John C. Calhoun, Speech on the Revenue Collection [Force] Bill [February 15–16, 1833] in John C. Calhoun (ed.), *Union and Liberty: The Political Philosophy of John C. Calhoun* (Liberty Fund, 1992), 401.

Carlos Closa, Interpreting Article 50: Exit, Voice and… What about Loyalty in Carlos Closa (ed.), *Secession from a Member State and Withdrawal from the European Union. Troubled Membership* (CUP, 2017a) 187.

Carlos Closa (ed.), *Secession from a Member State and Withdrawal from the European Union. Troubled Membership* (CUP, 2017b).

Carlos Closa in this volume.

David Copp, 'International Law and Morality in the Theory of Secession' (1998) 3 *The Journal of Ethics* 219.

Julie Dahlitz, *Secession and International Law: Conflict Avoidance—Regional Appraisals* (Asser, 2003).

Philpott Daniel, 'In Defense of Self-Determination' (1995) 105 *Ethics* 352.

Giacomo Delledonne and Giuseppe Martinico (eds.), *The Canadian Contribution to a Comparative Law of Secession. Legacies of the Quebec Secession Reference* (Palgrave, 2019).

Bonaventura de Sousa Santos, 'Stato e diritto nella transizione post-moderna. Per un nuovo senso comune giuridico' (1990) 3 *Sociologia del diritto* 5.

Giancarlo Guarino, *Autodeterminazione dei popoli e diritto internazionale* (Jovene, 1984).

Mattia Guidi, Mattia Casula in this volume.

David Haljan, *Constitutionalising Secession* (Hart, 2014).

Hurst Hannum, 'Rethinking Self-Determination' (1993) 34 *Virginia Journal of International Law* 1.

Natalino Irti, *Norma e luoghi. Problemi di geo-diritto* (Laterza, 2001).

Hans Kelsen, *Das Problem der Souveränität und die Theorie des Völkerrechts: Beitrag zu einer reinen Rechtslehre* (J. C. B. Mohr, 1920).

Claire Kilpatrick, 'The EU and Its Sovereign Debt Programmes: The Challenges of Liminal Legality' (2017) 1 *Current Legal Problems* 337.

Jan Klabbers, 'The Right to be Taken Seriously: Self-Determination in International Law' (2006) 1 *Human Rights Quarterly* 186.

Karen Knop, *Diversity and Self-Determination in International Law* (CUP, 2002).

Marcelo G. Kohen (ed.), *Secession: International Law Perspectives* (CUP, 2006).

Peter A. Kraus and Joan Vergés Gifra, Introduction in Peter A. Kraus and Joan Vergés Gifra (eds.), *The Catalan Process: Sovereignty, Self-Determination and Democracy in the 21st Century* (Institut d'Estudis de l'Autogovern, 2017) 195.

Susanna Mancini, Secession and Self-Determination in Michel Rosenfeld and Andras Sajó (eds.), *The Oxford Handbook of Comparative Constitutional Law* (OUP, 2012) 481.

Susanna Mancini, 'Ai confini del diritto: una teoria democratica della secessione' (2014) 3 *Percorsi costituzionali* 623.

Costanza Margiotta, *L'ultimo diritto. Profili storici e teorici della secessione* (Il Mulino, 2005) (*The Ultimate Right. Theoretical and Historical Profiles of Secession*).

Costanza Margiotta, Introduzione in John C. Calhoun (ed.), *Secessione e libertà*, edited by Costanza Margiotta (La Rosa, 2007).

Costanza Margiotta, 'Sulla (im)possibilità della secessione. Per una legalità «liminale»' (2017a) 2 *Ordines* 43.

Costanza Margiotta,'Perchè la secessione fa paura? Un aggiornamento su «l'ultimo diritto»' (2017b) 3 *Governare la paura* 37.

Costanza Margiotta, '(Dis)ordine sovrano: Brexit e la sentenza Wightman' (2019a) 1 *Nuove Autonomie* 19.

Costanza Margiotta, Questa casa non è un albergo! A proposito della sentenza Wightman (2019b). Available from: http://www.diritticomparati.it/questa-casa-non-e-un-albergo-proposito-della-sentenza-wightman/.

Giuseppe Martinico, 'Le costituzioni come strumento di gestione del rischio: il caso della secessione' (2017) 3 *Governare la paura* 19.

Giuseppe Martinico in this volume.

Robert W. McGee, 'A Third Liberal Theory of Secession' (1992) 1 *The Liverpool Law Review* 45.

Wayne Norman, *Negotiating Nationalism: Nation-Building, Federalism, and Secession in the Multinational State* (OUP, 2006).

Stefan Oeter, Self-Determination in Bruno Simma, Daniel-Erasmus Khan, Georg Nolte and Andreas Paulus (eds.), *The Charter of the United Nations: A Commentary*, vol. I (OUP, 2012) 313.

Francesco Palermo, Towards a Comparative Constitutional Law of Secession? in Giacomo Delledonne and Giuseppe Martinico (eds.), *The Canadian Contribution to a Comparative Law of Secession. Legacies of the Quebec Secession Reference* (Palgrave, 2019) 265–282.

Gianluigi Palombella, 'Interlegalità. Ripensare l'interconnessione tra ordini giuridici' (2018) 2 *Diritto e Questioni Pubbliche* 325.

Aleksandar Pavković and Peter Radan, *Creating New States: Theory and Practice of Secession* (Ashgate, 2007).

Aleksandar Pavković and Peter Radan, *The Ashgate Research Companion to Secession* (Ashgate, 2011).

Matt Qvortrup in this volume.

Matt Qvortrup, 'The «Neverendum»?: A History of Referendums and Independence' (2013) 2 *Political Insight* 4.

Matt Qvortrup, 'Referendums on Independence, 1860–2011' (2014) 1 *The Political Quarterly* 57.

Milena Sterio, *Secession in International Law: A New Framework* (Edward Elgar, 2018).

Cass Sunstein, 'Constitutionalism and Secession' (1991) 2 *University of Chicago Law Review* 633.

Antonello Tancredi, *La secessione nel diritto Internazionale* (Cedam, 2001).

Christian Tomuschat, Secession and Self-Determination in Marcelo G. Kohen (ed.), *Secession: International Law Perspectives* (CUP, 2006) 23.

Neus Torbisco Casal, National Minorities, Self-Determination and Human Rights a Critique of the Dominant Paradigms in the Catalan Case in Peter A. Kraus and Joan Vergés Gifra (eds.), *The Catalan Process: Sovereignty, Self-Determination and Democracy in the 21st Century* (Institut d'Estudis de l'Autogovern, 2017) 195.

Neil Walker, Internal Enlargement in the European Union: Beyond Legalism and Political Expediency in Carlos Closa (ed.), *Secession from a Member State and Withdrawal from the European Union: Troubled Membership* (CUP, 2017) 32.

Christian Walter, Antje von Ungern-Sternberg and Kavus Abushov (eds.), *Self-Determination and Secession in International Law* (OUP, 2014).

Norman Wayne, Domesticating Secession in Stephen Macedo and Allen Buchanan (eds.), *Secession and Self-Determination* (NYU Press, 2003).

Daniel Weinstock, 'Constitutionalizing the Right to Secede' (2001) 2 *Journal of Political Philosophy* 182.

Mark Weller, Secession and Self-determination in Western Europe: The Case of Catalonia (2017) in *Blog of the European Journal of International Law*. Available from: https://www.ejiltalk.org/secession-and-self-determination-in-western-europe-the-case-of-catalonia/#more-15619.

Christopher H. Wellman, 'A Defense of Secession and Political Self-Determination' (1995) 24 *Philosophy and Public Affairs* 142.

Christopher H. Wellman, *A Theory of Secession. The Case for Political Self-Determination* (CUP, 2005).

Reuven Ziegler, Jo Shaw and Rainer Bauböck (eds.), *Independence Referendums: Who Should Vote and Who Should Be Offered Citizenship?* (2014) RSCAS Working Paper 2014/90. Available from: http://cadmus.eui.eu/bitstream/handle/1814/32516/RSCAS_2014_90.pdf.

3 Secession v forceful union

A provisional enquiry into the right to decide to secede and the obligation to belong

Joxerramon Bengoetxea[1]

I. Introduction: concept of, and approaches to secession

Secession is a deeply contested issue, not only in politics, but also when discussed in academic circles. To begin with, reason and emotions are not always easy to sever. Next, public opinion tends to be quite polarized around secession, and political debates are most heated. Even in the courts, very rarely, does the issue get a serious argumentation, going beyond constitutional dogma.[2] Furthermore, descriptive approaches tend to be rich in comparative detail (Qvortrup, 2014; Roeder, 2018) but, being casuistic, do not always inform the normative debate, except in the claim that every case is, normatively and contingently, different. Yet, engaging in normative discourse is essential. Secession is a question of practical reason; it provides an answer to the question, "what is to be done in a political community facing a tragic choice?" as regards the decisions on practical action made and the courses of action taken by a people concerning their legal and political status and affecting their relations with other peoples. And then, there is the issue of demarcation of territories and defining the correlative peoples. Approaches to secession differ, depending on individual and collective outlooks, and normative disciplines vary: morality-ethics (divorce, separation, splitting a group), politics (secessions, factions, breakaway), economics (markets, new barriers), law and religion, where it is a classic in Western cultures (schisms). Within law, one can again distinguish different approaches: International Law (IL), Constitutional Law, Jurisprudence and, a late and odd newcomer, the criminal justice system, notably criminal procedure, criminology and criminal law.

This chapter approaches secession from the legal perspective, more particularly, from Jurisprudence. But, within Jurisprudence, one can, again, find different conceptions or approaches, depending on whether one follows natural law positions – secession as a natural right of peoples, pursuing the just cause of freedom from oppression and alienation, seeking emancipation and freedom – positivism

1 Professor in Jurisprudence and Sociology of Law at the University of the Basque Country (UPV/EHU), Research Group GI IT1190-19 "EU and Fundamental Rights."

2 *Pace* Martinico, 2017. I wish to thank Giuseppe for very helpful and sharp comments on an earlier draft of this chapter.

or rule-formalism – where secession is part of the law on self-determination either in IL instruments or in some constitutions, normally studies by comparative constitutional scholars – realism – where the practice of key legal actors is taken as ground for making predictions on their future behaviour – sociological Jurisprudence – where social and political conceptions of secession and sovereignty inform the legal apparatus – analytical Jurisprudence – where the use of the terms related to secession and their interactions as legal institutions give us an insight into our normative constructions – hermeneutical theories of law – where the pre-understanding of secession is shaped by our practices, themselves understood in terms of our normative aspirations regarding secession and its related concepts[3] – or critical studies, where the power relationships and knowledge conditions of discourses related to secession are related to issues like state power and state formation, subtle forms of domination in IL, and the critique of judicial neutrality in the service of formalism, as a means of hegemony.

My jurisprudential position, which tends to combine most of the above jurisprudential schools of thought, gives conceptual and axiological priority to the norm-user perspective, as opposed to the norm-giver perspective.[4] This provokes a bottom-up understanding of law and politics, and of practical reason generally, starting from the sovereignty of the individual, next to the group or groups – communities – where individuals cooperate, and successively to the larger groups where these groups tend to federate, all the way up to the state-national, supranational and international levels. My own work, since the mid-1980s, has tended to critically question the prominence of the state as the Hegelian culmination of reason, and has constantly suggested the need to explore alternatives to the state when understanding, theorizing and practically constructing the *polity*. I do not therefore see myself as a prima facie supporter of secession, understood as separation from one state in order to create another. As it has been argued secession is, simultaneously, "the most revolutionary and the most institutionally conservative of political constructs."[5] It breaks up a state, only to seek a new state.

Secession can be defended more coherently, as a matter of principle, when its agenda seeks cooperating and sharing systems of governance with other peoples, rather than going-it-alone situations. That would be a powerful reason to support, for any polity, the status of a federated entity within a larger supranational federation. In my particular predicament as a European, I advocate for

3 The key concepts tend to be people, population, community, demos, citizens, nationals, referendum, state, institutions, administration, authority, independence, autonomy, self-government, status, annexation, dissolution, self-determination, right to decide, democracy, territory, territorial integrity, *statu quo*, negotiation, claims, rights, obligation, practice, recognition, accommodation, multinational polities, multicultural societies, international community, constitutionalism, federalism.

4 My Philosophy of Law is inspired by the late Neil MacCormick, especially his latest work, the tetralogy on Law Practical Reason published with OUP between 1999 and 2009, which I have summarized in a book on MacCormick and institutional practical reason, Bengoetxea (2015).

5 Mancini (2012), at 48; Margiotta (2005), at 9 ff.

all national and pluri-national polities to integrate in a European Federation. Secessions from existing Member States would be then seen as purely transitional and provisional measures towards greater integration. The multiple levels of government at which groups or peoples can cooperate – local, regional, state-national, supranational, international, transnational – and the new concepts of governance and diplomacy, make secessions even more complex, well beyond all or nothing, absolute formulae (Cornago, 2017).

The usual factual framework in secession is the existence of a community or people *p* concentrated in a territory *tp* that claims, or already has, recognition as such people, and is integrated into, or forms part of, a relevant polity with the form of a state *e* with its own territory *et,* and pretends to secede from such state:

"*p* (pt) secedes from *e (et)*" or "people *p* wishes to secede from state *e*"

This pretension to secede is based, normatively, on a more fundamental claim of sovereignty or self-determination. It is necessary to analyze the normative weight of positions both defending and opposing secession, in a sort of dialogue engaged in an ideal discourse situation (Habermas, 1992; Alexy, 1989). My analysis does not purport to reflect actual practice, or any concrete case, although recent, post 1989, events of the over 1200 recorded cases of secession since 1793 (Qvortrup, 2014) provide important testing grounds.

Historical studies can provide interesting lessons on claims and mobilization for secession. As Margiotta (Chapter 2, this volume) points out, the interactions between claims and recognitions of secession from the perspective of constitutionalism are not always straightforward.[6] Still, the debate on the *Ought*, the normative and practical reason dimensions of secession are not pre-empted by empirical or historical, or even constitutional generalizations. Empirical notions like the territory (land), the people, individually and collectively considered, the relevant states, the international community and the mechanisms for expressing collective will, the census, cannot be ignored in the practical normative analyses.

When it comes to the normative, practical philosophical debate, claim of sovereign right and the democratic will of the people is the most recurrent argument for secession, whereas defence of the *statu quo* of the affected polity, currently the state, is the most recurrent argument against secession. People *p* claims to have, or considers that it has, the right to decide on its own status *s*, i.e. as to whether it wishes to continue as part of the relevant polity, state *e* (thus maintaining the

6 See the contribution by Costanza Margiotta in this volume: "The history of modern states, and recently Brexit, has proven how the constitutionalization of secession (the attempt to neutralise a possible conflict), can end, at a given moment, encouraging it , while the lack of constitutionalization, which would make the process much more complex, even after a possible declaration of independence, may discourage secession or at least discourage the separatists' enthusiasm when a referendum is called (consider the results of the referendums in Québec and Scotland). It is for these reasons that the right to secede has not found an easy place in constitutional orders."

statu quo), or else to change its status (secession). But in either case, the underlying postulate is that "*p* decides on *s*", *p* is "sovereign" to, or as a matter of fact can, decide on its status *s*. Obviously, the normative framework is never so simple, because *p*'s decision on *s* is not made in the abstract or in a vacuum, it affects the status, the definition and the territory of a state *e* and its people, and also, as in the EU, of the supranational or international organizations *io* or polities where that state is a member, *em*. Secession of people *p* in such cases has a direct impact on the parent Member State *em* and on the International Organization, *io*, and all its Member States, *em1, em, 2, … em n*.[7]

At any rate, secession conceptually implies these features: a people, a territory, a status, a state, mobilization, and a change of status. A referendum is not a necessary feature of secession. On the other hand, a referendum, or an equivalent plebiscitary formula based on a census, is, arguably, a defining feature of self-determination. Like self-determination, secession is not a *status* but a *process*. In secession there is a constitutional moment where there is a change of status. The difference between secession and self-determination is precisely the change of status: in self-determination there is also a process of decision or expression of the will – determination – but not necessarily a change of status (Quebec referendums, Scottish referendum of September 2014). But in secession, there is always a change of status, otherwise there is no secession. Secession is one of the possible consequences of self-determination (SD), which can also be understood as a process of decision-making. The outcome of secession, the change of status, is normally framed in terms of independence, but this is not necessarily so; there is a conceptual difference between secession and independence (Mancini, 2012).

Independence means the creation of a new state, with full legal personality. Secession need not lead to an independent, new state. It could also lead to association with, or accession to, a preexisting state, or it can be an almost automatic process of separation from one state and annexation to another (Saarland in 1950 or, arguably, Crimea in 2012). Secession always involves separation of one community or people from a larger entity or polity, constituted as a state. As a matter of fact, it is possible to have secession, or annexation to another state without a formal process of self-determination. The former USSR experienced some instances of secession of the Baltic Republics, before its fragmentation and final dissolution. The Western Sahara has not yet exercised its right to SD called for by a UN resolution. Instead it was dis-occupied or decolonized by Spain and occupied by Morocco. The population that had a right to determine itself when the UN resolution was passed in 1975 was never franchized in a census, and in the meantime, the affected population has changed, is in exile or in refugee camps. In Crimea a "referendum," of sorts, was held, in order to secede from the Ukraine and annex the Russian Federation (Roznai and Suteu, 2015). It is also possible to

7 See Closa, 2017. I do not follow Closa in his call on TEU: 49 to apply in all circumstances of internal enlargement, nor in his insistence on the original member state's consent without considering the normative value of the original state's reluctance toe ven engage in a debate on the right of its internal nations to decide on status.

have a (factual) process of self-determination through a referendum, where secession and independence is the option preferred by a large majority of the population and yet no change of status occurs. The September 2017, referendum in the Iraq part of Kurdistan, arguably, has not so far produced actual change of status, the reference state being considered somewhat 'failed.' The Catalan case could, arguably, be considered one such case. The conditions regulating the process of self-determination or the right to decide need to be agreed to by the relevant actors involved for the process to have any relevant consequences.

Secession is, like self-determination, normatively, analyzed in terms of a "right" assisting a people. A right of a people simply to decide on status, or a right to actually sever bonds of statehood with the larger state where the people legally belong or where it is embedded, along with other peoples *p', p'', ... pn* (as in multinational, con-federal models) even if those other peoples make no special rights-claims, or where it is considered as part of the same *demos* (as in unitary nation-state models). Of course, the question who is a people, and under what conditions can the people be considered a demos, is key, as we examine in Section III. But the empirical study of secession (Roeder, 2018) can give some guidance on the normative debates, especially as regards the self-constitution of the demos. In other words, a hermeneutic understanding of secession illuminates.

II. Stages in the process of secession

Secession, like self-determination, is best understood and analyzed as a discursive process comprising different stages or moments, rather than a status, or a fixed point in time. Secession is always a critical and tragic constitutional process of rupture: the state of things, relations between a people and the polity within which it is embedded, the matrix or parent, state have to get to a very difficult and critical point for secession to be envisaged. This perspective is also adopted by Roeder (2018) who focusses on national secession campaign's ability to coordinate expectations within a population on the common goal of independence. This process comprises several important temporal phases or stages that we identify according to a dialectic, agonistic, scheme of arguments for and against.

Stage One. The initial stage is one where secession is imagined. This can be the political proposal of a select, elite, group of intellectuals or politicians within a community. At this stage, political and practical arguments are put forward in favour of secession, in order to engage the people in a territory in a shared normative discourse that leads to awareness and to a claim regarding the necessity or desirability of secession. Only a limited number of actors will put secession forward as a desirable step. A political party or faction or movement may be formed to pursue the independence or secession agenda. Empowerment of the people is the challenge at this stage, focused on raising the awareness of the population. The (majority of the) people may already see themselves as nation or a demos, but not contemplate secession in a serious way. Counterarguments at this stage, to oppose secession, can be already articulated in normative discourses defending the *statu quo*. The "national majority" will normally find it rather expedient to dismiss the secessionist claims made by a "few radicals" or by unrealistic claims of a minority. The claims to secession tend to appear in narratives, discourses, political tracts, academic articles, press and media opinion, but the deliberative process has not yet taken place. The majority of the people in a territorial community has not yet been mobilized towards secession. Secessionist claims are only emerging, and they are not widespread yet. The "national" malaise will be perceived by a few, and it is not sufficiently momentous for secession to become a shared agenda in public opinion.

Stage Two. In the second stage, social movements and political parties mobilize in favour of secession (or independence) calling for a referendum to be held on the desired status of a people and for negotiations with the referent state on holding such a referendum, at some point in time. Secession is always a radical step. Things have to get really bad for this radical moment to be even conceivable at the popular level, well beyond the theoretical fabrications of Stage One. At this stage, the referent state can oppose such moves and decide to block the claims, and deny the possibility of any referendum or change of status, but it will already be engaged into some form of debate. The referent state would probably do better to recognize the, a priori, right of a people to decide on its status, but insist that the necessary conditions do not obtain to exercise this right, thus trying to weaken the momentum and bring the process back to Stage One. The reference state can also (try to) impose rather demanding conditions in order for the people to exercise the right to decide. At this deliberative stage the international community can also be engaged, to some degree.

Stage Three. This third stage is the referendum itself, or any equivalent instrument, depending on the success or failure of the negotiations at Stage Two. This is the political moment producing legal and constitutional consequences, depending on the result of the consultation and on the agreements reached or the confrontations accumulated in the previous stages, between the people and the reference state, and also the international community. This stage need not be a single moment where a referendum, a particular electoral mandate or a vote by representatives is taken. It can be a process involving more than one decision or moments of direct democracy or representative democracy mechanisms.

Stage Four is the post-referendum moment where consequences and effects are being deployed in different directions, depending on the continuation of the mobilization or the results, and the reactions of the reference state and the international community of states. The actors involved in the negotiations will keep confrontation and the process can take a long time and, in this sense, it can also be an instance of Stage Three, where different moments of decision take place: referendum, parliamentary votes, new referendum. Brexit is an interesting example.

Any of these stages can be superseded or overlapped, but analytically it is possible and useful to distinguish them. The arguments for and against secession are present throughout the process, but their intensity and procedure changes, depending on the moment.

The burden of argument is normally placed on whoever claims the right to secession and, once accepted, on the limits and conditions for the exercise of this right. There is a burden of justification on those who claim the right to secede, because there is a normative preference for *statu quo* solutions. Even where there is no coercion, no turmoil, no violence, stability and continuity are still favoured options. Normatively, from the ethical and political point of view, it is important to factor in the possible existence of violence and war along the process. Peaceful mobilization by a people does not guarantee peaceful negotiation between the people seeking secession and the reference state, any more than the use of violence does. Ethically, the implications are overwhelming, but legally, peaceful mobilization does neither guarantee peaceful reaction nor does it rule out coercive responses by the reference state, even by a state considered to be democratic. Change of status need not involve use of force, coercion or violence (Brexit, Slovakia and the Czech Republic), but it always requires serious and complex negotiation of an institutional, legal, economic and constitutional nature, the more so in the context of increased and enhanced interdependence.

Leaving, seceding is a serious and drastic decision. The consequences of a decision to secede affect large numbers of persons and people, some who did, and some who did not take part in the process or in the deliberations, some who wanted secession, and some who did not, and if the proportions are even, extreme care is necessary to preserve societal cohesion before and after Stage Three. It can also affect supranational structures of cooperation, as in the case of secession from a Member State of the EU. Therefore, no-change, momentum, default positions are systematically favoured over change of status, and the onus is usually on the claim for secession. Especially powerful arguments are called for, in order to engage in such a momentous and impactful process. The arguments usually put forward at Stage One are probably insufficient to provoke the mass mobilizations needed at Stage Two and the type of decision-making involved in Stage Three. The arguments for secession will be examined in Section III, along the lines of just cause, and democratic sovereignty theories.

However, this normative preference for *statu quo* tranquility, continuity or stability is not absolute, it is only prima facie. In other words, *statu quo* normally defeats other considerations for change of status, but this indefeasibility is not absolute, only relative. This normally means that change of status needs to be justified beyond a threshold of argumentation and legitimacy that protects *statu quo* by way of presumption, the *onus probandi* is on the claim to secede, the presumption of right is on stability. But, when the burden is accepted and satisfied, overturned, beyond reasonable doubt, and the presumption is seriously challenged, the burden should shift to the state opposing secession: how can it reinstate its claim to the indefeasible nature of *statu quo*? What are the *rights* and the justifications of a given established state *e*, clinging absolutely to *statu quo* to oppose claims to secession made by people *p*, by one or several of its components? This is where more analysis and research are called for.

This twist of the argument opens up a new area for academic research and political debate. To my knowledge, this could be rather innovative. The two most important legal decisions on secession in the last 20 years, the Canadian Supreme Court in *re Quebec*, 1998, and the International Court of Justice opinion on *Kosovo* 2010 (Wouters, Hamid, 2016). They adopt the line of thinking here advocated but do not carry it further: no unilateral right of Quebec to secede based on democracy alone, but no right of the provinces and the federal government to force union based on rule of law alone; rather a process of political negotiation would have to take place, and normative considerations need to take into account the four major principles of the Canadian Federation: democracy, federalism, constitutionalism with rule of law and rights of minorities. Likewise, the Kosovo Unilateral Declaration of Independence (UDI) is not incompatible with IL, since no rule or principle of IL prohibits UDI, and the principle of territorial integrity is confined to the sphere of relations between states. In both cases, there seems to be a dialectical structure or system. The scheme does not look only at the right of a people to secede, but also at the right of a state to impose union on that people.

Because of the strong presumption in favour of *statu quo*, reinforced by IL, Constitutional Law, and Criminal Law, the secession debate has normally turned around the "claim of right" to secession by a given people *p*. A similar argument can be made in this sense about self-determination. Normative (constitutional, political) and analytical (descriptive or conceptual) discourses seldom turn on the issue of states' justifications for the *statu quo* once this presumption is seriously challenged, if not rebutted. Yet the alternate or correlative position needs to be tested and scrutinized as well: what are the *rights* and the justifications of a given established state *e*, clinging absolutely to *statu quo*, to oppose claims to secession made by people *p*, by one or several of its components? In other words, how can state *e* force people *p* to be permanently locked within that state *e*? What follows is a sketch for possible research programs and also for political action, taking this alternative perspective into account.

III. Identifying the people: the single-demos thesis

The most obvious and automatic response that the state representatives will give to (claims to) secession by people *p* in state *e* is to deny that there are any such constituent parts or peoples of the state, because a state is necessarily constituted by one single people, and this people cannot be divided. This is the single-demos, thesis. This thesis is a dogma, it is not up for discussion: "Only the people of the state are a demos; the state cannot be split into plural *demoi*." There is a circularity here: the demos constitutes the state, and the state predefines the demos. Once constituted, there is no question of any other demos within the state. Thus, the single-demos thesis is also the no-other-demos thesis, and it relies on non-recognition (Nootens, 2011). One who defends this view does not even need to look at the historical or political formation of states to argue that the current state is the fusion of peoples into a single demos. In fact, the existence of a demos is no longer an empirical or conceptual disagreement, but a normative decision. The answer is dogmatic. This position holds true even for (some) federations, unless they are multinational. There is a unique, unitary, indivisible, un-severable and indissoluble nation-state and this nation holds sovereignty and predefines the demos.

The constituent people is thus predefined, preconstituted. End of story! There is no normative discussion because there is no possible case to discuss. As the nation cannot be questioned, the will of the people does not really come into play, and if the will of the people is irrelevant, the democratic credentials of the nation are missing. The existence of the nation substitutes the will of the people. If the nation is a dogma then the demos cannot be questioned either, and the democratic principle dissolves: the *demos* does not decide on itself, it is pre-decided. Once the nation-state constituted, the demos needs no foundation. The demos is a sort of Grundnorm behind the constitution. The demos is the nation that gives validity to the constitution in a real or hypothetical referendum. Two hard cases question this legitimacy:

a) Territorial majorities. When the majority in the state as a whole becomes the minority in one territorial part of the state and the majority in the smaller territorial part of the state is the minority in the whole of the state, the state majority can block the territorial majority minority forever. Scotland under Brexit can be an example. This issue was the subject of the *Re Quebec* decision of the Canadian Supreme Court (para. 124):

    > It is clear that "a people" may include only a portion of the population of an existing state. The right to self-determination has developed largely as a human right, and is generally used in documents that simultaneously contain references to "nation" and "state". The juxtaposition of these terms is indicative of the fact that the reference to "people" does not necessarily mean the entirety of a state's population. To restrict the definition of the term to the population of existing states would render the granting of a right to self-determination largely duplicative, given the parallel emphasis within the majority of the source documents on the need to protect the territorial integrity of existing states, and would frustrate its remedial purpose.

b) Future generations. When a state population largely takes part in a referendum on the constitution that defines the pre-constituted demos, the question of the demos may be settled from the point of view of democratic legitimacy. Yet, this is the decision of a given generation at a historical moment. Can it bind future generations? Are future generations involved in the reinstatement of the demos?

When the possibility of discussing (the very existence of) the demos is denied, then the democratic nature of the process is lost. This nationalist dogma is not only projected inside or downwards, in order to deny the status of a people to the territorial minorities within a state, but it is also carried upwards to deny the possibility of a demos at the supra-national level, or any plural democratic legitimacy to that higher level. On the opposite side, when the single-demos thesis loses its dogmatic character, and is open to scrutiny, the possibility opens, conceptually, for more than one demos to make up a state, a pluri-national state, thus recognizing the existence of diverse peoples. When this happens, then either the single thesis is reinterpreted, adjusted to accommodate ***national-cultural*** diversity but still with the discourse of the single-political nation, or the plural demos thesis is accepted and the single demos or no demos objection is abandoned.

(I) The single-demos thesis can be reaffirmed, in a milder version, accepting internal diversity of national cultures, or moves towards a softer revised version of the single demos based on the majority will of its constituents, making no allowances for territorial differences. One way to establish that will is to require a sort of constant or permanent plebiscite (Ernest Renan), a need to re-affirm the demos. The permanent plebiscite thesis assumes support for the single-demos thesis, inferred from the fact that people *p* normally take part in the electoral processes and constitutional life of state *e* (an internal self-determination postulate). However, it can be difficult to postulate if it ignores political facts or situations like the majority of people *p* in a territory of state *e* consistently expressing support for self-determination in its voting patterns, thus expressing a will to constitute itself.

(II) A plural demos (demoi) thesis is accepted, a ***demoicracy***. With the plural demos,[8] normative discourse on secession is not excluded. This is essentially how the Supreme Court (SC) of Canada explains the make-up of its confederation, by recognizing the provinces as parties to the federation. It is very hard to move to the recognition of plural demos in a state and still deny their (sovereign) right to decide on status, if the state is to retain democratic legitimacy. That can explain why, for the SC of Canada, secession of a province, under the constitution, will not obtain unilaterally without principled negotiation with the other participants in the confederation; these could not forego their duty to engage in discussion.

(III) Another possibility is to allow for secession, purely theoretically, by postulating that the union is voluntary, but no exit is procedurally possible (the USSR or Yugoslavia were, arguably, of this type).

8 On *demoicracy* in the EU, see Nicolaidis, 2013; see also Errasti, 2017. Plural demos points to the existence of an internally diverse demos, a people who is actually diverse from different standpoints – ethnic, religious, linguistic, territorial – and embraces such diversity, whereas plural demoi is a redundant demos in the plural, sharing some common platform or level of governance.

IV. Denial of claims to secession

Two major scenarios emerge from the previous discussion. One persists in denying the existence of people who can decide on status, since there is one demos only in the state, and that is the only people who can decide as a whole. The other recognizes the existence of a people, and a theoretical right to decide on status; in which case, further normative argumentation will be necessary to deny serious claims to secession. The first position can be a sufficient argument in positive law to deny the claims to secession. Debates, often, stop right there. This position fails to engage with the debate in the wider forum of practical reason, and cannot appease peoples' demands for recognition and determination.

In the first case, the strategy, after denying the existence of a people *p* who can aspire to become a demos and decide on status *s*, is to develop normative strategies and theories to deny any possible right to secession of people *p*. No-other-demos proponents put any of these arguments forward:

1. State integrity argument. State unity and territorial integrity is a paramount value and defence of the *statu quo* imposes a rule of no change, enhancing the value of stability. If this argument were absolute, there would neither be any changes of states nor any new states.
2. *Territorial integrity* argument. Unity and territorial integrity of states mean unity, completeness and uniformity of the state; the state cannot possibly break-up from within (but see Kosovo Opinion).
3. *Raison d'état* argument. This is a dogma based on state necessity: the interests of states – security and continuity – justify everything, even the use of force or criminal action; there are no limits. State interests override the rule of law and democracy and the factual situation of preeminence of the state is the source of legitimacy.
4. Hard version of the rule of law argument. The law overrides the democratic principle. The rule of law is only an approximation of the continental concept of *état de droit, Rechtsstaat, Estado de Derecho*, Stato di diritto, which, in their soft versions require that all state action be grounded in law, i.e. on pre-established legal norms and procedures. In the stronger versions, only *raison d'état* can override legality; or, rather, circumvent it. These strong versions relate to the single demos as the source of authority and law. The law that constitutes the state denies any other demos within the state. Postulating the existence of another demos within the state thus violates the rule of law. The *Rechtsstaat* then becomes the state imposed by the law, rather than the state based on the law. Respect for law requires respect for the state, upon which it is based.
5. Milder rule of law argument. Softer versions of these theories are a little more sensitive to the limits of sheer force, or national interest, as the source for a legitimate state. They deny *raison d'état* and elaborate on legal obstacles – unconstitutionality – and lack of procedural provision: if there is no procedure for claiming and negotiating secession, then law rules out secession or

self-determination: No remedy, no law! (Montilla, 2016). This begs the normative question, "Should there be such a procedure, and can the law actually be changed to provide for such a procedure given the territorial division of majority in the demos v majority in the people?"

In the second scenario, democratic principle prevails. There can be a formalistic answer based on rule of law or a principled answer, inspired by democracy, as in paragraph 90 of the Re Quebec decision. Taking democracy seriously is normally the way for a state to accept, theoretically at least, that its single-demos thesis is debatable. The most important justification for secession relies on the democratic principle, especially when based on a general consensus (Bossacoma, 2015). The state may thus reach to accept the hypothetical case of secession. The following arguments engage state *e* with the recognition to people *p* of the right to decide on status *s*:

6. Democratic rule of law argument. This is the legitimation for the position of states when *raison d'état*, or even the strong version of *état de droit* is considered too crude, from a democratic theory challenge. Such procedure can proceed according to the principles of a democratic constitution, since the rule of law is necessary, but not sufficient in itself, to warrant legitimacy. The law needs to be based on the democratic will of the people, and this cannot be taken for granted. Popular will has to be reinstated, and if there are parts of a state where a sufficiently large (internal) majority challenges this forced belonging to the state, then the majority of that state cannot permanently reduce the will of the internal majority (state minority). A process needs to be devised (a reform of the constitution), and democratic constitutionalism calls for mechanisms and processes where procedural obstacles to claims to democratic self-determination can be removed. In other words, the constitution should be malleable, rather than a straight-jacket (Gagnon, 2014).
7. Self-determination argument. Other theories are open to conditions for self-determination. Colonial situations in the process of decolonization, undemocratic states, states denying its people(s) any form of self-government through the structures of the state (internal SD), can all justify external self-determination in IL. This dominant understanding on Self-Determination in International Law is the subject of restrictive interpretation to favour the *statu quo* (Martin, 2015). As a result, self-determination has a liminal structure as a legal concept, it provides no normative weight for a new status in contentious cases (Walker, 2015), and it is taken for granted in clear colonial cases. Colonial situations and lack of internal self-determination in totalitarian regimes normally imply a direct route to secession and independence, where the process of self-determination goes almost unnoticed.
8. Right to decide argument. The modern, non-colonial version of the right to self-determination comes in the guise of the democratic right to decide on status, or a right to be taken seriously (Klabbers, 2006). Under agreed conditions, some theories defend the free adherence of a people to a union, in which case the *statu quo* is simply the continued will to belong. These theories are

open to democratic self-determination and secession and normally accept the pluri-national and multicultural and (con)federal nature of the polity: the EU is precisely in this position as regards its Member States (Article 50). Brexit is a good example. Perhaps this is also the position in Canada (Quebec referendums, and Supreme Court 1998 opinion in case Re secession of Quebec), Belgium and the UK (Scottish referendum, and the Good Friday Agreement contemplating the possibility of a referendum) as well.

Arguments 1–5 tend to correspond, roughly to strategies of *containment*, whereas arguments 6–8 would fit better with strategies of *contentment* strategies (Gagnon, 2014).

V. Claims to right to secession: burden of proof on claims to secession

Once the possibility for normatively discussing secession is accepted (options IV: 6–8), a new set of questions opens up. The questions regarding secession have been focussing on the three temporal stages involved in the secession discourses. To frame the question in terms of the stages identified under Section II, we now have the "claim of right" stage (Stage One) and the mobilization stage (Stage Two), all the way to the actual decision stage (Stage Three), and the post-decision stage (Stage Four). We shall briefly mention the main moments or stages.

1) Democracy: On what terms can people *p* have a right to secede from state *e* and when is it reasonable to seek secession? Can we distinguish this question from the question: Can a people *p* decide on its political status *s*? At the awareness-raising stage, discussions will turn on the need for people *p* to change status *s*, and union in state *e* under the *statu quo* will be a suboptimal status or state of affairs *s*. Different reasons explain this judgment, most significantly a real, or perceived, absence of recognition and insufficient empowerment of people *p* under state *e*. This deliberative stage will see through different arguments, for and against. It will normally be elite-driven: Key players from people *p* and from state *e* will lead the deliberative process. Intelligentsia, public opinion makers, think tanks, research and academia and politicians will offer arguments for deliberation. The key arguments supporting change of status will deal with the interpretation of the status *s* of people *p* as suboptimal, and change of status will be presented as a remedy to improve status (hence, remedial theories, as in Buchanan, 1997). Support for the change of status will invoke the democratic will of the majority of people *p* as broadly accredited throughout several electoral processes and other community claims for recognition and empowerment, and arguments will underline the need to ensure the democratic legitimacy of the claims.
2) Mobilization: From the deliberative stage, the seeds for mobilization can grow into something more substantial. Direct democracy movements, referendums from below calling for a process of determination to take place

will lead to stronger arguments in favour and against secession at this stage. Arguments will focus on the rational merits of the reasons offered (justification) and on practical action. Often these processes create a public sphere of sorts, and take place besides, or alongside, the public institutions. Not in confrontation with public institutions but rather as citizen-led initiatives and demands that will ultimately reach the institutions and political parties representing the people in parliament. How does people *p* actually secede from state *e*? Arguments for change of status *s* will intensify at this stage, stressing the suboptimality of the current status, stressing the merits of an alternative status *s'*, enhancing the democratic legitimacy of the will of a majority. It is crucial, at this stage, to engage with those who are not in favour of change of status, to persuade them of the legitimacy of the majority claim, and to convince them about the seriousness of the guarantees devised to control the expression of the will of the people, and to respect the rights of the minority.[9] The rational justification of the claim could argue, for instance, that change of status is actually the best way to protect human rights, especially those of a minority. The protection of minorities will be a crucial issue, especially if minorities relate to a territory (if they are a majority in a smaller part of the territory). It is also crucial to respond to arguments based on the non-reversibility of a change of status. One can achieve this by negotiating, beforehand, confirmation of the decision to change status. A sort of corroboration. Many decisions affect people who cannot take part in the decision process. Cosmopolitan solutions pending, it is important, at least to address the question of those identifiable minorities locked in larger territorial majorities.

3) The actual decision, the act of deciding on a change of status. Here we find several options or answers depending on whether the act of deciding and voting, i.e. the referendum is or is not the result of a process agreed between people *p* and state *e*:
   a) Suboptimal answer: Unilateral move by people *p* to create new status *s* with contestation by state *e*, disagreeing on the process or on the specific way the referendum or consultation takes place. The result can be a unilateral declaration of independence or the holding of a referendum that is not recognized or the suspension and repression of a referendum. This can turn out to be not only suboptimal but also a worst-case scenario. The calculation probably depends on a tactic to force the reference state *e* into negotiation after the *fait accompli* of a referendum makes it clear that a people *p* is serious about self-determination and, eventually, secession. However, the conditions for holding such a unilateral referendum and the practical normative consequences that the organizers derive from such a move can also backfire from the point of view of democratic legitimacy.

9 I happen to agree, on this point with Carlos Closa, Chapter 4, this volume.

b) Optimal answer: Agreed consensus after negotiation, leading to normative agreement between people *p* and state *e* so that people *p* are no longer forcefully part of state *e* and can opt to change their status, create a new state e', become part of a different, already existing, state *e*'', or not change their status, and freely remain as part of state *e*. As Costanza Margiotta (Chapter 2, this volume) puts it, "The Scottish case can be considered an excellent example of the secession process through the accomplishment of a consensual … referendum." The test of liminal legality between the internal legal system (which did not recognize secession) and the international legal system (which does not yet recognize secession as such) would have certainly been possible in the case of the success of Scottish independence.

4) The negotiation process: What happens next, after the decision made by a clear majority of people *p* to secede from state e? Again, this depends on the question of whether the referendum was agreed or not. If the referendum was not agreed, then state e will contest the validity and legitimacy of the result and people *p* may use it as an argument to bring about a further negotiation, or may insist on the result and pursue a unilateral agenda. This process, again, may or may not manage to gather recognition by the international community of states.

   If the result was agreed, the actual agreement between representatives of people *p* and state *e* will most likely have foreseen the steps to follow in case of a majority decision of people *p* to secede. A process of negotiation will follow towards a new status for people *p*, which can be the new state *e'* or the accession to existing state *e''* and the question of the recognition by the community of states, *e1, e2, … en.*

   The risk of recursiveness, or infinite redress, will apply at this stage. As Costanza Margiotta (in this volume) argues, if one accepts the secession of a territorial group from a State, one must also accept the secession of another territorial group within the seceding State.

The analysis of secession could also examine the claim that a people can be forced to stay in the parent state it wishes to leave.

VI. Conclusion: shifting the burden of proof

This contribution has argued that questions concerning secession become clearer when the burden of proof is shifted and one looks at the issue from the perspective of the correlative position, i.e. at the claims of the reference state *e* to block secession. The suggestion is to enquire on what grounds state *e* can normatively defend its *statu quo s* to oppose the claims of secession made by people *p*. In stronger terms, the question becomes to what extent state *e* can legitimately force people *p* to be part of it, regardless of their political will, and with no real chance to change status. The claim would be that people *p* is under an obligation to belong to state *e*.

A state opposing secession would probably not put the question in such crude terms as forced belonging. Belonging will be presented as a positive historical experience, as participation in a higher objective. Glorification of empire has often used such "civilizing" strategies. But the question remains, "On what terms can state *e* oppose secession and force people *p* to stay in a Union?" This question takes us back to any of the possible answers advanced above, like the single-demos thesis, i.e. the denial of the separate demos character of people *p*, or its most absolute version, i.e. denial of the very existence of a people. Even where a people is acknowledged, the key argument will be the lack of recognition of the very possibility of the claim to the right to secede. The argument here returns to the no-demos thesis: there is a people *p* but it is part of state *e* representing the whole people as the demos *d*, in other words, *p* is a part of demos *d*, and cannot possibly choose to sever itself from *d*. However, once we are already at this stage other arguments are necessary. These arguments will be based on the rule of law: secession is ruled out because the law does not contemplate it, and if the argument from democracy were to be stretched so far as to contemplate the right to decide as a matter of principle, it would be ruled out because no procedure is available. In other words, *statu quo* is presented as an absolute impediment.

Assuming mobilization towards secession is nevertheless powerful, and assuming the majority of people *p* feels political union in state *e* as an imposition, how can state *e* actually stop secession by people *p*, and force union? Assuming the normative objections to secession by state *e* and its claim that a people *p* has to be forcefully tied to this particular state *e* are not being shared by (a considerable majority of) people *p* and that people *p* persists in claiming the right to secede, and mobilizes to achieve a new status *s′* or a new state *e'*, what further arguments can state *e* provide to prevent people *p* from pursuing the secessionist agenda and force them to remain as part of state *e*; in other words, "How does a state preserve the *statu quo*?" The arguments are explored in this contribution. There are two opposing poles:

A. *Engaging in discursive strategies to seek consensus*

- Discussion and negotiation, seeking consensus by showing how interdependence makes it almost impossible to secede, in practice.
- Risk of losing stability: a stable, predictable and ordered society in which to conduct human affairs is necessary, and an orderly framework within which people may make political decisions is essential for democracy, secession moves may imply risks.
- Questioning the legitimacy for a move to secession (lack of sufficient democratic mandate, or need for a specially strong mandate to take such a radical move).
- Need to consider democratic will, not in the abstract or in isolation of the democratic principle, but alongside other constitutional principles like federation, constitutionalism, rule of law and protection of the rights of minorities.

- Especially these difficult equilibria protecting minority language, religion and education rights, which are often the product of delicate historical compromises in a context of national and cultural (religious, socioeconomic) pluralism.

B. *Imposing solutions by way of coercive means or pressure*

- Imposing union through the courts (constitutional courts, exactly the opposite of the restrained stance adopted by the Canadian Supreme Court, in Re Quebec, paras 100–101)
- Criminalizing any act leading to secession,
- Calling in the international consensus to oppose secession, by using allies,
- Threatening with non-recognition, embargo and full isolation.

Coercion and punitive responses may be lawful, a priori, according to a normative system of law where democracy is brought under the rule of law. This lawfulness does not decide the question of legitimacy in other domains of practical reason. Legality is a necessary but not sufficient justification in rational argumentation across normative systems. "Arguments" that defend the use of coercion by the criminal justice system in order to impose political union, are in need of further justification in rational discourse. Necessity, proportionality, alternative responses need to be considered.

Assuming state *e* is actually successful in its strategy to keep people *p* as part of state *e*, what happens after mobilization, when the *statu quo ante* is re-affirmed? Is secession ruled out for the future? How can state *e* prevent people *p* from trying again? Can people *p* be prevented permanently from claiming and pursuing a right to secession and create a new state *e'* or any new status *s*? This would be a sort of estoppel argument. The answers vary depending on whether one adopts strategies under A or under B. The arguments tend to be pragmatic. State *e* may want to stress that it is in the best interest for people *p* not to secede and to preserve its *statu quo*. The interests will refer to international support to state e and lack of support for people p to establish a state, or to a loss of citizenship (nationality of state e) for the citizens of people p. The interests can also relate to the complex negotiation of responsibilities, treaty succession and public debt in the event of secession (the complexity of the withdrawal agreement between the UK and the EU is a powerful reminder). Another powerful version of the best interests argument is the difficulty in getting back into the polity which is being exited (state or international organization). Exiting treaties is hard but entering back again may be even harder, since conditions for entrance can get harsher.

State *e* can also put forward the seemingly paradoxical argument that preserving political union will protect and defend national diversity better. The corollary would be that a smaller state based on people *p* would reduce diversity, become more homogenous and potentially less federal and less plural. A certain degree of pluralism, a sustainable diversity in law and governance would thus be an enriching factor in any polity (Glenn, 2014). This argument is worth considering in practical philosophy. A polity aspiring to self-government but also embracing federalism and cultural pluralism should take it very seriously. Secession in this sense is a form of going-it-alone, exclusive self-rule, whereas federalism implies a commitment to *shared rule*, participating in the joint making of the rules (Elazar, 1991). The counterargument would insist that forcing political union is incompatible with defending diversity and plurality and smacks of cultural and political uniformity. But this counterargument does not secure that the new polity formed by people p would actually aspire to preserve internal political and national diversity, or itself force other internal minorities to belong. Recursive situations are indeed endemic. In our current modernity, the new polity has to factor in the need to diffuse authority, the accommodation of significant claims to recognition, the deep pluralization of societies, and the emergence of some democratization movements at the trans-state level. Here, ideas of federalism and consociations may be appropriate and rule out the search of some form of unity based on the suppression of national diversity for the sake of the polity (Nootens, 2011).

Finally, pragmatic arguments are worth reckoning. These can be positive or negative. Positive arguments will stress the prospects for a better future together, once the claims for secession are abandoned and union is embraced, a new relationship based on trust can make a difference. The strength of such arguments depends on the historical record and on the perceptions of the actors. The negative pragmatic arguments will emphasize the destructive and divisive consequences that would follow from secession, or even from attempts to claim secession. The fear of sanctions, the loss of what (little) you already had by way of self-government, and the criminal responses to all those involved in secession claims are some of the examples of negative consequences in the Catalan case. In the case of Brexit, chaos, internal division, infighting, loss of trust, polarization, economic crisis, political instability and loss of prestige.

Secession is *ultima ratio*. Secession, divorce and schism are often brought into a conceptual family. Divorce provoked a schism in the Catholic Church in the Renaissance, and these processes led to the creation of new states in Europe and elsewhere. They are a reaction against a forced or imposed cohabitation. They are moments of strife, grief and pain. Divisions are always tragic experiences, whether they take place in a marriage, in a family, in the larger family groups, in the circle of friends, in the village or in the community. When living together, forced union, becomes so difficult or so unbearable that a radical step of separation or secession is contemplated, the search for mechanisms that try to bring the parties together may come too late. Procedural means to prevent getting to the point of secession gain special relevance, but mechanisms to deal with the actual process in a civil manner become even more relevant. Identifying the different stages in the process and the responses that constitutional democracy can devise to address them is even more important than trying to enquire into the reasons that led to the breakup of the relationship. Reasons will end up confused with the will. De-dramatizing secession is easier when the parties involved agree to share a new relationship. If the proposal is to share this relationship in a larger federal entity or cooperative group, outwith the forceful binds of hierarchical power, then interesting forms of mutual trust can even develop from the new relationship.

References

Robert Alexy, *A Theory of Legal Argumentation* (OUP, 1989).
Joxerramon Bengoetxea, *Neil MacCormick y la razón práctica institucional* (Grijley, 2015).
Allen Buchanan, 'Theories of Secession' (1997) 1 *Philosophy and Public Affairs* 31.
Pau Bossacoma I Busquets, *Justícia i legalitat de la secessió. Una teoria de l'autodeterminació nacional des de Catalunya* (Institut d'Estudis Autonòmics, 2015).
Carlos Closa, 'Changing EU Internal Borders through Democratic Means' (2017) 39 *Journal of European Integration* 515.
N. Cornago, 'Beyond Self-Determination: Norms Contestation, Constituent Diplomacies and the Co-Production of Sovereignty' (2017) 2 *Global Constitutionalism* 327.
Daniel Elazar, *Exploring Federalism* (University of Alabama Press, 1991).
Ander Errasti, *Nations and Nationalism in a Cosmopolitanized World. Some Lessons from Ulrich Beck's Work*, Phd thesis at the UPF, Barcelona, 2017.
Alain Gagnon, *Minority Nations in the Age of Uncertainty* (University of Toronto Press, 2014).
Patrick Glenn, *Legal Traditions of the World, Sustainable Diversity in Law* (OUP, 2014).
Jürgen Habermas, *Between Facts and Norms* (MIT, 1992).
Jan Klabbers, 'The Right to be Taken Seriously: Self-Determination in International Law' (2006) 1 *Human Rights Quarterly* 186.
Susanna Mancini, 'Secession and Self-Determination' in Michel Rosenfeld and Andras Sajó (eds.), *The Oxford Handbook of Comparative Constitutional Law* (OUP, 2012) 481.
Costanza Margiotta in this volume.
Costanza Margiotta, *L'ultimo diritto. Profili storici e teorici della secessione* (Il Mulino, 2005).
José Martin y Pérez de Nanclares, *Reflexiones jurídicas a propósito de una eventual declaración unilateral de independencia de Cataluña: un escenario político jurídicamente inviable* (Real Instituto Elcano, 2015).
Giuseppe Martinico, 'Courts and Identity Conflicts in Federal and Regional System' (2017) 21 *Revista General de Derecho Público Comparado* 1.
José Antonio Montilla Martos, 'El referéndum de secesión en Europa' (2016) 26 *Revista de derecho constitucional europeo* 24.
Kalypso Nicolaïdis, 'European Demoicracy and Its Crisis' (2013) 51 *Journal of Common Market Studies* 351.
Geneviève Nootens, 'On the Feasibility of Plurinational Democracies: The Problem of the Demos' in Filibi Igor, Noé Cornago and Justin Orlando Frosini (eds.), *Democracy With(out) Nations? Old and New Foundations for Political Communities in a Changing World* (Universidad del Pais Vasco, 2011) 109.
Matt Qvortrup, *Referendums and Ethnic Conflict* (University of Pennsylvania Press, 2014).
Philip G. Roeder, *National Secession, Persuasion and Violence in Independence Campaigns* (Cornell University Press, 2018).

Yaniv Roznai and Silvia Suteu, *Eternal Territory? The Crimean Crisis and Ukraine's Territorial Integrity as an Unamendable Principle* (2015) University of Edinburgh, School of Law, Research Paper Series 15.

Neil Walker, 'Beyond Secession? Law in the Framing of the National Polity' in Stephen Tierney (ed.), *Nationalism and Globalization* (Hart, 2015) 155.

Jan Wouters and Linda Hamid, 'We the People: Self-Determination v. Sovereignty in the Case of De Facto States' (2016) 1 *Inter Gentes* 53.

4 A critique of the theory of democratic secession[1]

Carlos Closa

La democracia va primero, antes que la ley

Joaquim Torra, President of the Generalitat de Catalunya[2]

The scholarly consensus on theories of secession divides them into two broad categories (Buchanan, 2017), although authors label them differently. These labels serve the purpose of emphasizing specific characteristics of each approach. On the one hand, the so-called "*just case theory*" or *remedial right only theory* (Buchanan, 1991) argues that any legitimate right to secession must respond to an egregious injury or harm committed against the seceding entity for which secession is the remedy of last resort (see also Baubock, 2019). Although some have spoken about just case theory as *acceptable secession* under international law (Cassese, 1995:119–120), the most widespread consensus is that international law does not permit or legitimates secession (Tancredi, 2001; Margiotta, 2006). I will not discuss just cause theories since I assume that such egregious violations might justify legitimate secessions.

A particular variant of the just case is the *alienation* argument (Oberman, 2017): since states impose coercion upon individuals, this coercion must have some acceptance base even if this is a shallow one. Consent, then, becomes the basis for determining whether a "just case" exists: if the sectors of the population feel alienated, this alienation creates a justification for seeking secession. Using similar assumptions to the one of the alienation argument, Patten (2014) has argued that the *failure of recognition* (i.e. the failure of a polity to properly recognize the rights of specific groups) creates a requirement that renders acceptable democratic secession. Given that the appeal to failure to recognition speaks of some wrong being committed against the seceding unit, I believe that versions of the alienation argument are, in reality, soft versions of the just cause theory. Because of this, its discussion and criticism belong to a different domain (theory of justice), although it constructs a fairly unilateral right: the

1 I am in debt to Costanza Margiotta and Giuseppe Martinico for their comments to earlier version of this chapter. Responsibility remains exclusively mine.

2 13 February 2019. Declarations to Onda Cero. Available at https://www.ondacero.es/programas/mas-de-uno/videos/quim-torra-democracia-primero-antes-que-ley_201902135c63dc710cf2cb42a35882af.html

existence of a failure of recognition is not an objective process but it depends on the subjective perceptions of those demanding recognition. Consider, for instance, the cases of Catalonia and Scotland and take the level of devolved powers as a measure of recognition and the level of political conflict as an indicator of failure of recognition. While in objective terms, the level of devolved powers to Catalonia is vastly superior to those devolved to Scotland, the perception of a failure of recognition is fairly superior in Catalonia than in Scotland. Bengoetxea (Chapter 3, this volume) argues a variant of this position: on what terms can you oppose secession and force a people to stay in a union? In other words: on what terms is *status quo* an absolute impediment? (the same line of criticism against *status quo* prevalence in Walker, 2017).

My criticism to these theories is straightforward: they have valid arguments. Non-oppression, non-alienation etc. are legitimate requirements within democratic states. However, in purity, alienation theory speaks more to the notion of legitimate domination and it only becomes a secession theory *when and if* connected to a territory and/or people. But the theory does not theorize the subject entitled to secession. Either territory and/or a people could be the subject of secession but both are factors exogenous to the theory. Given the absence of this theorizing, the non-oppression theory becomes in reality a theory on legitimate resistance to power. Constructed in this way, the alienation argument connects with the classical "right of resistance" that Francisco de Victoria upgraded to the level of natural right from its traditional Middle Ages foundation. Feeling of alienation may explain the bandwagon effect in Catalan secessionist movement with the adhesion of collectives gathered around very specifically defined identities that are unconnected to the territorial dimension (feminists, environmentalist, etc.) but share their perception of state authority as unacceptable or illegitimate if exercised in specific ways (e.g. denying an independence referendum).

The alternative "*choice theory*" or "*primary right theory*" (Buchanan), "*plebiscitary theory*" (Philpott, 1995; Wellman, 1995; Beran, 1998; Nielsen, 1998, Patten, 2014) constructs its justification by appealing to a majoritarian notion of decision-making perceived as the essential democratic procedure. In some versions of the theory, the procedure to construct such a majority and attain secession (be this referendums or mass mobilization) takes the central role. For the sake of expediency, I would call this theory of *democratic secession*. This term emphasizes that secession is the substantive object in the theory although reasoning switches to the procedure.

In a nutshell, this theory argues that groups within polities are entitled to a general right of secession, as long as it is grounded in the will of the seceding majority. The "choice" argument argues, in essence, that secession is legitimate if it results from a democratic process. In this conception, there is no need of a "teleological justification" and the procedure (democratic means, normally associated with a referendum and a given majority) legitimates secession. The will of a majority suffices for the constitution of a new independent sovereign subject and the most characteristic procedure for the identification of such a majority is holding a referendum. International law scholarship has conclusively established that "*there is no unilateral right to secede based merely on a majority vote of the population of a given sub-division or territory*" (Crawford, 2006: 417). Baubock (2019) has vigorously argued a general democratic presumption against secession on grounds of territorial stability, democratic diversity and mutual recognition. Whilst these criticism oppose either legal or prudential arguments, my own criticism targets the fundamentals of the theory: conflating democracy and majoritarianism, the weakness of its theoretical construction of the demos and the associated lack of response to the issues of symmetric divisibility, externalities and reversibility. Modern attempts of secession (in Quebec, Scotland and Catalonia) appeal systematically to democracy as a self-legitimizing mantra: by labelling "democratic" the process, this and its outcome become automatically legitimate without further need of justification.

1. An unlimited notion of democracy

The first criticism refers to the unbound and unlimited conception of democracy within this theoretical construction. Since theory of democratic secession relies mainly on the procedure (democratic majorities) at the same time that moves to a secondary position the need for justification (inherent, instead, in the "just case" theory), it basically relies on the assumption that democratic means justify *any* end whatsoever: for secessionists, the end that democracy may justify is secession. This approach aligns itself with the notion of aggregative democracy that does not require people to justify their preferences, but only seeks to combine them (Gutmann and Thompson, 2004: 13).

By doing this, this conception, however, releases democracy (but, by extension any form of politics) from any constraint: since the application of democratic procedure spares the need for justification, we could conclude, in line with the assumption of such a theory, that any end may be legitimate if achieved by democratic means or, in other words, if a majority supports them. This sounds plainly absurd if we were to discuss such ends as suppressing female voting rights, introducing the death penalty or legalizing slavery within European constitutional structures. Many would argue that secession is not the same as these horrendous ends. Yes, but why is it then different? The counterargument would be to say that secession may have a different moral value. But the appeal to this different moral value and acceptability of different democratic ends reveals precisely that secession must contain some kind of "just cause" theory since an end does not become morally acceptable just because it can be democratically attained. Behind majoritarianism as the foundation of secession there may be some moral foundation; for instance, the alienation argument. But for the theory of democratic secession, means in themselves provide enough moral foundation. Rather, recourse to majoritarianism (i.e. voting) becomes the proof of the moral wrongdoing that justifies secession. Justification for and means to secession melt without solution of continuity.

Democracy becomes unlimited when it transforms itself into "extreme majoritarianism" (Wind, 2019), in which the set of values and constitutional principles associated with the contemporary notion of democracy, such as the rule of law and respect for fundamental rights become subordinated to the will of undefined majorities (see Martinico and Beaulac, Chapters 6 and 7, respectively, this volume). The absurdity of the extreme majoritarianism thesis emerges clearly in the following example: the supreme council of Mafia can decide by majority but this does not turn their decisions into democratic decisions. Majority then must emanate from rule of law and respect from fundamental rights and this obligation unfolds in the associated constitutional principles of legality and due process in the production of norms, at a minimum. In particular, the principles of legality and respect for the due process in the production of norms is unavoidable since majority is a legal construct (Steinbeis, 2017): nature does not provide "majorities" and, in fact, legal rules define what (a) majority is. Legal rules define who counts and in which ways. They also establish legal safeguards of liberty, equality and diversity of opinion. More importantly, those legal rules determine what the majority will be able to do, which necessarily implies that the majority gets to tell what it is not allowed to do. Majority (and democracy) need constitutional law. By relegating rule of law (legality), "democracy as majoritarianism" breaks the axiological balance that characterizes democratic constitutionalism: the synthesis between the rule of majority and the rule of law (Murphy, 2007). This axiological balance results difficult to fix and it is often challenged. Thus, some have perceived that, in the Spanish model of liberal democracy, the liberal component (i.e. rule of law) weights more than the democratic element producing a "legalistic" interpretation of democracy: the state opposes the law to (legitimate) political vindications (Sánchez Cuenca; 2018: 129). Certainly, lack of political engagement and dialogue with political vindications may be criticized but, by no means, this is an antidemocratic position if backed by a majority and formulated within the limits of the law. Because of this, refusal to engage with a majoritarian claim for secession is a legitimate position even if we could disagree on its lack of wisdom.

Implicitly acknowledging the necessity of framing majority within legality, some pro-secessionist author has appealed instead to "revolutionary legality" *in a revolutionary situation like* (the Catalan one), *there is no way of knowing which of the competing legalities is "the law in force"* (Krisch, 2017). In short, the decision to go revolutionary suffices to create a new legality that becomes legitimate *if and when secession triumphs.* This *Schmittian* decisionist position results are only palatable because the author turns into a seemingly variant of the "just cause": lack of adequate recognition and negotiation from Spanish government did not offer any alternative to the Catalan people (sic): In fact, extreme majoritarianism ends turning towards the assertion of the will of the people as the final legitimizing aspect for majorities. And this begs the question: Who is the seceding people for theory of democratic secession? (see also Margiotta, Chapter 2, this volume).

2. The boundaries of the seceding demos

The second criticism to "choice theory" or "theory of democratic secession" refers to their incapacity or lack of concern[3] to resolve a central problem of the-

3 Some theorist (Innerarity and Errasti, Chapter 5, this volume) explicitly propose to move away from the definition of the subject to focus instead on the "what" and the "why" of the decision. However, they come, in fact, to an explicit identification of the so-called "national political fact" under which it is difficult to see anything different to traditional nations.

ories of democratic self-determination: the delimitation of the demos (Song, 2012). To be fair, this is not exclusively a problem of secession theories but rather, a central problem for democratic theory; as Whelan (1983:13) summarized "*any democratic theory must face the logically prior and in some ways more fundamental question of the appropriate constitution of the people or unit within which democratic governance is to be practiced.*"

The contours of the polity, society or group of individuals called to decide whether they want to become sovereign depends on a *previous* aggregation of these collectivities. Scholars have tackled the definition of the group entitled to secession through two alternative theoretical avenues (Buchanan, 2017): the **ascriptive group** and the **associative group**. *Adscriptive characteristics exist independently of any actual political association that the members of the group may have forged. Certain nonpolitical characteristics of the groups provide the justification for the group's right to an independent political association.* In a nutshell, this group usually responds to some kind of ethnic, linguistic or religious delimitation established on a given territory and, precisely, those characteristics ground a valid and legitimate claim on that territory (Margalit and Raz, 1990). This thesis roots its normativity in communitarianism and it has been contested in practical terms. For instance, Judge Yusuf, in an obiter dicta in the Kosovo Case, opined that "a radically or ethnically distinct group within a state, even if it qualifies as a people for the purposes of self-determination, does not have the right to unilateral self-determination simply because it wishes to create its own separate state."[4] A clear weakness of the ascriptive group theory relates to the tight implicit association between a group (and its characteristics) and a given territory. This connection is merely assumed and places in a disadvantageous situation claims from adscriptive groups without connection with a territory, such as the Roma.

The aggregation of individuals to become a seceding entity does not result from the aggregation of separate individual decisions to make part of such a community. Paradoxically, proponents of democratic secession attack the assumption that the constituent power of the original polity (i.e. the one from which secession is sought) is pre-constituted (i.e. does not result from the aggregation of democratic decisions) and, hence, closed to normative criticism. In this way, adscriptive group theory falls into some of the same weaknesses that it criticizes: normativity on the value of the community depends on some kind of preliminary characteristic that antecedes (and is even condition of) democratic decisions. Given that the boundaries of the seceding communities result from historical accident rather than voluntarily and freely expressed choice (very much in the same way as the community of the original state), the claim for having a right to

4 Re Kosovo (2010), ICJ Advisory Opinion, International Law Materials, 1410. As Margiotta explains in Chapter 2, the automatic identification between secession and self-determination is wrong since the latter is firmly connected to de-colonization and *unlike secession, the object of self-determination is not to draw new borders, but to choose by whom to be governed and not to have an alien government in a given territory.*

independent existence is not morally superior than the one of the original state community from which secession is exercised.

An attempt to vary on the adscriptive theory side is the theorization on the basis of the so-called "national facts." In their search for conceptual innovation to reflect increased social complexity, Innerarity and Errasti (Chapter 5, this volume) propose an alternative conceptualization of the demos around the notion of "social fact": an intersubjective practice that, while not being material, acquires factual category. Thus, intersubjective practice provides the basis for any kind of aggregation. Then, following Cheneval and Nicolaidïs (2017), they take a step further to construct the notion of *political* fact: i.e. an intersubjective practice that meets three requirements. First, those that constitute the social fact recognize and value it as such. In other words, they self-reflectively recognize themselves in their intersubjective practices. Second, a defined set of rules and laws will rule the social facts. Nothing is said on the origin and nature of these rules and, more importantly, their legitimacy and fit with eventually competing rules form other alternative/competing/overlapping social facts. Third, those belonging to the social fact show the will of projecting the social fact towards the future, i.e. of ensuring its progress. Nothing is said on the procedures to register this will which resembles the everyday plebiscite on the nation of Renan. Not surprisingly Innerarity and Errasti (Chapter 5, this volume) conclude that these criteria conflate "national political facts" with nation-states. But they do not reveal at any point in their argument the procedure by which political social facts turn "national" facts. They, instead, indicate two additional requirements to ensure that a political fact should be considered a national political fact beyond nation-states. The first is *the existence of an institutional framework within a territory that could potentially act autonomously*. The second is that *the individuals within that territory (for various reasons that vary from place to place and through time) identify and value a certain bond with those institutions, i.e. they value their citizenship in those institutions)*. They conclude that, therefore, the definition of national social facts is not necessarily restricted to nation-states. The origin of institutions, the bond with the territory and the autonomous activity are all exogenous to the theorization, are "given" and we may assume that given by history.

To contest this reliance on the "national" element, alternative **associative group** theories (Beran, 1998; Wellman, 1995) focus on the voluntary political choice of the members of a group as expressed by the majority of them to form their own independent political unit. Within this approach, the basic premise holds that any group, no matter how heterogeneous, can qualify for the right to secede. The theory does not set any requirements, nor even the minimum one of having any common connection, historical or imagined, to the territory that they they vindicate as their own state. The only relevant criterion is that the members of the group voluntarily choose to associate together in an independent political unit of their own. Associative group theories, then, assert that there is a right to secede that is, or is an instance of, the right of political association.

Lacking a foundational element that defines group membership, the challenge for associative group theories is how the group is formed/defined. Who belongs to the group and how are the boundaries of the group established? Given the voluntary character associated to the group, associative theory does not provide a response to this. Rather, it relies vicariously on territory on which some form of connection/control already exist. I think that this creates two objections to associative group theories. First, implicit reliance on territory morphs subtly pure associative character into "historical contingency" and, finally, into an adscriptive theory. Would we accept, for instance, that a group of Germans in Mallorca could "secede" a piece of the island? Rather than examining the validity of their associative claim, the absurdity of the claim derives from their lack of (historical) connection and control of the territory of the island. Lack of territorial control explains why claims to secession from nomadic people, such as the Roma, for instance, or a hypothetic claim to secede in a given territory by a group of people connected via cyberspace do not make part of the cases in which such associative right is built. The associative right is, in reality, *the associative right of groups historically established in a territory on which they have a claim of control.* Obviously, this is an inherently unfair theory since groups lacking a connection with a territory will not be entitled to secession. In conclusion, associative theories rely vicariously on adscriptive theory.

Secondly, the associative group delimitation of the demos does not resolve what could be labelled as "symmetry of majority claims" problem. In purely democratic terms (i.e. majority of a group), there is not *prima facie* criterium to assert that the democratic right to secede of a group must prevail over the equally democratic rejection of this right expressed by a majority of the wider demos which comprises the seceding one. In other words, taking Catalonia as an example, the majority in Spanish institutions is, at least, as legitimate as the one that may exist in Catalonia. So, how could one association prevail over alternative ones (which could even overlap?). The only logical mechanism is to establish some kind of exclusionary association: being associated to a group excludes *ipso facto* being associated to an alternative one. But even in this case, there is no clear logical argument why the will expressed by an associative majority logically prevails.

3. The symmetric divisibility issue (the anti-*status-quo* argument)

The lack of a conclusive solution to the delimitation problem raises a complementary issue: the question of "symmetric divisibility" or "recursive character" of secession (Wellmann, 1995; Margiotta, this volume). If an existing democratic state accepts that it may divide itself as a result of democratic processes of self-determination, the seceding territory must logically and consequently (i.e. symmetrically) accept the same principle. This means that groups within the seceding territory must also be able to secede. Proponents of the theory of democratic secession make a central normative point of the critique to the preference and prevalence of the *status quo* (i.e. why should existing communities enjoy the presumption that they are the most legitimate ones to claim and exercise sovereignty). Because of this, consistency and consequentiality require that the theory of democratic secession reproduces a similar requirement on the divisibility of the seceding group. In practical terms, this result is unavoidable since there will always be "minorities within minorities" even within a seceding minority. Thus, unless 100% of the voters back the decision to secede, the outcome (i.e. independence) will be imposed on a given percentage of the voters (a minority).

Now, the claim made in favour of secession is that a structural minority within a state will always be a structural minority and, hence, they must have the right to self-determine. But, on the other hand, the decision to secede is imposed to 100% of the population. Those voting in favour of not seceding may feel alienated from the new state. More importantly, that minority does not see their right to secede from the seceding territory recognized unless they control some part of the seceding territory (see above the discussion on the boundaries of the seceding demos).

Secessionism proponents have addressed this logical objection by recourse to the notion of "economic viability": whilst the right to secede can be recognized to majorities that decide so, it can only be acknowledged if economic survival of the seceding group is viable (López, 2015). The (prudential) origin of this limitation within democratic theory is nevertheless nowhere established, though. Some additional conclusions can be logically deduced from the respective positions on the boundaries of the seceding group. For adscriptive group theorists, divisibility of the seceding group would be possible on the basis of some symmetrical criteria to the ones that determined the boundaries of the seceding group. This means identifying some pre-existing characteristic of the group-within-the-group. For instance, the Catalan independentist process has reflected this approach by recognizing that the Valley of Aran, a small area in the Pirynees, could opt for secession from a hypothetically independent Catalonia because of the recognition of its specific linguistic identity.

For the ascriptive group theory, symmetric divisibility raises a large challenge since, in logical terms, any given aggregation of citizens expressing by majority a wish not to adhere to a seceding territory should have their wish respected. In Chapter 5, for instance, Innerarity and Errasti use the adscriptive theory to ground their justification of secession. Thus, following Isaiah Berlin (1999: 84), they argue that

> insofar citizens within a democratic regime raise those claims (i.e. about secession), we have the duty of considering them the same way as we consider any other claims: neither accepting them nor rejecting them a priori. Refusing a priori to even consider them will violate these citizens' political equality, which is, by definition, incompatible with a democratic regime.

While these authors have written this thinking on the justification of secession from the original group, this justification logically applies within the seceding group after secession. The effect of this logical foundation is to keep the group permanently opened for definition and redefinition.

4. The isolated demos assumption: the all affected principle and externalities

The delimitation of the seceding group leaves an additional question pertaining to whether the decision to secede can be restricted to those seeking secession or, else, the subject of such a determination should be different. Restriction to the seceding group requires first, assuming that those groups (i.e. communities) are perfectly separated with no overlap among them. If communities intersect, the logic of separating groups for decision-making does not seem self-evident. In any case, one could imagine this perfect separation. But none could deny that these kinds of decisions affect others beyond the group taking them. In a situation of high interdependence, effects of decision affect others. To respond to this practical challenge that raises normative questions on the boundaries of the demos, some modern theorization has advanced the all-affected notion of the demos: anyone whose interests are affected by a decision should participate in taking the decision (Whelan, 1983; Warren, 2002: 678; Held, 2005; Goodin, 2007; Näsström, 2011). As Robert Dahl (1970:64) eloquently argued, the Principle of Affected Interests is very likely the best general principle of inclusion that you are likely to find. The all-affected principle nuances the normative requirements for democracy that holds that accountability requires the justification of democratic decisions *just* in front of the citizens bound by the law. In purity, the justification of democratic decisions should expand to all affected by them.

International affairs is the area that more clearly illustrates the normative dilemmas associated with restrictive configurations of the demos: state decisions in policies such as war, trade, immigration or economic development clearly affect people in other countries. In fact, decisions apply often more constrainingly on "*the citizens of foreign countries than on the citizens who are legally bound by them*" (Gutmann and Thompson, 2004: 37). In such cases, it is fair to assume that democratic policies should be accountable to people whose fates are significantly influenced by them. Secession fits easily within the category of events that even if democratically decided, may affect third parties beyond the one taking the decisions.

In more radical terms, democratic decisions may have the explicit and declared intention to influence third parties. Discussions on secession within the EU around the cases of Scotland and Catalonia illustrate perfectly how democratic decisions may surreptitiously acquire the property of automatically translating the effects (and costs) of decisions on third parties. In both cases, almost all political forces favouring secession did so on the assumption that gaining independence goes hand in hand with retaining or acquiring EU membership (Closa, 2016 and 2017). What those arguments assumed is that being democratic, external (affected) actors could not deny the effects of the decisions that the seceding group sought to create for third parties. In other words, since secession was a majoritarian decision, instant membership of the EU was an obvious consequence. Implicitly, these arguments also assumed that member states ought to recognize the statehood of the new independent territory (since it resulted from democratic decisions). The prevalent interpretation has consolidated the opinion that precisely because the EU and its member states are affected, secessionist territories could not gain EU membership as a by-product of democratic decisions on independence.

5. The democratic reversibility paradox

The central assumption behind the association of majority rule and democracy is that majorities and minorities are not permanent in democracy and both will define and redefine themselves once and again through electoral processes. And when a minority becomes structural, constitutional protection must be afforded. The constitutional protection of minorities is behind recognition theories, as presented above. Leaving aside structural minorities' constitutional protection, the central assumption of democratic majoritarianist secession translates into a very intuitive effect: whatever a majority decides, a similar majority can reverse it. Reversibility, thus, is tightly associated with democracy.

Within this framework, the theory of democratic secession faces a paradox: while a majority may take the decision to secede, a similar majority may not retract the original decision. The consent of the original group will be required to revert secession and, needless to say, the seceding group cannot determine the will of the original one. The democratic reversibility paradox goes beyond secession itself to affect any democratic decision: in fact, decisions (any decision) transform reality in some way. Hence, full reversibility to an identical situation to the original one may look as a futile pretension. Because of this, non-reversibility may lead to the absurd situation that a group may decide to avoid taking decisions because of the impossibility of reverting to the original situation.

While the theory of democratic secession should not be burdened with more stringent criteria than a general theory of democracy, non-reversibility results in a much more evident and acute problem in case of secession. This inspires two considerations to factor into the theory of democratic secession. First, slim majorities (i.e. 50% + 1 of votes) result in a hugely unfair decisional principle. Second, restricting the democratic decision to secede to the departing group automatically closes the gate to any *fair* reversibility claim (in theoretical terms): excluding the original group from the decision to secede transforms reversibility in an equally eventual unilateral future decision of the original group: there is not founding contract between both groups. This may transform secession into a irreversible process.

6. Conclusion

The theory of democratic secession, on its own, does not provide a solid irrefutable justification for secession. Majoritarianism alone cannot justify secession and the delimitation of the demos (the group asserting its right to secede) raises theoretical difficulties: namely either it appeals to the nation or, in associative theories, it opens up to additional obstacles. These are the following: the issue of symmetric divisibility (whether groups within the seceding group can also secede), the externalities issue (questioning a unilateral decision to secede) and the problem of symmetric reversibility (the possibility to return to the current status quo). Because of these limitations, the legitimizing discourse of secessionism quite often conflates the democratic argument with some combination of an essentialist (i.e. adscriptive notion of the group/community) and the addition of some "just cause" argument.

The normative obstacles for a theory of democratic secession purely and simply imply that secession cannot be constructed as a "right." But this is not the same as to say that there is no possible democratic secession. Rather, within democracy, this requires, first, a strict adherence to the framing principles of constitutional democracy (rule of law and respect for fundamental rights). Second, this also requires seeking agreements that go beyond the mere assertion of a majority may lead the path to an agreed process of secession. In the absence of such an environment, secession may emerge out of facticity (e.g. support of a huge proportion as, for instance, 99% of the population). Facticity can be transformed into normativity as an *ex pots fact* exercise, of course. But none could claim it as a legitimate democratic process.

References

Bauböck, Rainer (2019) 'A Multilevel Theory of Democratic Secession', *Ethnopolitics* 18, 227–246. doi: 10.1080/17449057.2019.1585088.

Beran, Harry (1998) 'A Democratic Theory of Political Self-Determination for a New World Order', in Percy Lehning (ed.), *Theories of Secession* (London, UK: Routledge), pp. 32–59.

Berlin, Isaiah (1999) *Concepts and Categories*, edited by Henry Hardy (Princeton, NJ: Princeton University Press).

Buchanan, Allen (1991) *Secession: The Morality of Political Divorce From Fort Sumter to Lithuania and Quebec* (Boulder, CO: Westview Press).

Buchanan, Allen (2017 [2003]) 'Secession', Stanford Encyclopedia of Philosophy, https://plato.stanford.edu/entries/secession/

Cassese, Antonio (1995) *Self-Determination of the Peoples: A Legal Reappraisal* (Cambridge, MA: Cambridge University Press).

Cheneval, Francis and Kalypso Nicolaïdis (2017) 'The Social Construction of Demoicracy in the European Union', *European Journal of Political Theory* 16, 2.

Closa, Carlos (2016) 'Secession from a Member State and EU Membership: The View from the Union', *European Constitutional Law Review* 12(02), 240–264. doi: 10.1017/S1574019616000146.

Closa, Carlos (2017) 'Changing EU Internal Borders through Democratic Means', *Journal of European Integration* 39, 515–528. doi: 10.1080/07036337.2017.1327525.

Crawford, James (2006) *The Creation of States in International Law*, 2nd edition (Cambridge, MA: Cambridge University Press).

Dahl, Robert A. ([1970] 1990) *After the Revolution?: Authority in a Good Society* (New Haven, CT: Yale University Press).

Goodin, R.E. (2007) 'Enfranchising All Affected Interests, and Its Alternatives', *Philosophy & Public Affairs* 35(1), 40–68.

Gutmann, Amy and Dennis Thompson (2004) *Why Deliberative Democracy?* (Princeton, NJ: Princeton University Press).

Held, D. (2005) 'Democratic Accountability and Political Effectiveness from a Cosmopolitan Perspective', in D. Held and M. Koenig-Archibugi (eds.), *Global Governance and Public Accountability* (Boston, MA: Blackwell Publishing), pp. 240–267.

International Court of Justice (2010) Accordance with international law of the unilateral Declaration of Independence in Respect of Kosovo Advisory Opinion of 22 July 2010, https://www.icj-cij.org/files/case-related/141/141-20100722-ADV-01-00-EN.pdf

Krisch, Nico (2017) The Spanish Constitutional Crisis: Law, Legitimacy and Popular Sovereignty in Question, 7 October 2017, https://verfassungsblog.de/the-spanish-constitutional-crisis-law-legitimacy-and-popular-sovereignty-in-question/

López, Jaume (2015) 'El derecho a decider', in B. Mercè, C. Mercè, L. H. Jaume, G. B. Alfonso and J. M. Vilajosana (eds.), *El derecho a decidir. Teoría y práctica de un nuevo derecho* (Barcelona: Ed. Atelier).

Margalit, Avishai and Joseph Raz (1990) 'National Self-Determination', *Journal of Philosophy* 87, 445–447.

Margiotta, Costanza (2006) *L'ultimo diritto. Profili storici e teorici della secessione* (Milano, Italy: Il Mulino).

Murphy, Walter F. (2007) *Constitutional Democracy: Creating and Maintaining a Just Political Order* (Baltimore, MD: Johns Hopkins University Press).

Näsström, S. (2011) 'The Challenge of the All-Affected Principle', *Political Studies* 59(1), 116–134.

Nielsen, K. (1998) 'Liberal Nationalism and Secession', in M. Moore (ed.), *Self-Determination and Secession* (Oxford, UK: Oxford University Press), pp. 103–133.

Oberman, Kieran (2017) 'Does Catalonia have a Right to Secede?', *Open Democracy*, 10 October 2017, https://www.opendemocracy.net/can-europe-make-it/kieran-oberman/does-catalonia-have-right-to-secede

Patten, A. (2014) *Equal Recognition: The Moral Foundations of Minority Rights* (Princeton, NJ: Princeton University Press).

Philpott, Daniel (1995) 'In Defense of Self-Determination', *Ethics* 105, 352–385.

Sánchez-Cuenca, Ignacio (2018) *La confusión nacional. La democracia española ante la crisis catalana* (Libros de la Catarata).

Song, S. (2012) 'The Boundary Problem in Democratic Theory: Why the Demos Should be Bounded by the State', *International Theory* 4(1), 39–68.

Steinbeis, Maximilian (2017) 'Majority Is a Legal Concept', *Verfassungsblog*, http://verfassungblog.de/majority-is-a-legal-concept

Tancredi, Antonello (2001) *La Secessione nel Diritto Internazionale* (Milano, Italy: CEDAM).

Walker, N. (2017) 'Internal Enlargement in the European Union: Beyond Legalism and Political Expediency', in C. Closa (ed.), *Secession from a Member State and Withdrawal from the European Union. Troubled Membership* (Cambridge, MA: Cambridge University Press), pp. 32–47.

Warren, Mark E. (2002) 'What Can Democratic Participation Mean Today?', *Political Theory* 30(5), 677–701.

Wellman, Christopher (1995) 'A Defense of Secession and Political Self-Determination', *Philosophy & Public Affairs* 24, 142–171.

Whelan, Frederick G. (1983) 'Democratic Theory and the Boundary Problem', in J. R. Pennock and J. W. Chapman (eds.), *Liberal Democracy* (New York: New York University Press), pp. 13–47.

Wind, Marlene (2019) *The Tribalization of Europe – A Defense of Our Liberal Values* (Madrid, Spain: Espasa Calpe).

5 Decide on what? Addressing secessionist claims in an interdependent Europe[1]

Daniel Innerarity and Ander Errasti

Introduction: "Right to decide" claims beyond clichés

On 18 February 2006, a demonstration wound its way through Barcelona with one main slogan: "Som una nació i tenim el dret de decidir" ("We are a nation and we have the right to decide"). Since then, a significant part of the debate on Catalan secession has focused greatly on this idea of the "right to decide." Contrary to what the title might suggest, this chapter does not aim to address the recent but extensive literature on this normative framework.[2] Neither does it present an analysis of the independence movement in Catalonia and the legal and political conflict it has generated. Instead, it presents some reflections that focus on the way these kinds of conflicts should be politically addressed in a context of interdependencies such as the one in Europe. Therefore, while this reflection is influenced by cases linked to sub-state nationalist claims, including the recent events in Catalonia, it does not apply specifically to any one set of facts.

Even though the aim of this chapter is not to address the right to decide theory, it does engage to a certain extent with this way of addressing secessionist claims. Nevertheless, rather than focusing on the traditional ways of dealing with sub-state independence movements, this reflection corresponds to the so-called democratic theories of secession and the latest evolutions connected with nationalism.[3] Alternative approaches, the ones centred on clarifying the subject and scope of the right to self-determination, fail to adequately address secessionist conflicts in democratic contexts. This applies both to the primary right and to remedial approaches towards self-determination.[4] First, because both require identifying the subject of that right, which usually leads to a sort of unending

1 We want to thank Sandra Kingery for her excellent language review of the chapter. Our thanks are also due to the colleagues at the University of Edinburgh's Centre on Constitutional Change for their comments to an early outline of this chapter.

2 Tejada (2015), Lopez (2018), González et al. (2015).

3 Kymlicka (1995), Patten (2002, 2016), Seymour (2010), Weinstock (2001).

4 We are not claiming that primary and remedial right approaches do not provide a valuable framework (particularly in terms of discussing the positive right to self-determination), but that they do provide clues to answering these claims politically in consolidated democracies (as opposed to post-colonial or post-authoritarian contexts).

ontological debate regarding what can be considered a nation beyond the current status quo. Second, because these views encourage a focus on the cases that fall within their clauses, thereby deviating the debate from the underlying political elements that generate the claim in the first place.

This chapter holds that we should analyze and address that which is of value in the claims that fall under the umbrella of the right to decide theory regardless of the conception we may have about the subject raising the claim. That is why we focus on claims linked to the "will to decide" rather than the right to decide. The reason these claims should be analyzed and addressed is, therefore, the equal citizenship status[5] of those who are raising the claims. That is, insofar as those claims are raised by citizens within a democratic regime, we have the duty of considering them the same way as we consider any other claims: neither accepting them nor rejecting them a priori. Refusing a priori to even consider them will violate these citizens' political equality, which is, by definition, incompatible with a democratic regime.[6] However, this leads to a very challenging paradox: the normative need[7] of granting the political equality of those who claim the will to decide opens the door to potentially breaking the political equality of citizens within the state if there is majority support for secession. Little wonder, if those claims lead to the breakup of the demos, political equality will no longer apply between the members of the remaining and seceding *demoi*. In spite of this, we take as our point of departure the idea that there is no other option to deal with this paradox.

Why are there no other options? First, because any other course of action would de facto violate these citizens' political equality. That is, if we consider these citizens' claims, there is the possibility that the result might be the breakup of the demos and the subsequent distortion of political equality. On the other hand, if we simply ignore their claims, that violation will not be a potential risk but a fact. Second, because any other response may make the situation politically unsustainable. When a democratic regime will not even consider the claims of its citizens, those citizens may end up believing that the regime is not open to their interests or preferences. Subsequently, they could support political options that not only make those claims but also amend the whole system. The same applies when it comes to inequalities. As José Fernández-Albertos has argued,[8] the rise of inequalities has generated a political schema where there are no incentives to address the needs and preferences of certain social groups. As a result, those social groups tend to vote for political options that go against the system, even when they know that those options will not necessarily address their needs and interests. The will to decide claims vary among different contexts and, for that reason, they do not have a univocal reading. However, this reaction seems, at the very least, a plausible consequence if political regimes choose to ignore a priori any will to decide claims.

5 There are many definitions, but we may say that it broadly refers to equal participation in the process of choosing the principles and rules by which they would be governed.

6 Berlin (1999).

7 Nässtróm (2013).

8 Fernández-Albertos (2018).

This is related to another normative debate that, while critical when analyzing these claims, cannot be addressed here due to space constraints: the interaction between principles of justice and the potential depiction of sub-state nationalist claims, in general, and secessionism, in particular. In this regard, we may state three elements that often condition reactions vis-à-vis secessionist claims that we judge unfair.[9] The first refers to the term nationalism. While the literature on nationalism studies has shown widely that there are multiple types of nationalism,[10] normative approaches to secessionist claims coming from other disciplines (moral philosophy, legal theory, political science or sociology) tend to use the term nationalist as if it were unambiguous. This understanding makes it difficult to provide a balanced analysis. For that reason, we will introduce two other related concerns that we consider key premises for a balanced analysis. First, that not all nationalist expressions are necessarily essentialist and exclusive. While many expressions of nationalism have, indeed, generated homogenizing trends, others have been based on liberal and cosmopolitan principles of openness, mutual recognition and inclusiveness[11]. Moreover, in most cases, both dimensions coexist within the same nationalist expression (be it majoritarian or minoritarian). Applying essentialist patterns to all expressions of nationalism would be as analytically misguided as rejecting socialism as such based on the way socialism was fostered in a given historical context. This is related to the second concern, which posits the allegedly selfish character of nationalism, especially when it comes to distributive justice. While this judgment leads to a more complex normative debate, it is fair to say that there are reasonable arguments to claim both that it is compatible with a cosmopolitan duty of justice[12] and that it is not.[13]

To summarize, we take as a starting point the notion that there are democratic reasons why claims that fall within the right to decide umbrella must not be ignored, even if they could be connected to nationalist expressions. This is far from implying, as we will explain, that democratic regimes must favour secessionist movements: most of the time the will to decide framework shows claims that do not necessarily require focusing the debate on the possibility of constituting independent states. This is even clearer within the context of shared sovereignties (as imperfect as they may be) and interdependencies such as the European Union. While we will not provide definitive answers, we will to a certain extent try to provide a different perspective that may help encourage the consideration of will to decide claims, even if those claims originally arise as part of an independence movement. We will also offer alternative tools to address these claims beyond the pure-conflict dynamics that characterize these cases nowadays. That is, these claims must be addressed from the point where a party's claims are not

9 Weiler (2017).

10 Breully (1993), Seymour (1999), Keating (2001), Gans (2003), Gagnon (2014), Tamir (2019).

11 Parekh (2000), Guibernau (2013), Uberoi (2015), Kymlicka (2015), Torbisco (2016).

12 Gagnon (2009), Sanjaume (2016), Boucher et al. (2015), Van Parijs (2015).

13 Caney (2005).

considered a necessary loss for the other party (or parties) in conflict, excluding a priori any win–win solution. Alternatively, we propose a perspective change that may lead to rather cooperative scenarios. To that aim, we will first introduce the renewal of a conceptual framework.

1. A conceptual renewal for a complex democracy in Europe

When the description of a conflict is introduced and the necessary result is a dichotomic or polarized frame where there is no field for nuanced or intermediate positions, we should be aware that the diagnosis is most certainly not correct. If, in addition, it happens that, in that allegedly objective description of a conflict, one party is entirely right while the other party (or parties) are either unintelligent, then it is the one making the analysis who should reflect on his or her bias. Conflicts, in this sense, tend to become unsolvable when they fall into the hands of those who oversimplify them, reducing political problems to a single dimension: legality, public order, procedural justice, stability, legitimacy, etc. The same happens when we consider that one party in a conflict is in sole possession of some of those dimensions, either in positive terms ("the democrats," "the constitutionalists," "the cosmopolitans") or in negative terms ("the populists," "the nationalists," "the radicals"). Underlying this approach, there usually is a tendency to address political conflicts in terms of a dichotomic "us" versus "them" framework, where there is no sign of plurality both within and among the different parties in conflict. It is not until we manage to overcome these simplifications that potential solutions for overcoming the conflict begin to arise. It is not surprising that finding an adequate way of approaching a problem is usually the first step to overcoming it.

Interpretations of reality that provide linear, binary or moralizing[14] explanations are usually simplistic. The same happens with explanations that overestimate one's capacity to intervene in the reality that we may wish to modify, ignoring the usual tragic and comic dimension of historical progress: the interference of principles and values that overlap and displace each other, fight each other or make peace in an inevitably precarious equilibrium. Nevertheless, sociopolitical realities, particularly in democratic states, reflect a plurality of interests and preferences that hardly coexist. Pretending that a perfect and absolute equilibrium is feasible would imply denying the need for democracy itself. That is why simplistic depictions of social facts, binary or moralizing approaches that essentialize social facts are not capable of recognizing the social divisiveness inherent to any democratic (ergo pluralistic and free) society in a constructive manner. Simplistic solutions produce a temporal detente of the conflicts and the perplexity of those

14 This statement does not refer, in any case, to the fundamental task of moral philosophy in general and the specific debate on moral objectivism in particular. Neither to the debate about the translation of these highly sophisticated debates particularly in analytical philosophy, into political practice.

witnessing them, but end up worsening the situation, both in the fields of knowledge and action, as they worsen our cognitive capacities and practical potential paths.

That is precisely why addressing the complexity of sociopolitical conflicts, although it is not the complete solution, is an important part of democracy and a necessary requirement to channel them in a civilized manner.[15] We should be suspicious of those ways of governing our societies that take for granted that legitimacy is easily obtained, that societies are easily controllable and obedient when confronted by the decisions of an authoritative figure, that punishment in the short term can replace trust-building efforts in the long term, that identifying the allegedly guilty actors will solve the problem or that "the people" is an incontestable reality. One of the mechanisms that contributes most to the rise of political conflicts is their immediate translation into moral terms. If something does not work properly, there should be a culprit; if there is a disagreement, there should be someone refusing to accept the evidence that will unblock the situation. In contrast to this view, if political analysis and decision-making want to address political complexity, both analysts and the parties in dispute should avoid pathologizing the opponent; not because there are no people with pathologies, including in politics, but because the difficulties in building trust and common understanding in politics are not necessarily a matter of ill will. If politics only focuses on the wrongs done by the parties in conflict, the minimum empathy required to understand each other's reasons (as minimal as they might be) will not arise and, thus, we will not be capable of engaging in a constructive deliberation. Thus, democratic societies reveal the difficulties that impede progress when they practice politics in such a way that each party in the conflict takes for granted their interpretation of reality and considers those who see reality differently as irrational or immoral.

This also applies to the exclusive use of "democracy" and "democratic" that parties in conflict tend to apply, particularly when the controversy refers to a fundamental element of the political system such as the territorial distribution of power. This is the case for conflicts regarding will to decide claims, particularly when they lead to claims for independence: some parties appeal to democracy to defend their right to vote for secession, while others hold that there is no democracy without the rule of law. This sort of debate, however, is far from unusual in politics, as all around the world democracy is used to defend different or even antagonistic positions. As Gerhard Lehmbruch stated, this results in the paradox that we may end up concluding that all political paths lead to the "Rome of democracy."[16] It is true that some aspirations and procedures that are held to be democratic are not democratic at all. Moreover, the limitations to many social and political conquests that are inherent to democratic regimes nowadays (with women's right to vote being the clearest example) were democratically accepted

15 Bejan (2011).
16 Lehmbruch (1987), at 3.

and defended in the past. However, when we refer to the way of addressing secessionist claims in a democratic society, this ethos rarely applies.[17] Nevertheless, within a democratic regime, both statements are to a certain extent true: it is hard to hold that a regime is democratic if people do not have the final words (substantive requirement), but it is equally true that this decision cannot plainly ignore the legal framework (procedural requirement). There is no democracy when the status quo cannot be changed, but neither is there democracy if change is merely subjected to the popular will. At least, this is the case if we agree with a republican understanding of democracy,[18] and agree that democracy is not a procedure to foster the majority's decisions but one to avoid the domination of minorities. How, then, do we overcome this dilemma?

To begin with, we must understand that democracy is a set of complex values and procedures that we need to articulate. The problem is not that the claims might not be democratic but that it lies in ignoring the fact that democracy cannot absolutize one of its moments or features. Instead, we should assume that democracy is the set of values and dimensions that are diversely articulated depending on the type of issues we may be dealing with, the historical moment when decisions are made and the type of society making the decision. As Jürgen Habermas rightly pointed out,[19] we should avoid replacing democratic legitimacy for some of its concrete moments (rule of law, plebiscite, responsibility, deliberation, transparency, respect for minorities, etc.). Democratic maturity consists of adequately balancing all of those factors. Will to decide claims are problematic precisely because this limitation often presents their expression and understanding in purely plebiscitary terms (as mentioned earlier, it is not the aim of this chapter to engage with the scholarly debate on the right to decide theory, which has a higher level of sophistication than its popular version). It often appears as if deciding were a sort of magical concept, linked to an inaugural momentum, eluding the fact that societies exert self-government, legitimize their institutional frameworks and balance the plurality of internal identities in a continuous way.

That is the case, for instance, for polities that, de facto, encompass a plurality of national social facts that identify as national political facts. We may define a social fact as a group of individuals who interact in a way that could be identified, although they do not necessarily need to be identified, both by the internal participants and the external observers, as constituting a social fact. The supporters of a football team, people who share a sexual orientation, people who have the same level of income or people visiting foreign cities for a short period of time

17 We could discuss, indeed, if this also applies to internal self-determination claims within a democratic regime, particularly when they come from a historically oppressed minority nation. Nevertheless, there are sound moral, political and legal arguments to hold that a democratic regime has the normative duty of recognizing its internal diversity. However, that is not the case we are addressing in this chapter.

18 Pettit (2015).

19 Habermas (2011), at 54.

could constitute social facts. People who share a language may also constitute a social fact. That is, a social fact is an intersubjective practice that, while not being material, acquires factual category: regardless of which precise definition and borders each of us may apply, we can talk about social facts such as "tourists" or "Manchester City fans" in the same way we can talk about apples and buildings. When we talk about social facts that become political facts, it is often the case that those willing to oppose the political fact tend to use the strategy of denying even the social fact. However, this does not make the social fact less factual.

If we follow the definition of a political fact used by Kalypso Nicolaïdis and Francis Cheneval,[20] a political fact is a social fact that meets, at least, three requirements: (1) those who constitute the social fact recognize and value the status of the social fact as a social fact, (2) there is a defined set of rules and laws that will rule the social fact, and (3) those belonging to the social fact show the will of projecting the social fact towards the future, that is, of ensuring its progress. However, in Nicolaïdis and Cheneval's definition, when we deal with national social facts, the application of these requirements automatically equates "national political facts" with "nation-states." While we agree that not all the social facts that become political facts can be considered national political facts (municipalities, for instance, are social facts turned into political facts, but not national political facts), we hold that national political facts cannot be limited to nation-states either. Instead, we introduce two additional requirements to ensure that a political fact should be considered a national political fact: (1) the existence of an institutional framework within a territory that could potentially act autonomously and (2) that the individuals within that territory (for various reasons that vary from place to place and through time) identify and value a certain bond with those institutions, i.e. they value their citizenship in those institutions). Therefore, the definition of national social facts is not necessarily restricted to nation-states.

Of course, even this broad definition of national political facts could be contested: this might happen with small nations that we may not differentiate from a city or province but that are still considered national political facts (San Marino, Luxembourg), with diasporic peoples who are considered nations (gipsy communities), indigenous groups who do not necessarily have the institutional framework to act autonomously (first nations in Canada), alleged nations that are settled in different institutional frameworks (the historical understanding of the Basque Country defended by some nationalist groups) or even the case of huge cities that, while they could eventually meet all the requirements, are far from being considered national political facts (Tokyo, Shanghai). However, as mentioned in the introduction, the focus of this chapter is not on discussing the subject or scope of an alleged right to secession, but on how to deal politically with independence movements framed under the right to decide ethos. To that aim, we can simply consider that however disputed they might be, it is plausible to identify a plurality of alleged national political facts that coexist and even

20 Cheneval et al. (2017).

overlap within a single state, just as we could identify the will to decide claims arising from those national political facts.

The problem arises, precisely, as those national political facts are overall disputed and overlapping. That is, within the same national political fact there are a number of citizens who prioritize the encompassing national political fact (i.e. the nation-state) and a number of citizens who prioritize the encompassed national political fact (i.e. the minority nation) instead. Therefore, some citizens within the encompassed national political fact would like to share the decision with the rest of the citizens of the encompassing national political fact (i.e. the nation-state), and others would like to restrict the decision to the citizens of the encompassed national political fact (i.e. the minority nation). Both positions, given that all of them are citizens of the same national political fact where the will to decide claims have been raised (i.e. minority nation), are equally legitimate. That is, the aspiration of deciding on the smaller or bigger decision-making framework are both equally democratic: no position aims to exclude their co-citizens from the decision-making process. The sole difference is the framework of citizenship that each side prioritizes (assuming that citizenship is, in any case, always restricted to a defined group). Of course, there are plenty of arguments in favour and against the virtue and desirability of each of these positions. However, neither of those arguments make any of the positions less democratic than the other (i.e. both are democratic aspirations regardless of which one we consider normatively and politically superior).

In other words, if we take this reasoning further, we may synthesize the issue as follows: accommodating the will to decide implies the squaring of the circle in the sense that we need to satisfy to the greatest extent possible two positions that have radically different decision-making frameworks. That is, materializing the will to decide claims coming from the encompassed national political fact should include both disputed wills. This is even more important in a context such as European integration, where we are trying to elaborate a framework of co-decision with the rest of the Europeans: it will not make sense to accept co-decision in one case but to reject it in the other. That is, autarchic frameworks of decision-making, while still existing in the practice of some nation-states,[21] are increasingly obsolete.[22] Little wonder, while any national political fact has an imaginary dimension,[23] they are also operative fictions.[24] In the European context, this effectiveness becomes decreasingly factual (and more imagined) as the national political facts regarding existing interdependencies become more closed. Thus, while European national political facts continue to be relevant (and there is, in this sense, no reason to consider nation-states to be more relevant than minority nations, even while acknowledging their empirical asymmetry and normative differences), the truth is that we are moving towards a new equilibrium where some issues are decided autonomously and others are co-decided through a process of delegation and

21 Innerarity (2015).
22 Breen et al. (2010).
23 Billig (1995), Gellner (1998), Anderson (2006).
24 Calhoun (2007).

sovereignty transfer. This process, while far from perfect, is being progressively settled through a common institutional framework at the European scale.[25]

Consequently, taking the political exercise of the will to decide seriously should imply assuming it to the full extent of its radicality: defending every citizen's decision-making power. That is, formulating it in such a way that it integrates all the decision-making models that are implicit in the diverse types of national identifications that conform multinational societies. Only if this radicality is assumed will claims over the will to decide become a meeting point, an authentic shared decision, rather than the imposition of a veto. Nevertheless, it is a basic democratic principle that political facts – particularly when we refer to national political facts, as they are the result of historical struggles to build free democratic institutions, can freely decide their own destiny. However, this is a principle exerted in contexts of pluralism, and respect towards this pluralism is an equally relevant democratic principle. Consequently, any position that defends the relevance of addressing the claims underlying the will to decide should make clear that it accepts this pluralism not as an intermediate step towards unanimity (as if the diversity of opinions and interests were the result of ideological deformations or ill wills). Plurality exists insofar as reality is not a set of previously given facts: if that were the case, dialogue would be a waste of time and democratic procedures unnecessary. Institutionalizing political pluralism constitutes the guarantee of our freedom vis-à-vis those who aim to impose a triumphant majority.

An adequate management of the will to decide requires a more complex and nuanced political culture. One of the main pathologies of today's politics comes from the fact that when societies polarize over simple counter positions (such as the positions that could arise around independence movements or defenders of the status quo's unchangeability), adequate democratic processes rarely apply. How can we foster a political culture where nuances and complex proposals are not systematically penalized with inattention or even contempt? How do we avoid allowing oversimplification and mere confrontation to become politically viable? Why do political values such as rigour, responsibility or mere civility[26] remain so unrecognized? An adequate response to these questions is a fundamental requirement to provide democratic answers to will to decide claims, as only a complex democracy is a complete democracy.

2. The demos problem: unrivalled issue?

Most of the concepts we tend to use in politics have aged more than in other areas of social life, such as arts, technology or the economy, where the necessary renewal has been arranged. Adequate politics require more than adequate concepts, of course, but without a proper critical reflection on the theoretical realm, we will remain unable to understand the ongoing transformation of societies[27]

25 Nicolaïdis (2017).

26 Bejan (2016).

27 Albrow (1996), Beck (2006), Castells (2000), Innerarity et al. (2019).

and the best way to govern them. This reflection is particularly necessary to understand and manage issues related to territoriality, identity or sovereignty, where the main practical changes coexist with the most anachronistic concepts. We are witnessing the birth of a new political logic that contrasts with the previous simplistic understanding of power. Thus, we need a new vocabulary that makes this new complexity visible. Politics often become exhausted on the essentialist use of obsolete concepts or ideological derivations for rigid premises. We would like to understand the peculiarities of our times, but this is imperilled by inadequate language and useless models. The concepts that we have at our disposal to describe and order our surrounding reality, including the evolving social and political facts, are not adequate for the plural, intercultural, irregular, changing and discontinuous world in which we increasingly find ourselves.

That is the case, for instance, when we reflect upon the notion of sovereignty. Territorial integrity of the states is a feature that is (more or less explicitly) granted by most of the democratic nation-state's constitutional regimes in Europe. However, they do not state that sovereignty itself is unbreakable. That is, they do not ban a variety of ways of distributing sovereignty over the state's territory. In this regard, affirming an exclusive, vertical, hierarchical and monopolistic understanding of the state implies a purely ideological position about the nation rather than a solid normative standpoint. Nevertheless, this understanding of sovereignty does not take into account the modifications experienced by a reality where the concept is being applied, particularly through the European integration process.[28] This is especially true if we consider the ways in which, despite some reluctance, European member states come to terms with sharing the nation-state's sovereignty with other European member states. Unsurprisingly, if member states had understood their sovereignty regarding the EU in a similar way as it is often conceived regarding internal territorial affairs, European integration would not have been possible.[29] It is this transfer of sovereignty towards Europe which shows that, while reality evolves in a certain direction, mindsets often remain unaltered. As a consequence, sharing sovereignty beyond the nation-state ends up appearing less harmful than sharing it within the nation-state: not as a result of a theoretical impossibility, but due to ideological resistances.

In a compound or multinational state, loyalty is not built unless diverse political identities and wills of self-government are recognized instead of subordinated. That is, unless the diverse national political facts (minority nations) within the encompassing national political fact (nation-state) are mutually recognized and avoid any form of domination, both within and towards each other. As the most advanced reflections on compound states show,[30] it is not effective to conceive political power in states where different national political facts coexist as if citizens have a single national affiliation or belonging. It is necessary to provide an

28 MacCormick (1999), Krisch (2010), Isiksel (2016).

29 Sánchez Cuenca (2018), at 118–122.

30 Fossas et al. (1999), Nicolaidis (2001), Gagnon et al. (2006), McEwan (2006), Moreno (2012) at 185–199.

innovative answer to the question of legitimacy incorporating other elements – mostly linked to recognition of collective rights, shared rule and shared power – that may grant the usual ethos of "united in diversity." A goal that is, in fact, incentivized by a transnational context where the monopoly over a territory is far from operative. That is why it is necessary to generate new coherences for multiple spaces[31] that equilibrate each other beyond the constrictive and hierarchical views that block the democratic resolutions of will to decide claims.

In order to reach this point, we need, among other issues, to make an effort of conceptual renewal, as the old political notions and legal tools do not allow the reconfiguration of political spaces required by democratic communal living in compound polities. While this conceptual renewal requires more extensive work, we may already anticipate which principle could guide this process: mutual recognition of difference instead of imposition, subordination, exclusion or autarchy. As previously mentioned, the application in practice of conceptual renewal will require from the work a variety of disciplines that fall beyond the scope of political philosophy (e.g., legal theory, political science, economy). However, this political transformation will require new concepts to evolve towards a rescaling of democracy[32] in at least two ways: new ways of conceiving legitimacy and institutional innovation.

On the former, legitimacy in contexts of interdependence will revolve around citizens' free adhesion, identification and implication. As opposed to previous periods of "container societies" where those elements were given a priori,[33] in interdependent societies, the consent of citizens will become the core of democratic decision-making. However, this consent will not refer to aggregated or majoritarian wills, but to expressions of transactions and pacts. That is, the focus will be on elaborating procedures that may channel these transactions of the citizens' will in such a way that no interests are completely excluded or disregarded. That brings us to the second way in which the conceptual renewal should be applied: the institutional innovation of shared sovereignties. Given that the reality of differentiated political facts, particularly in the case of national political facts, is as persistent as the need to build common institutions, we should think about new ways of decision-making that imply a certain level of co-decision. That is, institutional frameworks where the right to address claims to decide over a certain political fact are combined with the duty of reaching agreements with those who will be affected by those decisions. The world is not moving towards disintegration, but towards differentiated integration. This does not imply, as those opposing sub-state nationalism often hold, defending the current nation-state's status quo, as the actors who need to integrate in this new dynamic are much more diverse than the ones recognized in the present-day 'nation-state centred' status quo. Nevertheless, the multilateralism requested by the more progressive

31 Nicolaïdis et al. (2017).
32 Keating (2013).
33 Beck (2016).

understandings of global governance should apply equally to domestic political dynamics.

Still, there is a key concept that we cannot avoid when we refer to the issues related to the will to decide, given its democratic dimension: the demos. Traditionally, the demos could be defined, in its simplest definition, as the populace of a democracy, as a political unit. In our account, if we want to maintain the traditional understanding of the demos, this will imply conceiving of the demos as a political fact. Moreover, regarding the case that we are analyzing (the claims around the will to decide that are often expressed as movements for independence), it will imply conceiving of the demos as a national political fact. However, if we agree that this "populace of a democracy as a political unit" is relevant for democracy insofar as it is the subject making democratic decisions, we should also renew the concept so that its understanding may better capture ongoing increases in complexity. How does this complexity apply to the demos? There are plenty of authors who have thoroughly addressed this debate,[34] proposing diverse theoretical alternatives to reconfigure the demos in an age of interdependencies. These alternatives[35] include theories such as *all citizenship stakeholders*, *all affected interests* or *all subjected to coercion*. However, they all refer to a broader principle that we need to reconfigure: the notion of democratic inclusion.

One of the fundamental distinctions of this debate would be, from this chapter's perspective, the difference between the agreement of the decision-making process and the agreement of the decision-making subject. The reconfiguration of the demos in terms of democratic inclusion affects, in the debate concerning this chapter, the latter. That is, when we talk about reconceptualizing the demos in such a way that we may exclude unilateral decisions that have consequences beyond the decision-making framework, we refer to the need for the procedure and implications of the decision to agree. To make it clear, in the case of democratically accommodating the will to decide of a national political fact within a democratic state, this implies different decision-making stages that constitute the act of co-deciding. If the decision-making process really wants to result in a co-decision, these stages will depend on the plurality of political facts involved, which transcend the dichotomy of the encompassing and encompassed national political facts, both internally and externally. However, for the sake of the argument and to illustrate its ethos, let us reduce it to two stages. The first decision implies agreeing to the terms, procedures and implications of the different ways in which the will to decide about the future of the national political fact could materialize. As we know, particularly in a dêmoicratic institutional realm, such as the one in the EU, this materialization could have many different shapes: federal state, confederal state, autonomous region, nation within a nation or, as independence movements may claim, an independent (member[36]) state.

34 Young (2000), Goodin (2006), Fraser (2009), Goodin (2016).

35 Bauböck (2018), at 22–47.

36 Álvarez (2015), Bengoetxea (2016), Waker (2017), Cetrà et al. (2018).

There are at least two major reasons to think that, in a democratic context, this decision cannot be taken unilaterally. First, a unilateral decision would imply excluding those co-citizens of the encompassed national political fact (minority nation) who prioritize their attachment to the encompassing national political fact (nation-state). This is particularly clear in the case of secession, as a unilateral decision could affect issues as valuable for the individuals as nationality and citizenship. Even if the seceding national political fact would grant political equality and grant whichever necessary group rights to those opposing secession, it seems reasonable to state that unilaterally removing their citizenship would be normatively problematic. However, as a second reason, there is an even stronger motive, more connected to the complex understanding of the demos, that invalidates unilateral decisions in democratic regimes: the fact that whichever decision the encompassed national fact (minority nation) makes on the relationship between the encompassed national political fact (minority nation) and the encompassing national political fact (nation-state), it will have an impact on the encompassing national political fact (nation-state). If we agree that, in an interdependent world, we are moving towards schemes where the plurality of demos or demoi should avoid these dynamics, the argument applies even more so when the different demoi share a common institutional framework such as a state. The clearest example would be the redistributive impact of secession: an encompassed national political fact, particularly when its average wealth is greater than that of the encompassing national political fact, cannot legitimately request seceding without considering the impact of this decision on the rest of the former encompassing national political fact. This dynamic, according to the principle of mutual recognition of difference, also applies the other way around: the encompassing national political fact cannot make decisions without considering the impact of those decisions over the encompassed national political fact.

Therefore, whichever materialization of the will to decide prevails (which will not necessarily mean constituting an independent state: as we will explain in the third section, this seems an unlikely outcome when those claims are addressed democratically), it will require an agreement between the different parties regarding the procedure, terms, implications, etc., of the decision. That is, it should exclude a unilateral decision that will entail an oversimplified understanding of the demos. However, once an agreement is reached on this first and necessary stage, a second decision will necessarily involve only the national political fact whose future is actually being decided.[37] Otherwise, the majority of the encompassing

37 One could argue that this first stage of the procedure is rather similar to the one applied, for instance, to the process for updating the Statutes of Autonomy in Spain. Indeed, the renewal of these constitutional agreements by national political facts is a possible, but not unique, way of addressing claims of the will to decide. People might then ask whether the failure of the first stage of that specific way of addressing will to decide claims (i.e. the one used to update the Statutes of Autonomy) could not lead to "just cause" justifications for secession, arguing that there is a lack of recognition. This question has given rise to a sophisticated debate (see, for instance, Seymour 2007). However, even if the answer, in theory, were that

national political fact will always impose their will to decide over the minority of the encompassed national political fact. That is, there will be a domination of the hegemonic state demos over the minority demoi. This is often portrayed as a lack of inclusion of the encompassing national political fact's interests. However, this would only apply if there had not been the first stage of the decision-making process where an agreement was reached on the terms, implications and procedures for the second stage of decision-making. In other words, anyone who aimed to determine the encompassed national political fact's future unilaterally would be employing a notion of the demos that was as oversimplified as a person who aimed to impose the decision of the encompassing national political fact. Moreover, the perspective that denies the subject of this second decision-making stage ends up promoting pure conflict dynamics, hindering win–win outcomes, as the national political facts will lose any incentive to reasonably negotiate in the first decision-making stage. This creates a pure conflict dynamic where, once again, oversimplified dichotomies will arise, thus fostering a situation in which the only foreseeable outcome of the will to decide claims are either secession or an unchanged status quo.

3. Negotiating secessionist claims

Avoiding a pure conflict dynamic requires, in the first place, accepting that the conflicts between national political facts that dispute the same territory do not have a logical but a pragmatical solution. That is to say, there is a contingent agreement that aims to promote common existence rather than the imposition and open conflict dynamics it generates. This is a Gordian knot that is based on the paradox that we cannot define the deciding subject until someone decides who this subject is. As Robert Dahl stated,[38] democratic procedures tend to presuppose that the given deciding subject is the correct one. However, in a context of interdependencies such as the compound polities in Europe, with all their underlying conflicts and disputes, this assumption is far from self-evident. Some may state that this is false, as they would like to have a less conflictive environment where cooperation may arise endogenously. Others may hold that these conflicts are the result of past injustices yet to be repaired, as if the non-conflict arcadia is something that will arrive in the future. Whatever the correct answer, the truth is that politics is not exerted in either of these ideal scenarios, but in a reality where national political facts exist and interact whether we like it or not. Therefore, the only alternative is to assume that the demoi underlying those national political facts are a reflexive, arguable, reviewable and open reality. That is why the first

Just Cause Theories might apply, in practice this path has very little feasibility, at least if the context remains democratic and there is no intervention by third parties to compensate the power asymmetry. Therefore, the only feasible way forward would be to continue working politically in the first stage until the parties reach an agreement. Not based on normative arguments, but for purely pragmatic reasons.

38 Dahl (1983), at 103.

stage of decision-making regarding the claims on the will to decide is fundamental: because it is the only way to renew, update or modify the existing pacts that constitute our political coexistence without ignoring, a priori, any conceptions of the national political facts implied in the dispute. That is, accepting the impossibility of conceiving the features of national political facts as irrefutable data. In other words, we cannot impose an aprioristic framework of absolute legitimacies as if it were an unquestionable fact. That is why the majority rule on decision-making only applies at a second stage of decision-making, once all the interests, perspectives and political identities at stake have been duly recognized and balanced during the first stage of decision-making. That is the only way of overcoming the pure conflict dynamic where one party imposes its will on the other, the dynamic where the winnings of one party imply automatic loses for the other.

Assuming the requirement of renouncing unilaterality by accepting the requirement of the first stage of decision-making and thus insisting on the relevance of an agreement over a victory, the playing field is radically changed. Because, in that way, the confrontation is not between those who hold an aprioristic and absolute view of the encompassed national political fact (minority nation) and those who hold an aprioristic and absolute view of the encompassing national political fact (nation-state), but between those who seek agreed solutions and those who prefer imposition. If this perspective is changed, the terms of the conflict are also modified: the dispute will no longer be between one national political fact and another, as the first stage of the decision-making departs from recognizing both, but between those who seek encounter and those who seek confrontation. Once we assume this frame of analyzing the conflict, the debate around the claims linked to the will to decide will stop being focused on the "who" and the "how" and centre on the "what." In this way, more rational ways of channelling this will to decide democratically may prevail.

It might be the case that, even in that scenario, the "what" is so divergent that there is no way to duly address it within the same institutional framework. That is, it could be that federal, confederal and other types of solutions are not capable of dealing with such a divergency on the "what." One could wonder whether that was the ethos behind the evolution of the will to decide claims in Scotland: evolving from a claim for devolved institutions to claims on external self-determination as a result of a series of deep discrepancies with the majoritarian United Kingdom's political preferences represented in Westminster (first with the aftermath of the Thatcher vs Scottish Labour dispute, later with the Brexit vs pro-EU Scottish National Party dispute). However, even in that scenario, the fact that the claims on the will to decide were democratically addressed, contributed to channelling the issue without falling into a pure conflict dynamic. Such is the case that Scottish independentists even accepted that a favourable result in the independence referendum would not necessarily imply the rupture of several common institutions, such as common defence polities, the British Monarchy, the monetary union or, even, a sort of double citizenship arrangement, among others. We can see that the case was far from a pure conflict dynamic that not only was the referendum preceded by an overarching deliberation process among citizens and civil society representatives supporting almost all the parties in dispute, but that immediately after the result, both national political facts managed to keep addressing the will to decide claims, internally and externally, through the Smith Commission that resulted in the 2016 Scotland Act.

The underlying lesson is that if we address conflicts regarding will to decide claims by assuming their inner complexity, we will not see polarized groups but citizens who want to make compatible a common existence with their diverse institutional attachments. Assuming these lenses allow us to overcome seeing reality as comprising homogeneous confronted blocks, but rather of nuanced differences. If we interiorize this complexity of the demos, its inherent political (not merely cultural or administrative) pluralism, we will be able to promote decision-making processes that aim to include diverse plurality rather than impose a majority. It is true that it might seem that real-life politics (the Catalan case, mentioned in the introduction, being a clear but not unique example) tend to illustrate apparently irreconcilable disputes. The short-termism of the currently existing incentive schemes, the accumulation of perceived or actual historical grievances, asymmetries of power either on the encompassing or the encompassed national political fact that led to impositions and even unhelpful geopolitical dynamics may complicate this cooperative approach in the short- and even mid-term. However, in a democratic context and an interdependent Europe, the only way of addressing claims linked to the will to decide of a national political fact is through negotiation and agreement.

In the end, if we assume the contingency of the national political facts and their interaction, we also need to assume that their political accommodation in a democratic context should also be subjected to negotiation. It is not the plurality of nations that stands in the way of achieving this goal, but the way in which those national political facts are politically expressed. If we agree that secession is a case of last resource, as it denotes the impossibility of defining a minimum set of common areas for a cooperation that is in itself desirable, we should neither deny national political facts nor promote their expressions in exclusive, homogenizing and hegemonic ways. In this sense, the idea that decision-making processes set two stages so that co-decision would be ensured fosters this open and pluralistic understanding of the national political facts. The key element is that, by requiring that the actual expression of the national political fact through voting should be preceded by an agreement, we make it easier to identify the claims linked to the national political fact's will to decide. Little wonder, in the search for an agreement based on the mutual recognition of the parties, claims will necessarily be on the table, because otherwise the parties will not be able to agree on the best way to accommodate that will to decide. If, on the contrary, the parties do not recognize each other, any path for negotiating a successful method for addressing these claims will not be fruitful. That is why, adapting Wayne Norman's statement[39] to a context of interdependent demoi, we could state that the plea for

39 Norman (2006), at xii.

multinational states is also in part a revulsion with the idea that it is impractical or otherwise undesirable for distinct but overlapping national political facts to cooperate within the same institutional framework.

This is a goal that necessarily requires the promotion of negotiating skills that are not always compatible with the ongoing political dynamics. The increasing request for transparency, although it may have justified motivations (particularly in the aftermath of an economic crisis where inequalities were on the rise), does not always contribute to the purpose of inclusiveness. Negotiation requires combining accountability with discretion: citizens should have mechanisms to ensure that the plurality of claims that answer to their will to decide are actually considered by their representatives, just as they should have the opportunity to decide whether the agreement reached by those representatives answers to their will. That is, citizens should continue to be the last bearers of sovereignty.

However, we should not confuse this democratic principle with an obsession with publicity that introduces incentives for exclusive positions among the parties in dispute. That is also, and even particularly (given the emotional dimension linked to national political facts[40]), the case when we refer to conflicts between and within national political facts. That is, democratically addressing claims around the will to decide using negotiation skills during the first decision-making stage not only contributes to the generation of more inclusive dynamics, but also to the raising of underlying claims in such a way that differences are alleviated. In this way, agreement might be more plausible, and it may be easier to generate wider consensus. That is, it will be more probable that a wide majority of citizens may accept the agreement in a second stage of decision-making. Nonetheless, the negotiating approach in the first stage of decision-making opens the possibility to non-binary solutions (such as those that portray conflicts in terms of status quo vs secession) that may bring together wider and more pluralistic majorities. This approach, in sum, complements the competitive dimension of democracy with a negotiating dimension that allows a more accurate, nuanced and cooperative construction (first) and processing (second) of the popular will. Without the combination of both dimensions, conflicts such as those arising in multinational states may result in winning majorities but will hardly generate the internal and external consensus required for a common and stable coexistence.

Conclusion: towards a politics of understanding

Charles Taylor[41] refers to the perversity of what he calls the neurotics' alliance, consisting of the dreams of some becoming the nightmares of others. According to Taylor, when conflicts escalate, each part tends to unconsciously act on the fears of the other. Therefore, difficulties in reaching agreements result from the dynamics in which any concession to the other parties in dispute lead to fear that

40 Cagiao y Conde (2018).
41 Taylor (1990).

it will be used in the path towards their destruction. In multinational states, this implies that the encompassing national fact tends to be afraid of never being able to satisfy the encompassed national political fact's will to decide claims. The latter, in turn, believes that the former's goal implies, ultimately, their absorption and disappearance as a differentiated political reality. Consequently, cooperative dynamics are almost impossible. That is even more usual in contexts of high polarization. The most perverse consequence of this dynamic is that the suspicion that the other parties will never change their position is often used to justify our own incompetence at reviewing our positions. On the contrary, European history shows that even in contexts of the highest escalations of conflicts, parties end up reaching agreements: the differences among cases reside, mostly, in the time and costs that were necessary to reach those agreements.

The agreement to engage in a negotiation, no matter how suspiciously it is seen by the parties, is more difficult than confrontation as it requires the elaboration of more sophisticated concepts and provides arguments where it was previously sufficient to make statements of principles. Nevertheless, the main requirement of a negotiation is the acceptance of entering an area of indeterminacy. There is no possible negotiation when the frameworks and procedures predetermine the result of that negotiation. As James Bohman rightly states,[42] the uncertainty of democratic decision-making procedures is not their flaw, but their normative strength. We should not confuse this with conceiving negotiations in terms of full equality. While we should aspire to a decision-making framework that compensates the de facto inequalities among the parties, we cannot completely avoid power asymmetries. However, we may overcome these contingent asymmetries by adequately choosing the best timing to begin negotiation, as well as limiting its effects to a manageable period (i.e. since no solution will imply absolutely overcoming the conflict).

Ultimately, as irreducible as national political facts might be, insofar as they involve individuals and their intersubjective experiences, whatever their contingent settlement might be, their interactions with the surrounding national political facts (either with or without an encompassing state, although mainly in the former) will generate interferences on the citizens' will to decide.These interferences, that increase in the current context of interdependencies, will require the different actors to find methods that provide mutual advantage, reciprocity, recognition and shared self-limitations. In democratic contexts such as the European context, one's survival does not result from the destruction or domination of the other (i.e. from the denial of its existence), but through mutual recognition. It might be the case that, especially for the neurotics, the possibility of engaging in negotiations to reach agreements may seem far-fetched or even impossible. However, as agreement will eventually be unavoidable (even for the final recourse of deciding about secession on a second stage), actors might better interiorize this perspective. Nevertheless, in the European democracy (or dêmoicracy[43]) the

42 Bohman (2002) at 81.
43 Nicolaïdis (2018).

key issue is not whether there will be an agreement or not, but how actors in conflict should prepare for a game that will be lost by those who seem in charge of delaying or blocking the possibility of reaching that agreement. In other words, the losers will be those who assume aprioristic views of their political reality and, therefore, impede the flourishing of de facto multinational states.

References

Alain Gagnon, *The Case for Multinational Federalism: Beyond the All-Encompassing Nation* (Routledge, 2009).

Alain Gagnon, *Minority Nations in the Age of Uncertainty: New Paths to National Emancipation and National Empowerment* (University of Toronto Press, 2014).

Alain Gagnon and R. Iacovino, *Federalism, Citizenship and Quebec: Debating Multinationalism* (University of Toronto Press, 2006).

Alan Patten, 'Democratic Secession from a Multinational State' (2002), *Ethics*, Vol. 112, No. 3, pp. 558–586.

Alan Patten, 'Self-Determination for National Minorities', in Fernando Teson (ed.), *The Theory of Self-Determination* (Cambridge University Press, 2016), pp. 120–144.

Alfonso González, Jaume López, Josep M. Vilajosana, Mercè Barceló and Mercé Correjta (eds.), *El derecho a decidir. Teoría y práctica de un nuevo derecho* (Atelier, 2015).

Benedict Anderson, *Imagined Communities: Reflections On the Origin and Spread of Nationalism* (Verso, 2006).

Bhikhu Parekh, *Rethinking Multiculturalism: Cultural Diversity and Political Theory* (Macmillan, 2000).

Chaim Gans, *The Limits of Nationalism* (Cambridge University Press, 2003).

Charles Taylor, *Rapprocher les solitudes. Écrits sur le fédéralisme et le nationalisme au Canada* (Presses Universitaires de Laval, 1990).

Craig Calhoun, *Nations Matter: Culture, History and the Cosmopolitan Dream* (Routledge, 2007).

Daniel Cetrà and Robert Liñeira, 'Breaking-Up within Europe: Sub-state Nationalist Strategies in Multilevel Polities' (2018), *JCMS: Journal of Common Market Studies*, Vol. 56, No. 3, pp. 717–729.

Daniel Innerarity, 'Transnational Self-Determination: Resetting Self-Government in the Age of Interdependence' (2015), *JCMS: Journal of Common Market Studies*, Vol. 53, pp. 1061–1076.

Daniel Innerarity and Ander Errasti, 'Cosmopolitan Public Space(s)', in Gerard Delanty (ed.), *Routledge International Handbook of Cosmopolitanism Studies* (Routledge, 2019, 2nd edition), pp. 287–298.

Daniel Weinstock, 'Constitutionalizing the Right to Secede' (2001), *Journal of Political Philosophy*, Vol. 9, No. 2, pp. 182–203.

Enric Fossas and Ferrán Requejo, *Asimetría Federal y Estado Plurinacional. El Debate sobre la acomodación de la diversidad en Canadá, Bélgica y España* (Editorial Trotta, 1999).

Ernest Gellner, *Nacionalismo* (Ediciones Destino, 1998).

Francis Cheneval y Kalypso Nicolaïdis, 'The Social Construction of Demoicracy in the European Union' (2017), *European Journal of Political Theory*, Vol. 16, p. 2.

François Boucher and J. Maclure, 'Fiscal Distributive Justice: Lessons from Canada', in J. F. Grégoire and M. Jewkes (eds.), *Recognition and Redistribution in Multinational Federations* (Leuven University Press, 2015), pp. 157–182.

Gerhard Lehmbruch, *Proporzdemokratie nach zwanzig Jahren. Überlegungen zur Theoriebildung in der komparatistischen Forschung über politische Strategien in der Schweiz* (unpublished manuscript, 1987).

Ignacio Sánchez Cuenca, *La confusión nacional. La democracia española ante la crisis catalana* (Catarata, 2018).

Iris Marion Young, *Inclusion and Democracy* (Oxford University Press, 2000).

Isaiah Berlin, *Concepts and Categories*, edited by Henry Hardy (Princeton University Press, 1999).

James Bohman, 'Internationale Regime und demokratische Governance. Gleicher Einfluss auf globale Institutionen', in Mattias Lutz-Bachmann (ed.), *Weltstaat oder Staatenwelt? Für und wider die Idee einer Weltrepublik* (Suhrkamp, 2002), pp. 75–103.

Jaume Lopez, *El derecho a decidir. La vía catalana* (Editorial Txalaparta, 2018).

John Breully, *Nationalism and the State* (Manchester University Press, 1993).

Jorge Cagiao y Conde, *Micronacionalismos ¿será que todos somos nacionalistas?* (Catarata, 2018).

José Fernández-Albertos, *Antisistema: Desigualdad Económica y Precariado Político* (Catarata, 2018).

Joseph H. H. Weiler, 'Secessionism and Its Discontents', in Carlos Closa (ed.), *Secession from a Member State and Withdrawal from the European Union* (Cambridge University Press, 2017), pp. 12–31.

Joxerramon Bengoetxea, 'From Nation-Regions to Member States: Internal Expansion of the European Union' (2016), *RIEV*, Vol. 12, pp. 104–121.

Juan José Álvarez, 'Europe and the Challenge of Internal Expansion: International Law and Democracy' (2015), *RIEV*, Vol. 11, pp. 58–77.

Jürgen Habermas, *Zur Verfassung Europas* (Suhrkamp, 2011).

Kalypso Nicolaïdis, 'Conclusion: The Federal Vision beyond the Federal State', in K. Nicolaïdis and R. Howse (eds.), *The Federal Vision: Legitimacy and Levels of Governance in the United States and the European Union* (Oxford University Press, 2001), pp. 443–484.

Kalypso Nicolaïdis, 'Sustainable Integration in a Demoicratic Polity: A New (or not so new) Ambition For the European Union after Brexit', in Uta Staiger (ed.), *Brexit and Beyond* (Cambridge University Press, 2017), pp. 212–221.

Kalypso Nicolaïdis, 'Braving the Waves? Europe's Constitutional Settlement at Twenty' (2018), *JCMS: Journal of Common Market Studies*, pp. 1614–1630.

Kalypso Nicolaïdis and Juri Viehoff, 'Just Boundaries for Demoicrats' (2017), *Journal of European Integration*, Vol. 39, p. 5.

Keith Breen and Shane O'Neill (eds.), *After the Nation? Critical Reflections on Nationalism and Postnationalism* (Palgrave Macmillan, 2010).

Luis Moreno, 'State and Stateless Nationalisms, Old and New Diversities, and Federal Governance', in Michelle H. Williams (ed.), *The Multicultural Dilemma: Migration, Ethnic Politics, and State Intermediation* (Routledge, 2012), pp. 185–199.

Manuel Castells, *The Rise of the Network Society* (Blackwell-Wiley, 2000).

Marc Sanjaume, 'Normative Arguments in Spanish Territorial Debate', in Xavier Cuadras (ed.), *Catalonia: A New Independent State in Europe?* (Routledge, 2016), pp. 56–69.

Martin Albrow, *The Global Age* (Blackwell Publishers Polity Press, 1996).
Michael Billig, *Banal Nationalism* (SAGE Publications, 1995).
Michael Keating, *Plurinational Democracy: Stateless Nations in a Post-Sovereignty Era* (Oxford University Press, 2001).
Michael Keating, *Rescaling the European State: The Making of Territory and the Rise of the Meso* (Oxford University Press, 2013).
Michel Seymour, 'On redefining the Nation' (1999), *The Monist*, pp. 411–445.
Michel Seymour, 'Secession as a Remedial Right' (2007), *Inquiry*, Vol. 50, No. 4, pp. 395–423.
Michel Seymour, 'Political Liberalism and the Recognition of Peoples', in M. Seymour (ed.), *The Plural States of Recognition* (Palgrave Macmillan, 2010), pp. 172–196.
Montserrat Guibernau, *Belonging: Solidarity and Division in Modern Socieites* (Polity Press, 2013).
Nancy Fraser, *Scales of Justice: Reimagining Political Space in a Globalizing World* (Columbia University Press, 2009).
Neil MacCormick, *Questioning Sovereignty* (Oxford University Press, 1999).
Neil Waker, 'Internal Enlargement in the European Union: Beyond Legalism and Political Expediency', in Carlos Closa (ed.), *Secession from a Member State and Withdrawal from the European Union* (Cambridge University Press, 2017).
Neus Torbisco-Casals, 'Multiculturalism, Identity Claims, and Human Rights: From Politics to Courts' (2016), *The Law and Ethics of Human Rights*, Vol. 10, No. 2, pp. 367–404.
Nico Krisch, *Beyond Constitutionalism: The Pluralist Structure of Postnational Law* (Oxford University Press, 2010).
Nicola McEwan, *Nationalism and the State: Welfare and Identity in Scotland and Quebec* (Peter Lang, 2006).
Oriol Tejada, *El pensamiento (in) dependiente: Veinticinco reflexiones sobre el proceso soberanista catalán* (Createspace Independent Pub, 2015).
Philip Pettit, 'The Republican Law of Peoples: A Restatement', *Domination and Global Political Justice: Conceptual, Historical, and Institutional Perspectives* (Routledge, 2015), pp. 37–70.
Philip Van Parijs, 'Fiscal Federalism and Solidarity: In Search of an Ideal Formula', in J. F. Grégoire and M. Jewkes (eds.), *Recognition and Redistribution in Multinational Federations* (Leuven University Press, 2015), pp. 183–192.
Rainer Bauböck, 'Democratic Inclusion: A Pluralist Theory of Citizenship', in David Owen (ed.), *Democratic Inclusion in Dialogue* (Manchester University Press, 2018), pp. 3–102.
Robert Dahl, 'Federalism and the Democratic Process', in J. R. Pennock and J. W. Chapman (eds.), *Nomos XXV: Liberal Democracy* (New York University Press, 1983), pp. 95–108.
Robert Goodin, 'Enfranchising All Affected Interests, and Its Alternatives' (2006), *Philosophy and Public Affairs*, Vol. 35, pp. 40–68.
Robert Goodin, 'Enfranchising All Subjected, Worldwide' (2016), *International Theory*, Vol. 8, No. 3, pp. 365–389.
Simon Caney, *Justice Beyond the Borders* (Oxford University Press, 2005).
Sofia Näsström, 'Normative Power of Political Equality', in Eva Erman and Sofia Näsström (eds.), *Political Equality in Transnational Democracy* (Palgrave McMillan, 2013), pp. 157–181.

Theresa Bejan, 'The Bond of Civility: Roger Williams on Toleration and Its Limits' (2011), *History of European Ideas*, Vol. 37, p. 4.

Theresa Bejan, 'Difference without Disagreement: Rethinking Hobbes on 'Independency' and Toleration' (2016), *The Review of Politics*, Vol. 78, pp. 1–25.

Turkuler Isiksel, *Europe's Functional Constitution: A Theory of Constitutionalism Beyond the State* (Oxford University Press, 2016).

Ulrich Beck, *Cosmopolitan Vision* (Polity Press, 2006).

Ulrich Beck, *The Metamorphosis of the World* (Polity Press, 2016).

V. Uberoi, 'The 'Parekh Report'–National Identities without Nations and Nationalism' (2015), *Ethnicities*, Vol. 15, No. 4, pp. 509–526.

Wayne Norman, *Negotiating Nationalism: Nation-Building, Federalism and Secession in the Multinational State* (Oxford University Press, 2006).

Will Kymlicka, *Multicultural Citizenship* (Oxford University Press, 1995).

Will Kymlicka, 'The Essentialist Critique of Multiculturalism: Theories, Policies, Ethos', in V. Uberoi and T. Modood (eds.), *Multiculturalism Rethought: Interpretations, Dilemmas and New Directions* (Edinburgh University Press, 2015), pp. 209–249.

Yael Tamir, *Why Nationalism* (Princeton University Press, 2019).

Part II

The instruments of the theory of democratic secession

6 Constitutionalists' guide to the populist challenge

Lessons from Canada

Giuseppe Martinico[1]

1. A constitutional approach to secession

This chapter looks at the populist use of secessionist arguments in divided societies and aims to explore the relationship between constitutional democracy and referendum in contexts characterized by new waves of populism. New lifeblood to the debate on this noble and yet complex instrument of the referendum has been given by the British events connected to the Brexit vote held on 23 June 2016 – the consequent request for a new referendum on Scottish independence and the burning Catalan scenario. Without analyzing all the above-mentioned phenomena and referring to the chapter by Qvortrup (Chapter 8, this volume) about a detailed overview of the use of referendums on secession, this chapter shall explore some comparative reflections concerning the risks connected to the "inappropriate" use of the referendum, especially in times of populism. As written in the Introduction, the new wave of populism has added another level to the complex scenario of secessionism in Europe by producing a powerful chemistry that risks jeopardizing the essence of constitutional democracy. In my view, the Canadian experience has offered an important contribution that can be used to tackle these issues. This chapter is divided into two sections. In the first section, I shall (briefly) explore the debate on how to proceduralize secession in light of the notion of "exit-related conditionality." In the second section, I shall highlight some reasons for prudence in the use of referendums in the contexts of representative democracy. Without denying or neglecting the political side of secession, this chapter maintains that it also presents legal aspects, and indeed courts have devised a set of techniques in order to cope with it (Martinico, 2017; Castellà Andreu, 2016). For many years, secession was understood as a sort of "constitutional taboo,"[2]

1 Associate Professor of Comparative Public Law at the Scuola Superiore Sant'Anna, Pisa. All websites accessed on 10 January 2019. Thanks to Giacomo Delledonne, Costanza Margiotta and Carlos Closa for their comments. This chapter is part of the Project Jean Monnet Module "Eur.Publ.IUS" (European Public Law-IUS), https://www.santannapisa.it/it/ricerca/progetti/jean-monnet-module-european-public-law-ius-eurpublius. giuseppe.martinico@santannapisa.it

2 "A paramount consideration in any secession-related discussion is that, irrespective of the nature of secessionists claims, secessions are not prima facie desirable, because they jeopardize

at least until 1998 when the Canadian Supreme Court broke the taboo, delivering its famous Reference regarding secession of Québec.[3] That was a pretty brave decision, because on that occasion the Canadian Supreme Court dealt frontally with the issue, accepting the challenge going beyond a formalist reading of its constitutional text(s), i.e. rejecting the argument according to which secession was banned since no written provision provided for that in the Canadian legal system. It did so by identifying the untouchable core of its constitution and reading the issue in light of the principles belonging to such a hard nucleus (federalism, democracy, constitutionalism and rule of law, protection of minorities). When offering its view, the Supreme Court of Canada did not limit its attention to domestic law only but, on the contrary, accepted to take international law into account. For all these reasons, this Reference has become a turning point.[4] Since then, a new debate has begun about how to constitutionalize secession,[5] how to tame something that had been considered for a long time as a sort of "beast" hard to domesticate (Mancini, 2012). Before proceeding, it is necessary to clarify what I mean by "constitutionalisation of secession." By this formula I mean the effort made by the Canadian Court to treat secession as a constitutional option, which may be carried out provided that the untouchable core of the legal system is secured. In other words, by means of this decision, the Canadian Supreme Court "rehabilitated" secession (that is why the Reference broke a taboo as I recalled above) as a legal option that may be used under certain circumstances. In this sense, by "constitutionalisation" I do not automatically mean the codification of a secession clause in a constitutional text, although as I will try to show the inclusion of a clause like this should not be seen as bad *per se*.

In order to tackle secession, the Canadian Supreme Court first contextualized it in a legal scenario, avoiding easy choices and facing the preliminary objections concerning the lack of legal relevance of the challenged acts or of the raised questions. This strategy was perceived to be necessary in order to compensate the passivity of the relevant political actors or to try to facilitate a dialogue that had not yet begun between the central and regional levels. Second, the Canadian

world stability. However, demonizing secession, turning it into a constitutional taboo, often adds fuel to secessionist claims," Mancini, 2012, 481, at 482. The origin of this taboo is linked to the story of John Calhoun. Calhoun was a man rooted in the culture of a country that was quickly moving from the end of the Revolution to the start of the Civil War. Although he passed away in 1850, Calhoun has always been seen as "the man who Started the Civil War," to cite the emblematical title of an article by Rafuse (2002). Being a man of his times of course implies that Calhoun also defended slavery and its importance for the Southern economy. However, he was also one of the most brilliant champions of the so-called compact theory. Nevertheless, the result of the Civil War marginalized him and his theories.

3 Canadian Supreme Court, Reference Re Secession of Quebec [1998] 2 SCR 217.

4 On the increasing importance of references in Canadian Constitutional Law see: McKay-Panos, 2014. As the author recalls: "A reference case is different than a regular civil or criminal case that involves litigating parties. In a reference, the federal or provincial government submits questions to the courts asking for an advisory opinion on major legal issue(s). Often, the question involves the constitutionality of existing or proposed legislation."

5 For instance, see: Haljan, 2014; Weinstock, 2001.

Court gave a complex notion of democracy, which cannot be reduced to mere majority rule. This is a very important point as we will see later; which makes this Reference also a powerful tool against populism. Third, it reconstructed the core of Canadian constitutional identity by recalling the untouchable principles that make the Canadian Constitution special. In so doing, the Canadian Supreme Court also presented the referendum as an instrument that needs to be mediated and which should not be considered as a source of automatic political or legal truth. This explains the deference that characterizes the Reference, which is also clear in giving political actors the task "to determine what constitutes a clear majority on a clear question."[6] This way the Canadian Court avoided treating the referendum as something alternative to representative democracy.

In light of these considerations, the legacy of the Canadian Reference is fundamental to challenge the constitutional counternarrative advanced by populists. In this regard, more recently, scholars tried to go beyond a conflictual analysis (constitutionalism versus populism) by showing that – to a certain extent at least – even populism "contains a (largely implicit) constitutional theory."[7] Even more recently, Fournier defined this relationship by relying on a "parasite analogy," saying that "the relation between populism and constitutional democracy is comparable to a process of parasitism where constitutional democracy would be the host and populism the parasite."[8]

In fact, one could say that the real aim of populist movements is to alter the axiological independence that characterizes constitutional democracies, for instance, by presenting democracy (understood as the rule of majority) as a kind of "trump card" which should prevail over other constitutional values,[9] such as the rule of law. To question this argument, one could recall one of the most important "lessons learned" thanks to the Canadian Reference, which instead proposed a richer understanding of democracy – i.e. – non-limited to its formal or procedural sense. Finally, it is important to recall that the Canadian Supreme Court did not recognize a proper right to secession, rather it treated secession as an option that may be tolerated only in presence of some important safeguards. In order to make this point, the Canadian Court came up with a sort of "exit related conditionality" as we will see in the next section, this way it guaranteed the respect of the constitutional identity of Canada.

6 Canadian Supreme Court, Reference Re Secession of Quebec [1998] 2 S.C.R. 217.

7 "Populism in a Constitutional Key" cit. "Constitutional theorists have not devoted a lot of attention to the phenomenon of populism [...] There may be two interpretations of this silence. Either constitutional theory has nothing to say about populism, in which case the silence is justified, or constitutional theory does have something to say, in which case the silence is unjustified and (potentially) problematic," Corrias, 2016, at 6.

8 Fournier, 2018. On populism and parasitism see also: Urbinati, 1998.

9 "Populist rhetoric can be defined as the political discourse aiming to convince a fictional majority that constitutional democracy gives rise to the tyranny of minorities. The choice of 'rhetoric' instead of 'discourse' is intentional," Fournier, 2018.

2. Exit-related conditionality and secession

Comparative lawyers have analyzed the provisions concerning the possibility of secession[10] and also legal and political theorists have dealt with the issue of how to justify the option of secession even in legal systems whose constitutions say nothing about that, including the Canadian one.[11] As said, the Canadian Reference has been crucial to rehabilitate – under certain circumstances – the idea of secession as a constitutional option. This does not automatically lead the codification of a constitutional clause on that. As we know, the outcome of that decision relied on a series of unwritten principles. However, without recalling the very huge debate already mentioned, I would like to briefly mention an element that in my view could justify the codification of a secession clause in the constitution of some federal/regional contexts. This element is linked to constitutional homogeneity: legal systems[12] tend to ensure a virtuous connection between diversity and unity with a series of mechanisms aimed at preserving loyalty and adhesion to the fundamental values of the national system. Evidence of this can be found in Art. 28 of the German Basic Law[13] and in Art. 51 of the Swiss Constitution which conditions, for example, the contents of the cantonal constitutions.[14]

10 Mancini, 2014 at 791. She also pointed out that "The charter of the Soviet Union had similarly constitutionalized the right of secession. Recognition of this right, in Lenin's opinion, in no way led to the 'formation of small States, but to the enlargement of the bigger ones—a phenomenon more advantageous for the masses and for the development of the economy [...] Analogously, the guarantee of the right of secession in the Ethiopian Constitution of 1994 seems largely motivated by the desire to strengthen cohesion by dissuading the component subunits of the state from following the example of Eritrea," Mancini, 2012, at 494–495. See also: Margiotta Broglio, 2005, at 37.

11 See: Norman, 2006; Buchanan, 1991.

12 Recently on this see: Delledonne, 2017.

13 Art. 28 of the German Basic Law: 1 The constitutional order in the Länder must conform to the principles of a republican, democratic and social state governed by the rule of law, within the meaning of this Basic Law. In each Land, county and municipality the people shall be represented by a body chosen in general, direct, free, equal and secret elections. In county and municipal elections, persons who possess citizenship in any member state of the European Community are also eligible to vote and to be elected in accord with European Community law.
In municipalities a local assembly may take the place of an elected body.

2. Municipalities must be guaranteed the right to regulate all local affairs on their own responsibility, within the limits prescribed by the laws. Within the limits of their functions designated by a law, associations of municipalities shall also have the right of self-government according to the laws. The guarantee of self-government shall extend to the bases of financial autonomy; these bases shall include the right of municipalities to a source of tax revenues based upon economic ability and the right to establish the rates at which these sources shall be taxed.
3. The Federation shall guarantee that the constitutional order of the Länder conforms to the basic rights and to the provisions of paragraphs (1) and (2) of this Article'.

14 Art. 51 of the Swiss Constitution: "Each Canton shall adopt a democratic constitution. This requires the approval of the People and must be capable of being revised if the majority of those eligible to vote so request. Each cantonal constitution shall require the guarantee of the Confederation. The Confederation shall guarantee a constitution provided it is not contrary to federal law."

Similar examples can be found even at the supranational level. Here it is sufficient to recall the criteria employed for the accession of new Member States to the EU. Reasons connected to homogeneity can always suggest forms of control and monitoring and even the possibility of activating forms of centripetal intervention in case of departure from the fundamental values of the constitutional pact. This is the case of Art. 155 of the Spanish Constitution and above all Art. 37 of the German Basic Law.[15] Against this background, in pursuing homogeneity these legal systems develop forms of conditionality aimed at ensuring a sort of structural compatibility between their different components.

How is this connected with the possible introduction of a secession clause? Even the clauses on exit/withdrawal from a federal union can be read as forms of "exit related conditionality," by ensuring an axiological continuity between the new order and the old one. This might appear paradoxical, but it is actually a process in which the old system accepts the detachment of the seceding entity by making it conditional upon the adhesion to its fundamental values. This way the constituent phase of the seceding legal system is partly guided and influenced by the values of the old constitution. This way the revolutionary character of secession is partly "exorcised." To understand what I mean by exit-related conditionality, recall the Canadian Reference according to which, in case of activation of the negotiations with Québec, "the conduct of the parties in such negotiations would be governed by the same constitutional principles which give rise to the duty to negotiate: federalism, democracy, constitutionalism and the rule of law, and the protection of minorities."[16] This axiological continuity would guarantee the rights of that population residing in the territory of the new state which had not voted for the independence. By constitutionalizing secession, in other words, the legal system could tame the violent side of secession and containing (which does not mean excluding, of course as legal norms may also fail) the risk of political abuses that might be produced by a contingent majority (Norman, 2006, at 178). The appeal to the will of a contingent majority and the risk of "extreme majoritarianism" (see Closa, Chapter 4, this volume) is the bridge connecting secessionism and populism and we will see in this chapter. A possible counterargument against the constitutionalization of a secession clause is linked to the threat of constantly exposing a legal system to the blackmail of the exit, in a sort of game to negotiate further forms of autonomy. Actually, the Spanish scenario shows that a risk like this exists even in the absence of a secession clause. In this sense, the lack of a provision like this has led to the explosion of a political crisis in the absence of constitutional paths other than the constitutional amendment.

15 Art. 37 of the German Basic Law: "(1) If a Land fails to comply with its obligations under this Basic Law or other federal laws, the Federal Government, with the consent of the Bundesrat, may take the necessary steps to compel the Land to comply with its duties.
(2) For the purpose of implementing such coercive measures, the Federal Government or its representative shall have the right to issue instructions to all Länder and their authorities."

16 Canadian Supreme Court, Reference Re Secession of Quebec [1998] 2 S.C.R. 217, para. 90.

Concerning how to design a norm governing the exit from the federal entity examples that could be taken into account are not absent. Many of the models recalled by comparative lawyers have given referendums an important role.[17]

This makes the Canadian Reference an important message of hope, since it recognizes a fundamental role to the law. Although the law cannot exclude the resolution of secessionist crises by means of violence, it has at least procedural advantage to oblige the institutional actors to treat – *prima facie* – secession as a legal issue before resorting to extra-legal measures, by offering some binding guidelines[18]aimed at protecting minorities. This is not a detail in my view: instead of leaving this process to politics or violence, legal norms can contribute to containing the political dialectic within the rule of law.

3. The constitutional risks of referendums: what can we learn from comparative law?

Comparative constitutional law[19] offers examples of provisions which give referendums an important role in the procedure devised to govern secession: Ethiopia,[20] Uzbekistan,[21] (former) Serbia Montenegro,[22] Liechtenstein,[23] Northern Ireland,[24] Nevis and Saint Christopher.[25]

In this part of the chapter, I shall recall the constitutional risks of referendums and suggest some prudence in their use, especially in populist contexts. Scholars have traditionally pointed out the ambiguities of referendum and the risks connected to an appropriate use of the instrument. It is a very long debate (Luciani, 2008, 2005, 1992; Di Giovine, 2005) and already Max Weber, for instance, recalled such risks and stressed how it can be used to deresponsibilize the political forces:

> The referendum does not know the compromise, upon which the majority of all laws is based in every mass state with strong regional, social, religious and other cleavages [...] Moreover, the plebiscitary principles weaken the autonomous role of the party leader and the responsibility of the civil servants. A disavowal of the leading officials through a plebiscite which rejects their proposals does not and cannot enforce their resignation, as does a vote of

17 Mancini, 2014, at 800; Ziegler, Shaw, Bauböck, 2014.

18 As Norman recalled "the perceived advantages of handling secessionist politics and secessionist contests within the rule of law rather than as 'political' issues that lie outside of, or are presumed (by the secessionists) to supersede, the law," Norman, 2006, at 189.

19 See also the 1947 Constitution of Burma at arts. 201-206. On this see: Gökhan Şen, 2015; Qvortrup, 2014; Frosina, 2017.

20 Art. 39 of the Ethiopian Constitution.

21 Art. 74 of the Constitution of Uzbekistan.

22 Art. 60 of the Constitution of Serbia Montenegro.

23 Art. 4 of the Constitution of the Principality of Liechtenstein.

24 Section 1 of the Northern Ireland Act 1998.

25 Art. 113 of the Constitution of Saint Christopher and Nevis.

> no-confidence in parliamentary states, for the negative vote does not identify its reasons and does not oblige the negatively voting mass, as it does a parliamentary majority voting against a government, to replace the disavowed officials with its own responsible leaders.
>
> (Weber, 1978, English edition)

These are considerations that have inspired generations of social scientists and that are dramatically topical nowadays. Comparative lawyers have reflected a lot on the complicated relationship on referendums and representative democracy (Carré de Malberg, 1931; Mirkine Guetzévitch, 1931; Schmitt, 2001, Italian edition; Butler and Ranney, 1994; Qvortrup, 2002; Uleri, 2003; Tierney, 2012; Lewis, 2013). British lawyers have reclaimed the topic in light of the recent debate on Brexit[26] and EU law scholars have also developed a mass of literature on that, due to the several examples of consultations that have taken place on European issues, starting from the referendum conducted in 1975, for instance (Mendez, Mendez and Triga, 2014, 2017; Özlem Atikcan, 2015; Closa, 2007).

The ideal starting point of this debate[27] is obviously the well-known exchange between Carré de Malberg and Mirkine Guetzévitch. According to the former, the referendum was compatible with parliamentary systems,[28] especially if understood as a way of solving the conflicts occurring between parliament and government and of limiting the parliamentary almightiness.[29] According to the latter, the referendum implied a tension that could hardly be solved with the idea of rationalization of parliamentarism.[30] It is necessary to recall that Mirkine Guetzévitch partly changed his mind, as observed by Morel.[31] Actually, as Luciani

26 Building on the seminal works by Dicey, 1890. On Dicey: Weill, 2003;. See also: House of Lords. 2010; Torre, 2005; Torre, Frosini, 2012.

27 Recently, Morel has identified at least two research strands in the debate on referendums and argued: "Theoretical accounts on referendums belong either to the constitutional debate or to democratic theory. What distinguishes the two debates in a rather precise way is the set of questions raised: while the classical, constitutional, debate questions the issue of the compatibility of the referendum with representative democracy and the extent and modalities of its use, the democratic debate rather focuses on the democratic quality of the referendum and whether its extension could help to improve the quality of contemporary democracies," Morel, 2012.

28 See also: Guarino, 1947.

29 Carré de Malberg, 1931, at 262.

30 Mirkine Guetzévitch, 1931, at 334. "The discussion of the Russian constitutionalist focused in particular on a new variety of referendums and popular initiatives aimed at solving conflicts between the executive and the legislative, which could lead to the dissolution of parliament or the revocation of the head of the state. Mirkine Guetzévitch regarded this as contradictory with the trend toward a 'rationalization' of parliamentarism, by means of a strengthening of executives, which he welcomed as the great novelty of these Constitutions." Morel, 2012, at 504.

31 "The author had, however, expressed a rather different position one year earlier, in *Les Constitutions de l'Europe nouvelle* (1930), where he wrote that 'the referendum is the logical conclusion of the process of rationalization of parliamentarism'," Morel, 2012, at footnote n. 9.

pointed out, the two scholars started from a common premise represented by the antiparliamentary flavour of the referendum (Luciani, 2008, at 33).

This debate is partly connected to the qualification of the referendum as an instrument of direct democracy. This position is, for instance, quite widespread in the Italian debate, but there are important scholars who have rejected this view by understanding the referendum as a device of popular participation on the basis of an interesting historical excursus (Luciani, 2005, at 163). It is the case of Luciani, for instance, who stressed the necessary physical coexistence as an essential connotation of direct democracy ("the assembled people" as Luciani wrote commenting on Rousseau).[32] Similar considerations have been shared by political scientists who argued that direct democracy does not exist as a modern form of government and is a misleading category (Uleri, 2003), also in light of the continuity that exists between referendum and political competition. If comparative law offers a variety of typologies of referendum (constitutional, legislative, conventional, preventive, successive, mandatory, optional, advisory; see Volpi, 1997, 2016) such a variety does not impede the finding of common concerns and trends. This does not deny the analytical validity of the distinction between experiences in which the referendum initiative belongs to constitutional bodies only and experiences where the initiative is, so to speak, diffused (as opposed to centralized/institutionalized) in civil society. In these contexts, referendums have been seen as a "counter-power" (Fois, 1978) or a manifestation of the "right of resistance" (Volpe, 1998).

However, all the legal systems know forms of limitation of the political risks connected to the referendum. For instance, in an essay devoted to the Swiss[33] and American experiences, Auer once recalled the fear of the American founding fathers towards "pure democracy"[34] and in light of that he went on to explain the lack of the referendum at the federal level in the US. These remarks do not

32 Luciani, 2005, at 11. On that occasion Luciani referred to Rousseau, 1762.

33 On Switzerland see also: Raible, Trueblood, 2017: "Exploring the interaction between voters and the representative branches of government is helpful. It is necessary to take into account that the influence of the representative branches of government is considerably more pervasive than is acknowledged. Consider how the Federal Assembly may respond to popular initiatives for instance; the relationship is an iterative one. The Federal Assembly may submit a counter-proposal to popular initiatives, that is, partial revisions of the constitution requested by the citizenry (art. 139(5)). Whenever such initiatives take the form of a specific draft of a provision (as opposed to a general proposal) the Federal Assembly may decide to take up some or all of the concerns expressed by the initiative to form the basis of its own draft. The electorate then vote on the initiative and the counter-proposal at the same time (art. 139b(1)). In addition to the two questions about the two different proposals, the ballot also contains a third question where the electorate are asked to indicate a preference in case both drafts are accepted (art. 139b(2)). The value of this example is that it demonstrates that there is nothing particularly direct about democracy in Switzerland. Of course, there are more referendums in Switzerland than in, for example, the UK. But it is not the volume of referendums that makes the system distinctive, and it should not be understood to make it direct."

34 Auer, 1992, at 64.

come as a surprise if it is true, as Elster argued, that constitutions are frequently the product of violence and fear (Elster, 2012). Obviously, the British experience is very particular due to the only partially written nature of its constitutional sources (Bogdanor, 1981, at 75) and to the relatively recent practice of an instrument which has been, however, studied by eminent British lawyers such as Dicey (1890). Dicey analyzed that in light of the well-known distinction between "political sovereignty" and "legal sovereignty."[35] However, there have been attempts to extend to the British case some of the considerations made with regard to Continental Europe (f. i. Calamo Specchia, 2012) and British constitutional lawyers have stressed that the UK peculiarity does not impede fruitful comparisons (Leyland, 2013). It is sufficient to refer to the continental discussion about the advantages and disadvantages of referendums (Luciani, 2005) with what was written by the Select Committee on the Constitution of the House of Lords some years ago (House of Lords, 2010). Although these cases are different, some of the arguments employed in this debate are identical and it is no coincidence that the issue of the referendum has given new lifeblood to the need for a (further) codification of British constitutional law (Leyland, 2013). Another element of comparability is given by the common influence exercised by the EU. This also explains why the first important consultation held in the 1970s in the UK was that on British membership in the European Economic Community. It is also known that the referendum in the history of European integration often goes back for seconds: this happened in Ireland and Denmark for instance, on the occasion of the ratification of some European Treaties (Özlem Atikcan, 2015). With regard to the EU, the "referendum on sovereign powers" ("referendum sui poteri sovrani"), as described by Baldassarre, have been trialled (Baldassarre, 1994) and, here again, it is possible to recall the different uses of the instrument. Within the almost 70 referendums held on European matters,[36] scholars have identified at least four groups: (1) "membership referendums"; (2) "treaty

35 Venn Dicey, 1959: "At this point comes into view the full importance of the distinction already insisted upon between 'legal' sovereignty and 'political' sovereignty. Parliament is, from a merely legal point of view, the absolute sovereign of the British Empire, since every Act of Parliament is binding on every Court throughout the British dominions, and no rule, whether of morality or of law, which contravenes an Act of Parliament binds any Court throughout the realm. But if Parliament be in the eye of the law a supreme legislature, the essence of representative government is, that the legislature should represent or give effect to the will of the political sovereign, i.e. of the electoral body, or of the nation. That the conduct of the different parts of the legislature should be determined by rules meant to secure harmony between the action of the legislative sovereign and the wishes of the political sovereign, must appear probable from general considerations. If the true ruler or political sovereign of England were, as was once the case, the King, legislation might be carried out in accordance with the King's will by one of two methods. The Crown might itself legislate, by royal proclamations, or decrees; or some other body', in the edition dated 2013 and edited by Allison this passage can be found at 429."

36 "To date there have been 60 referendums on EU-related matters making the referendum a key feature of the European integration process since the 1970s," Mendez, Mendez and Triga, 2017.

revision referendums"; (3) "policy referendums"; and (4) "third-country referendums" (Mendez, Mendez and Triga, 2017). Within these four groups it is possible to identify other sub-typologies based on the reasons that have led to the consultation and the subject of the question.[37] All this confirms not only the topicality of the issue but also the multi-functional nature of this device in European and comparative constitutional law.

Even in the UK, concerns about the use of the referendum have not been absent. First of all, in the UK there is legislative discipline which governs the use of this tool,[38] although it is not easy to understand what the formula "constitutional matters" means. Indeed, although it is unquestioned that "referendums undoubtedly have a constitutional role to play" (Leyland, 2013, at 146), in this context, as Bogdanor said, "the problem is that in Britain constitutional issues can easily arise out of seemingly non-constitutional legislation" (Bogdanor, 1981, at 73). Without mentioning that, "without clear rules referendums can be manipulated politically" (Leyland, 2013, at 146). The report of the Select Committee on the Constitution of the House of Lords gave an important contribution to this debate. First, it offered an account of the pros[39] and cons[40] in the

37 'Referendums on EU matters vary considerably in terms of (1) their functional properties or type and (2) the reasons for calling them. Taking into account these two dimensions is crucial to understanding the dynamics of EU-related referendums. There are four main types of EU-related referendum: (1) membership referendums (which can be divided between the frequently deployed accession referendum and the rarely used withdrawal referendum); (2) treaty revision referendums, which were generated by all six main rounds of treaty revision from the SEA to Lisbon; (3) policy referendums, which are held by EU Member States on an EU-related policy matter but are neither about membership nor treaty revision; (4) third-country referendums, which are held on the topic of European integration by states that are neither EU Member States nor are they Candidate States voting directly on an accession treaty; There are three broad categories of motives for referendums on EU matters which operate under distinct decisional logics: (1) the logic of constitutionality where referendums are either clearly constitutionally mandatory or at least considered to be; (2) the logic of appropriateness where the overriding rationale for deployment of a referendum is due to legitimacy concerns; (3) the logic of partisan calculus where the referendum is held for partisan motives whether to boost the popularity of an incumbent leader or to mediate divisions within a political party," Mendez, Mendez and Triga, 2017.

38 "The Election Commission is placed under a duty to advise on the intelligibility of any referendum questions and the legislation also establishes control over donations and expenses and many other issues. However, no clear rules have emerged to determine under what precise constitutional conditions referendums can be held," Leyland, 2013, 145.

39 "That referendums enhance the democratic process"; "that referendums can be a 'weapon of entrenchment'"; "that referendums can 'settle' an issue"; "that referendums can be a 'protective device'"; "that referendums enhance citizen engagement"; "that referendums promote voter education"; "that voters are able to make reasoned judgments"; "that referendums are popular with voters"; "that referendums complement representative democracy," House of Lords. Select Committee on the Constitution 12th Report of Session 2009–10.

40 Among others, "That referendums are a tactical device"; "that referendums are dominated by elite groups"; "that referendums can have a damaging effect on minority groups"; "that referendums are a conservative device"; "that referendums do not 'settle' an issue"; "that referendums fail to deal with complex issues"; "that referendums tend not to be about the issue

use of the referendum; second, it recalled some of the fundamental constitutional issues that would require the holding of a referendum (to abolish the Monarchy; to leave the European Union; for any of the nations of the UK to secede from the union; to abolish either House of Parliament; to change the electoral system for the House of Commons; to adopt a written constitution; and to change the UK's system of currency).[41]

There are, finally, two other considerations that make the referendum fascinating to comparative lawyers: the fact that many constitutional lawyers have changed their minds about this instrument. The first consideration can be explained in light of the fact that it is always necessary to look at it from the systemic impact that it might have on the context of representative democracy. This partly explains the changing position of Dicey.[42]

Many criticized Dicey for this change of mind; others have tried to find continuity in his thought by stressing the parliamentary disappointment that would have caused that (Weill, 2003, at 475).

This was due to the 1911 *Parliament Act* which had removed, in Dicey's own words, "[the] last effective constitutional safeguard" (Dicey, 1912, at 81), by recognizing the supremacy of the House of Commons over the House of Lords and creating a system where the majority of the Commons "can arrogate to itself that legislative omnipotence which of right belongs to the nation" (Dicey, 1912, at 91). In other words, according to Dicey, the referendums could compensate the new institutional scenario after the weakening of the House of Lords.

Because of the fact that the British institutional equilibrium had changed, Dicey's point was necessary to involve the people in the "constitutional changes."

The referendum has also had a chameleonic nature; it is sufficient here to notice what has happened in the UK where once Bogdanor defined the referendum as a "conservative device" (Bodganor, 1981, at 69):

> The referendum is generally seen as an instrument of popular sovereignty, an institutional expression of the doctrine that political authority derives from the people. Yet, as the history of the debate in Britain shows, the urge towards popular participation or self-government has not played a very important part in its advocacy. On the contrary, since first proposed by Dicey, the referendum has been suggested primarily as a means of checking disagreeable legislation [...] It has been, in the words of Beaverbrook, "not a spear but a shield," an adjunct to representative government and not a replacement for it.
>
> (Bogdanor, 1981, at 69)

in question"; "that voters show little desire to participate in referendums"; "that referendums are costly"; "that referendums undermine representative democracy," House of Lords, 2010.

41 House of Lords, 2010.

42 This point has been explored by Weill in a very important article which revolved around the reasons for this (apparent) departure from the principle of parliamentary sovereignty, Weill, 2003, at 475 and at 481.

This explains why referendums "could serve to increase its [the government's] power," and it is no coincidence that over recent years the debate has been focusing on how to discipline it to avoid possible abuses. This intuition was confirmed in the 1990s when it was used as an instrument to enfranchise the party leadership from the internal influences of the party and to create a direct connection with the people. This has led to forms of plebiscitary drift (Torre, 2012, at 73).

This explains why the referendum – once defined by Bogdanor as a "conservative device" as we saw – has become part of the reformist season (Carboni, 2012, at 40). While many perceive the only significant difference between the Scottish and the Catalan referendums as lying in the unilateral nature of the latter, what really makes the Catalan scenario inconsistent with the local constitutional framework is the fact that there, the Autonomous Communities have no competence to call these types of referendums, as scholars have clearly pointed out in the reading of Art. 149.1.32 of the Spanish Constitution.[43] This might appear as a procedural element but it affects the substance of the issue perhaps even more than the generic content of Art. 2 of the Spanish Constitution according to which: "The Constitution is based on the indissoluble unity of the Spanish Nation."[44]

4. An instrument to be handled with care: against a reductivist concept of democracy

The obsession of populist movements with the "politics of immediacy" (Corrias, 2016, at 12) inevitably results in questioning many of the instruments of representative democracy and in emphasizing the importance of instruments of direct and participatory democracy. This explains the importance that referendums play in the populist agenda as they offer charismatic leaders who have direct contact with the people. Frequently, the attack on representative institutions and the emphasis on referendums are taken as two sides of the same coin, since they are both emanations of that lack of mediation that political scientists frequently portray as one of the pillars of populism (Mény and Surel, 2004). As Canovan pointed out, "New Populists often call for issues of popular concern to be decided by referendum, by-passing professional politicians and leaving decisions to the people" (Canovan, 2005, at 76). Referendums also galvanize that dichotomous approach frequently endorsed by populists in the constant appeal to the people understood as a monolithic entity, in the sense that they tend to represent a part of the people as the people.[45]

43 Art. 149.1.32 of the Spanish Constitution: "1. The State shall have exclusive competence over the following matters [...] :32. Authorization of popular consultations through the holding of referendums."

44 Art. 2 of the Spanish Constitution.

45 "Brexiters, too, invoke the referendum as the 'will of the people', a phrase understood as a singular homogeneous monolith, conveniently ignoring that 62.5% of the electorate ('remainers', and those who abstained from participating) did not vote to leave the EU but are 'automatically' included in that will. That discursive populism has been voiced not

Against this background, the final part of this chapter revolves around three main points.

The *first one* is the idea of referendum as a graft transplanted into contexts of constitutional representative democracy. While referendums are normally seen by populist movements as a kind of "catch-all" appeal to the people which should be used to react against the corruption or passivity of the institutions, constitutional lawyers tend to handle referendums with care, looking upon them as a noble instrument whose compatibility with representative democracy must be guaranteed. This perspective can be justified in light of the political risks connected to excessive use of referendum, in other words referendums, if used as a full alternative to the instruments and institutions representative of democracy risk creating parallel channels of legitimation which could destabilize and delegitimize parliaments.

In order to prevent this, constitutions (even in contexts provided with partly written constitutions, for instance, the UK) come up with solutions designed to strike a balance between representative and direct/participatory (depending on how scholars understand referendums (Luciani, 2008) democracy.

The *second point* I would like to make is about the artificial concept of majority.[46]

It is possible to find confirmation of this in comparative law. Both the *Clarity Act* in Canada and Schedule I of the *Good Friday Agreement* give political actors an important role in detecting the existing majorities. The Clarity Act was a follow up to the secession Reference in the part in which the Canadian Supreme Court had said: "in this context, we refer to a 'clear' majority as a qualitative evaluation. The referendum result, if it is to be taken as an expression of the democratic will, must be free of ambiguity both in terms of the question asked and in terms of the support it achieves" (Canadian Supreme Court, Reference Re Secession of Quebec [1998] 2 S.C.R. 217).

In light of this, the *Clarity Act* listed some factors that should be taken into account by the House of Commons to verify *a posteriori* the existence of a majority:

> Factors for House of Commons to take into account (2) In considering whether there has been a clear expression of a will by a clear majority of the population of a province that the province cease to be part of Canada, the

only by UKIP members but by UK government ministers and governing party M.P.s; thus Priti Patel, Secretary of State for International Development, insisted in an interview on 16 October 2016 that 'the British people have spoken and we will deliver for them'," Freeden, 2017, at 7 .

46 "A majority is not something you will find in nature. It is an artifact of law. You need legal rules to determine who counts, and in which way. You need legal safeguards of liberty, equality and diversity of opinion. You also need legal rules to determine what the majority will be able to do, which necessarily implies that the majority gets told what she is not allowed to do. In short, you need constitutional law," Steinbeis, 2017.

> House of Commons shall take into account (a) the size of the majority of valid votes cast in favour of the secessionist option; (b) the percentage of eligible voters voting in the referendum; and (c) any other matters or circumstances it considers to be relevant.[47]

This has caused a harsh reaction in Québec as we know. A similar role, but to be played in the phase before the holding of a referendum, is granted to the Secretary of State by Schedule I of the *Good Friday Agreement*:[48]

1. The Secretary of State may by order direct the holding of a poll for the purposes of section 1 on a date specified in the order.
2. Subject to paragraph 3, the Secretary of State shall exercise the power under paragraph 1 if at any time it appears likely to him that a majority of those voting would express a wish that Northern Ireland should cease to be part of the United Kingdom and form part of a united Ireland.
3. The Secretary of State shall not make an order under paragraph 1 earlier than seven years after the holding of a previous poll under this Schedule.

These two examples show that the majority is not a neutral or easy concept (see Beaulac, Chapter 7, this volume); on the contrary, it is an artificial one which can be constructed through political and legal decisions, for instance by excluding or including particular groups of people in the right to vote. That is why procedural caveats are important, since they contribute towards ensuring the preservation of that core of untouchable values that is up to constitutionalism to defend. Finally, the *third point* lies at the heart of the alleged tension between formal and substantive democracy or, better still, between democracy and rule of majority. This aspect has been clarified – once again – in the already-mentioned Reference on Québec and secession by the Canadian Supreme Court in 1998 when it said that:

> Democracy, however, means more than simple majority rule. Constitutional jurisprudence shows that democracy exists in the larger context of other constitutional values… Canadians have never accepted that ours is a system of

47 An Act to give effect to the requirement for clarity as set out in the opinion of the Supreme Court of Canada in the Quebec Secession Reference S.C. 2000, c. 26, http://laws-lois.justice.gc.ca/eng/acts/c-31.8/page-1.html

48 "ANNEX A 1. (1) It is hereby declared that Northern Ireland in its entirety remains part of the United Kingdom and shall not cease to be so without the consent of a majority of the people of Northern Ireland voting in a poll held for the purposes of this section in accordance with Schedule 1.
(2) But if the wish expressed by a majority in such a poll is that Northern Ireland should cease to be part of the United Kingdom and form part of a united Ireland, the Secretary of State shall lay before Parliament such proposals to give effect to that wish as may be agreed between Her Majesty's Government in the United Kingdom and the Government of Ireland." The Northern Ireland Peace Agreement. The Agreement reached in the multi-party negotiations 10 April 1998, http://peacemaker.un.org/sites/peacemaker.un.org/files/IE%20GB_980410_Northern%20Ireland%20Agreement.pdf

> simple majority rule. Our principle of democracy, taken in conjunction with the other constitutional principles discussed here, is richer [....] While it is true that some attempts at constitutional amendment in recent years have faltered, a clear majority vote in Quebec on a clear question in favour of secession would confer democratic legitimacy on the secession initiative which all of the other participants in Confederation would have to recognize... However, it will be for the political actors to determine what constitutes "a clear majority on a clear question" in the circumstances under which a future referendum vote may be taken (Canadian Supreme Court, Reference Re Secession of Quebec [1998] 2 S.C.R. 217).

These inspirational words pronounced by the Canadian Supreme Court confirm the strong counter-majoritarian[49] nature of constitutionalism as such. Indeed, within the principles recalled by the Canadian Court there is also the protection of minorities. Although the Canadian Court focused on linguistic minorities in that case, the language used throughout the Reference allows this Reference to be connected to a broader concept of minority as clarified by the Court itself by insisting on the distinction between democracy and majority rule (para. 63). From that and other passages we can understand that democracy cannot be used as a "trump card" to alter the untouchable core that characterizes (liberal) constitutional systems, since there are values that cannot be decided by the majority in democratic systems. In this sense, the Canadian case shows that even in the absence of explicit constitutional clauses it is possible to attempt to proceduralize this phenomenon, by contributing to its domestication and in that the Canadian Supreme Court has indeed sent a message of hope: law – especially constitutional law – can and must have a role, avoiding delegating this issue to violence or politics only (Martinico, 2019).

References

Andreas Auer, 'L'esperienza del referendum in Svizzera e negli Stati Uniti', in Massimo Luciani and Mauro Volpi (eds), *Referendum* (Laterza, 1992) 61, at 64.

Antonio Baldassarre, 'Il «referendum» costituzionale' (1994) *Quaderni costituzionali* 235.

Alexander Bickel, *The Least Dangerous Branch* (Yale University Press, 1986).

Vernor Bogdanor, *The People and the Party System: The Referendum and Electoral Reform in British Politics* (CUP, 1981), at 75.

Allen Buchanan, *Secession: The Morality of Political Divorce from Fort Sumter to Lithuania and Quebec* (Routledge, 1991).

David Butler and Austin Ranney (eds), *Referendums around the World: The Growing Use of Direct Democracy* (AEI Press, 1994).

Marina Calamo Specchia, 'Quale disciplina referendaria nel Regno Unito? Brevi note su di un approccio sistematico per un modello a-sistematico', in Alessandro Torre and Justin Frosini (eds), *Democrazia rappresentativa e referendum nel Regno Unito* (Maggioli, 2012) 146.

49 Here the reference is of course to Bickel, 1986.

Margaret Canovan, *The People* (Polity, 2005), at 76.

Giuliana Giuseppina Carboni, 'I referendum mai realizzati e ancora da realizzare', in Alessandro Torre and Justin Frosini (eds), *Democrazia rappresentativa e referendum nel Regno Unito* (Maggioli, 2012) 39.

Raymond Carré de Malberg, 'Considérations théoriques sur la question de la combinaison du referendum avec le parlementarisme' (1931) 2 *Annuaire de l'Institut international de droit public* 272.

Josep M. Castellà Andreu, 'Tribunal Constitucional y proceso secesionista catalán: respuestas jurídico-constitucionales a un conflicto político-constitucional' (2016) 37 *Teoría y Realidad Constitucional* 561.

Carlos Closa, 'Why Convene Referendums? Explaining Choices in EU Constitutional Politics' (2007) 14 *Journal of European Public Policy* 1311.

Luigi Corrias, 'Populism in a Constitutional Key: Constituent Power, Popular Sovereignty and Constitutional Identity' (2016) 12 *European Constitutional Law Review* 6.

Giacomo Delledonne, *L'omogeneità costituzionale negli ordinamenti composti* (Editoriale Scientifica, 2017).

Albert Venn Dicey, 'Ought the Referendum to be Introduced into England?' (1890) 57 *Contemporary Review* 508.

Albert Venn Dicey, 'The Parliament Act 1911 and the Destruction of All Constitutional Safeguards', in William R. Anson, Frederick E. Smith and Lord Willoughby De Broke (eds), *Rights of Citizenship: A Survey of Safeguards for the People* (Frederick Warne, 1912) 81.

Albert Venn Dicey, *Introduction to the Study of the Law of the Constitution* (St. Martin's Press, 1959).

Albert Venn Dicey, *The Law of the Constitution* (OUP, 2013), edited by John Allison.

Alfonso Di Giovine, 'Referendum e responsabilità politica' (2005) *Diritto Pubblico Comparato ed Europeo* 1214.

Jon Elster, 'Constitution-Making and Violence' (2012) 4 *Journal of Legal Analysis* 7.

Sergio Fois, 'Il referendum come «contropotere» e garanzia nel sistema costituzionale italiano', in Ernesto Bettinelli and Luca Boneschi (eds), *Referendum, ordine pubblico, Costituzione* (Bompiani, 1978) 130.

Théo Fournier, *From Rhetoric to Action: A Constitutional Analysis of Populism* (2018) EUI Working Paper 2018/08, http://cadmus.eui.eu/handle/1814/51725.

Michael Freeden, 'After the Brexit Referendum: Revisiting Populism as an Ideology' (2017) 22 *Journal of Political Ideologies* 1.

Laura Frosina, 'Profili giuridici e aspetti problematici del referendum di secessione. Un'analisi comparata' (2017) 21 *Nomos* 1.

Giuseppe Guarino, 'Il referendum e la sua applicazione al regime parlamentare' (1947) 1 *Rassegna di diritto pubblico* 30.

David Haljan, *Constitutionalising Secession* (Hart, 2014).

House of Lords. Select Committee on the Constitution 12th Report of Session 2009–10, *Referendums in the United Kingdom. Report with Evidence* (2010), https://www.publications.parliament.uk/pa/ld200910/ldselect/ldconst/99/99.pdf.

Daniel Lewis, *Direct Democracy and Minority Rights: A Critical Assessment of the Tyranny of the Majority in the American States* (Routledge, 2013).

Peter Leyland, 'Referendums, Popular Sovereignty, and the Territorial Constitution', in Richard Rawlings, Peter Leyland and Alison Young (eds), *Sovereignty and the Law* (OUP, 2013) 145.

Massimo Luciani, 'Introduzione', in Massimo Luciani and Mauro Volpi (eds), *Referendum* (Laterza, 1992) 3.

Massimo Luciani, *Commentario della Costituzione. Art. 75 Referendum* (Zanichelli, 2005).

Massimo Luciani, 'Il referendum: questioni teoriche e dell'esperienza italiana' (2008) 37 *Revista catalana de dret públic* 15.

Susanna Mancini, 'Secession and Self-Determination', in Michel Rosenfeld and Andras Sajó (eds), *The Oxford Handbook of Comparative Constitutional Law* (OUP, 2012) 481, at 482.

Susanna Mancini, 'Costituzionalismo, federalismo e secessione' (2014) 18 *Istituzioni del federalismo* 779.

Costanza Margiotta Broglio, *L'ultimo diritto. Profili storici e teorici della secessione* (Il Mulino, 2005).

Giuseppe Martinico, 'Identity Conflicts and Secession Before Courts: Three Case Studies' (2017) 21 *Revista General de Derecho Público Comparado* 1.

Giuseppe Martinico, ''A Message of Hope': A Legal Perspective on the Reference' in Giacomo Delledonne and Giuseppe Martinico (eds), *The Canadian Contribution to a Comparative Constitutional Law of Secession: Legacies of the Quebec Secession Reference* (Palgrave, 2019) 249.

Linda McKay-Panos, 'The Increasing Importance of Reference Decisions in Canadian Law' (2014), http://www.lawnow.org/increasing-importance-reference-decisions-canadian-law/.

Fernando Mendez, Mario Mendez and Vasiliki Triga, *Referendums and the European Union: A Comparative Inquiry* (CUP, 2014).

Fernando Mendez, Mario Mendez and Vasiliki Triga (eds), *Referendums on EU Matters*, the Policy Department for Citizens' Rights and Constitutional Affairs, European Parliament's Committee on Constitutional Affairs (2017), http://www.europarl.europa.eu/RegData/etudes/STUD/2017/571402/IPOL_STU(2017)571402_EN.pdf.

Yves Mény and Yves Surel, *Populismo e democrazia* (Il Mulino, 2004).

Boris Mirkine Guetzévitch, *Les Constitutions de l'Europe nouvelle* (Delagrave, 1930).

Boris Mirkine Guetzévitch, 'Le référendum et le parlementarisme dans les nouvelles constitutions européennes' (1931) 2 *Annuaire de l'Institut international de droit public* 285.

Laurence Morel, 'Referendum' in Michel Rosenfeld and Andras Sajó (eds), *The Oxford Handbook of Comparative Constitutional Law* (OUP, 2012) 502.

Wayne Norman, *Negotiating Nationalism: Nation-Building, Federalism, and Secession in the Multinational State* (OUP, 2006).

Ece Özlem Atikcan, 'The Puzzle of Double Referendums in the European Union' (2015) 53 *Journal of Common Market Studies* 937.

Matt Qvortrup, *A Comparative Study of Referendums: Government by the People* (Manchester University Press, 2002).

Matt Qvortrup, 'Referendums on Indipendence, 1860–2011' (2014) 85 *Political Quarterly* 57.

Ethan S. Rafuse, 'John C. Calhoun: He Started the Civil War' (2002), http://www.historynet.com/john-c-calhoun-he-started-the-civil-war.htm.

Lea Raible and Leah Trueblood, 'The Swiss System of Referendums and the Impossibility of Direct Democracy' (2017), https://ukconstitutionallaw.org/

2017/04/04/lea-raible-and-leah-trueblood-the-swiss-system-of-referendums-and-the-impossibility-of-direct-democracy/.

Jean-Jacques Rousseau, *The Social Contract* (1762), English edition, https://www.earlymoderntexts.com/assets/pdfs/rousseau1762.pdf.

Carl Schmitt, *Democrazia e liberalismo. Referendum e iniziativa popolare Hugo Preuss e la dottrina tedesca dello Stato* (Giuffrè, 2001, Italian edition).

İlker Gökhan Şen, *Sovereignty Referendums in International and Constitutional Law* (Springer, 2015).

Max Steinbeis, 'Majority Is a Legal Concept' (2017), http://verfassungsblog.de/majority-is-a-legal-concept/.

Stephen Tierney, *Constitutional Referendums: The Theory and Practice of Republican Deliberation* (OUP, 2012).

Alessandro Torre, 'Un referendum per tutte le stagioni: sovranità del Parlamento e democrazia diretta nel Regno Unito' (2005) *Diritto Pubblico Comparato ed Europeo* 1339.

Alessandro Torre, 'Il referendum nel Regno Unito: radici sparse, pianta rigogliosa', in Alessandro Torre and Justin Frosini (eds), *Democrazia rappresentativa e referendum nel Regno Unito* (Maggioli, 2012) 11.

Alessandro Torre and Justin Frosini (eds), *Democrazia rappresentativa e referendum nel Regno Unito* (Maggioli, 2012).

Pier Vincenzo Uleri, *Referendum e democrazia. Una prospettiva comparata* (Il Mulino, 2003).

Nadia Urbinati, 'Democracy and Populism' (1998) 5 *Constellations* 110.

Giuseppe Volpe, 'Referendum abrogativo e diritto di resistenza', in Corte costituzionale (ed), *Il giudizio di ammissibilità del referendum abrogativo* (Giuffrè, 1998) 284.

Mauro Volpi, 'Referendum (dir. cost)', *Digesto delle discipline pubblicistiche*, IV edition, XII vol. (UTET, 1997) 434.

Mauro Volpi, 'Referendum e iniziativa popolare. Quale riforma' (2016), http://www.costituzionalismo.it/download/Costituzionalismo_201602_567.pdf.

Max Weber, *Economy and Society* (University of California Press, 1978, English edition), https://archive.org/stream/MaxWeberEconomyAndSociety/MaxWeberEconomyAndSociety_djvu.txt.

Rivka Weill, 'Dicey Was Not Diceyan' (2003) 62 *Cambridge Law Journal* 474.

Daniel Weinstock, 'Constitutionalizing the Right to Secede' (2001) 9 *Journal of Political Philosophy* 182.

Reuven Ziegler, Jo Shaw and Rainer Bauböck (eds), *Independence Referendums: Who Should Vote and Who Should Be Offered Citizenship?* (2014) RSCAS Working Paper 2014/90, http://cadmus.eui.eu/bitstream/handle/1814/32516/RSCAS_2014_90.pdf.

7 Sovereignty referendums: A question of majority?

Or how "majority" actually begs numerous questions

Stéphane Beaulac[1]

I. Introduction

Over the years, I have come to use the expression "law of independence"[2] to refer to the legal reality surrounding issues involved in the becoming (and being) of a state on the international plane. In ontological terms, this field of study would include both public international law[3] and comparative constitutional law.[4] For instance, statehood refers to a set of constituting elements, as codified in the *Montevideo Convention*:[5] defined territory, permanent population, effective government and the capacity to enter into relations with the other states.[6] These are international law issues; but they concern also constitutional law, as many of these criteria indeed refer to the domestic legal structures of states, for example the organization of governance within a federal framework.[7] Another field is the law of international recognition,[8] with the traditional distinction between the constituting and the declaratory theories[9] as well as the legally hybrid (and quite contested) concept of effectivity in international law.[10] These are downstream-type of issues, as regards states and statehood.

There are many other legal issues that are rather upstream, in a way, to the being of states on the international plane. They pertain to the becoming of states or, as often referred to,[11] the creation of states, although this expression gives the (false) impression that there is a kind of overarching authority responsible for statehood. In any event, here the legal rules gathered under the heading of the

1 Full professor (*professeur titulaire*) at the Faculty of Law, University of Montreal. Visiting professor at the University of Padua, spring 2018.
2 See Bérard and Beaulac, 2017.
3 For instance, among the vast international law literature, see Lecucq, 2017; Crawford, 1998.
4 See Palermo, 2019; Choudhry and Howse, 2000.
5 *Montevideo Convention on the Rights and Duties of States*, 26 December 1933, 49 Stat 3097, 165 L.N.T.S. 19.
6 See Brownlie, 2004.
7 See the classic by Wheare, 1963.
8 See Garcia (ed.), 2018. See also, generally, Dugard, 2013, at 35 ff.; Ryngaert and Sobrie, 2011.
9 See Talmon, 2004; and, generally, Verhoeven, 1975.
10 See Seymour, 2007, at 399–400; Mendes, 2019, at 23–24.
11 See Crawford, 2006; Radan, 2007.

"law of independence" are interested in both the substance and the process of becoming states. Indeed, how do international law and constitutional law, separately or together, deal with issues regarding the entitlement to or the possibility of statehood, as well as the processual aspects that bring about the becoming (or creation) of states. To use the terminology familiar to all, this normativity includes the right to self-determination[12] and the law of secession[13] – including doctrines like *uti possidetis juris*[14] – as well as the rules pertaining to sovereignty referendums.[15]

II. What "majority" entails in sovereignty referendums

This chapter examines a specific aspect of the last category of issues, namely the legal question of "majority."[16] Simply put, for the consultation of the population to bring a positive outcome to the initiative, in this case on statehood, what is required in terms of popular support? The short answer that comes to mind, intuitively, is "majority" support, of course.

What I want to demonstrate in this chapter, however, is that the word "majority" (or one may call it a concept, a notion, an idea) is not only problematic to capture what is required for a referendum to pass, but that it actually hides more than it reveals with regard to the process of popular consultation for the purpose of becoming an independent state. At the outset, let me address an epistemological point, a sort of preliminary objection to the very topic, perhaps: considering the question of majority in sovereignty referendums, in and of itself, before (or without) taking into account the right to self-determination and the law of secession, is it not like turning the whole thing on its head, or perhaps "putting the cart before the horse" as the saying goes?

On the contrary, I would submit that the idea of "majority" is so often intertwined with the legal reality of referendums – as well as self-determination and secession – that treating it as a separate object of study will help appreciate the complexity of the related issues and, indeed, allow to name many of the multifaceted elements, some obscure or less obvious, involved in ascertaining popular support for independence. Besides, be it through the prisms of international or constitutional law, scholarship has already defined and otherwise dwelled upon self-determination,[17] its

12 See Mancini, 2012.

13 See Margiotta, 2005; Wellman, 2005; Tancredi, 2001.

14 See Lalonde, 2002.

15 See Radan, 2012.

16 Indeed, "majority" is a legal construct, as Maximilian Steinbeis (2017) explains: "A majority is not something you will find in nature. It is an artifact of law. You need legal rules to determine who counts, and in which way. You need legal safeguards of liberty, equality and diversity of opinion. You also need legal rules to determine what the majority will be able to do, which necessarily implies that the majority gets to told what she is not allowed to do. In short, you need constitutional law."

17 See Buchanan, 1992; Buchanan, 2007.

internal and external dimensions,[18] the concept of secession[19] – which was said to be a word in search of a meaning[20] – even specific issues dealing with sovereignty referendums,[21] like the wording of an intelligible question put to a vote.[22] In a way, instead of attempting yet another definition,[23] bound to have shortcomings and be contested,[24] and given the numerous typologies in the domain already,[25] the objective here is to show that speaking of a "majority" in a narrative on sovereignty referendums actually begs numerous questions relating to popular support.

The method used for my demonstration may seem unorthodox at first blush, as it borrows from linguistics,[26] with a view to giving a meaningful structure in the discussion. In analyzing the English language, linguists distinguish two types of interrogations: (i) yes or no questions and (ii) WH-questions. The last category is also known as content-information questions, which contain interrogative pro-forms, aimed at gathering basic information.[27] These questions are why (reason), how (manner), which (choice), when (time), where (place), who or whom (person), what (object) as well as derivatives such as how much (amount, uncountable) and how many (quantity, countable). This is what I intend to do with "majority": asking these questions in order to show that the word – used within the narratives pertaining to self-determination, secession, referendum – is actually addressing (often concealing) a good number of materials, as well as contentious features of the law of independence.

III. The Canada-Quebec experience with "majority"

This author, of course, has a particular take on the law of independence – it is my hermeneutics, so to speak – because I first studied and conceptualized it in

18 See Cassese, 1995; Barten, 2015.

19 The Supreme Court of Canada in the celebrated *Reference re Secession of Quebec*, [1998] 2 S.C.R. 217, para 83, defined secession thus: "Secession is the effort of a group or section of a state to withdraw itself from the political and constitutional authority of that state, with a view to achieving statehood for a new territorial unit on the international plane. In a federal state, secession typically takes the form of a territorial unit seeking to withdraw from the federation. Secession is a legal act as much as a political one."

20 See Radan, 2016.

21 See Taillon, 2012; Choudhry, 2007.

22 See *infra*, under the sub-heading "The question of HOW MUCH."

23 For many decades now, scholars in many disciplines have attempted to define sovereignty, self-determination, secession, referendums, etc. See, for examples, these two classics: Hannum, 1990; Buchheit, 1978.

24 This idea could be linked to the philosophical theory by Gallie, 1955–1956.

25 For referendums, dating back to Scelle, 1934, at 277 ff., going to contemporary typologies such as the one in six categories of sovereignty referendums by Gary Sussman, 2012. See also Qvortrup, 2014a; Mendez and Germann, 2018.

26 See, generally, Quirk, Greenbaum, Leech and Svartvik, 1985.

27 See. Elson and Pickett, 1988, at 110 ff. A derivative of WH-questions are WH-movements, developed in theoretical linguistics, mainly by Chomsky, 1977; and also Cheng and Corver, 2006.

the Canada-Quebec context, not only having experienced the two referendums of 1980 and 1995, but also given the teaching of the Supreme Court of Canada in the 1998 *Quebec Secession Reference*.[28] It is interesting to note that a recent book, edited by Giacomo Delledonne and Giuseppe Martinico, highlights the contributions of this case to the study of secession, what were referred to as my country's legacies.[29] Thus I feel less shy (or presumptuous) to have this section recalling the celebrated contributions of our highest court, specifically in regard to the consultation of the population in a sovereignty referendum. The Canadian experience is meant not only to provide us with a factual background to help illustrate my different points, but the 1998 court case also proves useful to situate the role of "majority" within the bigger picture, as far as the processual law of independence is concerned.

The Supreme Court of Canada, in addressing the first issue about the legality of a UDI[30] in domestic law (the other issue was on UDIs in international law[31]), went beyond the black letter law[32] of the constitutional order and identified underlying (and unwritten) principles: federalism, democracy, constitutionalism and the rule of law and respect for minorities.[33] These were the legal justifications behind the statement that the Canadian constitution is not a "straitjacket."[34] Indeed, the Supreme Court audaciously held that

> the *clear* repudiation of the existing constitutional order and the *clear* expression of the desire to pursue secession by the population of a province would give rise to a reciprocal obligation on all parties to Confederation to negotiate constitutional changes to respond to that desire.[35]

Notice the decisive (and repetitive) use, already, of the adjective "clear," when referring to the support expected from a successful sovereignty referendum.

For the High Court, therefore, the consequence of such a clear indication of the population's will to secede is to bring the stakeholders (to force them) to sit down at the negotiating table. "The continued existence and operation of the Canadian constitutional order," it is said, "cannot remain indifferent to the *clear* expression of a *clear* majority of Quebecers that they no longer wish to remain in Canada."[36] The trigger of such a duty to negotiate a new constitutional deal is a

28 *Reference re Secession of Quebec*, [1998] 2 S.C.R. 217. See also Gaudreaut-DesBiens, 1999; Dumberry, 2006; Rocher, 2014.
29 Delledonne and Martinico (eds), 2019. See also. Walters, 1999.
30 Short for "unilateral declaration of independence."
31 See Toope, 1999. See also Tancredi, 2008.
32 See Gaudreault-DesBiens, 2019, at 38–39: "The Supreme Court's departure from a strictly positivist reading of the Canadian constitution allows it to elaborate tools from which to better grasp a potential provincial secession attempt."
33 See Gaudreault-DesBiens, 2006; and, generally, Leclair, 2002.
34 *Reference re Secession of Quebec*, [1998] 2 S.C.R. 217, para. 150.
35 *Ibid.*, para. 88 [emphasis added].
36 *Ibid.*, para. 92 [emphasis added].

referendum,[37] in which the Quebec population is asked to vote on a question, the result of which will determine whether or not there is a popular will supporting secession, all of which is justifiable by the underlying principles of the Canadian constitution. "Those principles," the court further explained, "must inform our overall appreciation of the constitutional rights and obligations that would come into play in the event that a *clear* majority of Quebecers votes on a *clear* question in favour of secession."[38] Note, time and again, the term "clear" is utilized in the reasons for judgment.

For better or worse, in analyzing the 1998 Reference, the focus of the discussion (if not the obsession) has been on what the High Court meant by "clear"[39] What is a clear referendum question? What is a clear majority? To concentrate on the latter, for present purposes, publicists[40] have highlighted that, in using the adjective "clear," the court is neither endorsing (nor rejecting, in fact) the idea of a simple majority (50%+1), nor is it necessarily speaking in terms of a qualified (or super) majority. The main other explicit indication in the reasons for judgment of what is meant by "clear majority" is when the Supreme Court writes this:

> In this context, we refer to a "clear" majority as a *qualitative* evaluation. The referendum result, if it is to be taken as an expression of the democratic will, must be free of ambiguity both in terms of the question asked and in terms of the support it achieves.[41]

It is noteworthy that the term "qualitative" is used only once by the High Court. Finally, the last passage that is deemed informative is towards the end of the judgment, summing up the reasons: "Democracy," it is said, "means more than simple majority rule." Is this a repudiation by the court of the 50%+1 hurdle for sovereignty referendums? The debate is still on, over 20 years strong!

This being so, by concentrating on what is meant by 'clear', when considering the issue of popular support (requiring a "clear majority"), publicists have in fact overlooked an important part of the equation: what do we mean by "majority"? Put another way, can there be different ramifications of the term "majority," when used to ascertain whether or not there is a will to secede? Here come the WH-questions, to help us navigate to the several elements linked to "majority": indeed, why, how, which, when, where, who or whom, what as well as how much and how many, in utilizing the word "majority."

37 See Haljan, 1999.

38 *Reference re Secession of Quebec*, [1998] 2 S.C.R. 217, para. 148 [emphasis added].

39 See Biglino Campos, 2016, at 453, who speaks of the need for a clear majority to a clear question as something that is now part of the constitutional patrimony in comparative constitutional law.

40 See, for instance, Derriennic, 1998.

41 *Reference re Secession of Quebec*, [1998] 2 S.C.R. 217, para. 87 [emphasis added].

IV. WH-questions to reveal the many facets of "majority"

These interrogations raise multifaceted features about having a "majority," thus pertaining to the quest for popular support in a sovereignty referendum. Gathered in three sub-sections, each question is considered below, with references to the Canada-Quebec experience, as well as to other relevant contemporary situations in the world.

(i) "Majority": WHY

In asking WHY a "majority" is required in a referendum, one is interested in the motivation, the reason behind the consultation of a population. In the present context, the focus is on sovereignty referendums – not on other types of referendums about internal governance,[42] such as in archetypes Switzerland and Italy[43] – but the question remains as to what popular support is meant in fact to accomplish. In other words, consulting about sovereignty brings up many different scenarios, secession being only one of them. In this first scenario, reaching a "majority" would be linked to the aspiration of becoming "a new state upon territory previously forming part of, or being a colonial entity of, an existing state."[44] The end goal is full-fledged statehood. Conversely, the motivation may be just to confirm the *status quo*, such as in Gibraltar in 2002 and in the Falkland Islands in 2014, having no expectation but to reiterate the actual constitutional arrangements with these territories. Having said that, when the literature suggests that, since the late eighteenth century, there have been more than 300 sovereignty referendums in the world – according to the Center for Research on Direct Democracy,[45] adopting a liberal concept of sovereignty[46] – the WHY has not always been secession or *status quo*. In numerous cases, the political project for which popular support was gauged was to move sovereignty, be it either in a centripetal or a centrifugal direction, with neither (initial) any intention of becoming a new state, nor disappearing from the international plane.

Counterintuitively perhaps for many, this was the situation for Canada-Quebec, where the WHY had nothing to do, at least not explicitly, with obtaining a "majority" for the purpose of statehood. The 1980 referendum was about sovereignty-association, as the question put to the people shows, referring to Quebec acquiring "[t]he exclusive power to make its laws, levy its taxes and establish relations abroad – in other words, sovereignty – and at the same time to maintain with Canada an economic association including a common currency." Precisely, the reason WHY a "majority" was sought in 1980 was to support the mandate for the government, in the words of the actual question again here, "to

42 See Butler and Ranney (eds), 1994; Qvortrup, 2005; Hamon, 2012.
43 See Grisel, 2004; Ryngaert, 1982.
44 Radan, 2016, at 18.
45 A web resource that may be consulted here: http://c2d.ch/.
46 See, generally, Qvortrup, 2014b.

negotiate a new agreement with the rest of Canada." Similarly in 1995, although the question was about Quebec becoming sovereign, the political project was linked to "a formal offer to Canada for a new economic and political partnership." In both 1980 and 1995, the WHY the "majority" was sought had much more to do with backing up a new autonomous arrangement within the parent state (as part of Canada) than with becoming a new state (for Quebec).[47]

The spectrum of centripetal or centrifugal transfers of sovereignty behind the WHY searching for "majority" support is wide. They range from new federative partnerships for sub-state entities seeking more autonomy, on the one end, to new inter/supra/trans-national arrangements pooling attributes of sovereignty, on the other end. Examples of the former category are the two waves of referendums in the UK[48] – in the late 1970s for Scotland and Wales, and again in the late 1990s for Scotland, Wales and Northern Ireland. In all these cases, popular support was tested for devolution of powers to regional parliaments. More recently, in the autumn of 2017, referendums were held in the two Italian regions of Veneto[49] and Lombardy;[50] both cases saw an overwhelming "majority" (Veneto 98.3%; Lombardy 95.3%) supporting the quest for more autonomy, which authorities have not yet acted upon, however.[51]

In highlighting the reasons WHY obtain "majority" support, on the other end of the spectrum, there are numerous illustrations of centrifugal political projects, putting together attributes of sovereignty. No doubt, the European Union is the best illustration, as there were numerous referendums held, at different points in time, within EU member states.[52] Adopting the typology of referendums on European integration suggested by publicists,[53] there would be three categories of them, all of which concerning sovereignty pooling. First, membership referendums, the most basic reason for them being to join the EU, or what was known before as the European Communities. Not all 21 accession referendums were successful though, with the notable case of Norway whose "majority" refused twice over to integrate the union. WHY seeking a "majority" in the EU context may have to do with reforming the union, that is to say, may concern the

47 This is in spite of what we learned following the 1995 referendum, that the leadership of the nationalist movement, especially then premier Jacques Parizeau, was apparently going to use the "majority" to make, at once, a unilateral declaration of independence. See Hébert and Lapierre, 2014.

48 See Kidd and Petrie, 2016.

49 The question was: "Do you want Veneto to be given further forms and particular conditions of autonomy?"

50 The question was: "Do you want the Lombardy Region, in the framework of national unity, to start the necessary institutional initiatives to ask the State the devolution of subsequent particular forms and conditions of autonomy, with the corresponding resources, in the way and for the purposes provided in Article 116, Paragraph 3 of the Constitution?"

51 See Delledonne and Monti, 2019.

52 See Auer, 2007; Shu, 2008.

53 See Mendez, Mendez and Triga, 2014.

ratification by member states of amending treaties. This is the second category of EU sovereignty pooling referendums, specifically the following instruments:

- *Single European Act* (1986)
- *Treaty of Maastricht Treaty* (1992)
- *Treaty of Amsterdam* (1997)
- *Treaty of Nice* (2001)
- *Constitutional Treaty of the European Union* (2004)
- *Treaty of Lisbon* (2007)

For each of these reform projects, some EU member states would hold consultations[54] – sometimes having to repeat the process twice to win a "majority" – with some 16 treaty ratification referendums being held from 1986 to 2009.[55]

To be complete, there is a third category of EU referendums, also illustrating the many different reasons WHY a "majority" may need to be ascertained. These are policy referendums, about specific issues, for instance monetary policy, fiscal policy or foreign policy (including the issue of enlargement).

Of course, still in the context of the EU, there is another example that is worth exploring to show WHY popular support may be sought, namely that of Brexit.[56] To put this current affair in a broader perspective, it would fall within the first category (above) of EU referendums, concerning membership in the union.[57] This time, it is not to join the EU, but the opposite – to withdraw from the EU. Interestingly, before Brexit was decided by a (slim) "majority" of the UK population in June 2016, there had been two instances of withdrawal referendums. The first one was also in the UK, in 1975, to decide whether to stay in the Common Market (or European Community), entered into two years prior; it was rejected by a "majority" of over two-thirds. Another withdrawal referendum took place in Greenland (a former Danish territory), in 1982, and this time proved to be successful, as a relatively thin "majority" of 53% of the voters decided in favour of leaving the union. Now, Brexit is the third experience in EU withdrawal referendums, although the first one conducted under Article 50 of the *Treaty of the European Union*, adopted via the *Treaty of Lisbon* in 2007,[58] provided for the possibility of withdrawal or renegotiation of EU membership status.[59] Although the actual vote on Brexit was often said to be a shot in the dark (or a blank cheque),[60] as the ultimate outcome was to be determined some two years down

54 On the reasons behind decisions by member states to hold EU referendums, see Closa, 2007.
55 See also, generally, Closa, 2013.
56 See, generally, Fitzgerald and Lein (eds), 2018.
57 See Hillon, 2015.
58 See Tatham, 2012.
59 See Łazowski, 2017b.
60 See Clarke, Goodwin and Whiteley, 2017, at 175 ff.; and, generally, Fabbrini (ed.), 2017.

the road – with a negotiated UK–EU accord, a hard or a no-deal Brexit[61] – the reason WHY a "majority" of the UK voted (52–48%) in favour of it was nevertheless known: to put an end to the current (and regular) form of membership of the EU.[62]

(ii) "Majority": HOW, WHICH, WHEN, WHERE and WHO or WHOM

The question HOW is interested in the manner in which support of the population is ascertained in relation to a political project involving sovereignty. Although it may just be about the process, this interrogation makes it explicit that a referendum is not the only possible procedure. Another option would be to have a vote in parliament, instead of[63] or along with[64] (*ex ante* and/or *a posteriori*) a referendum. HOW relates also to whether the verdict of the "majority" in a referendum is merely advisory or indeed binding.[65] As well, HOW is concerned with a possible pre-referendum agreement to provide a framework through which the existence of a "majority" will be determined, as in the Scotland–UK case with the *Edinburgh Agreement*.[66] Finally, HOW includes a role for courts to help with referendum processes of testing "majority,"[67] which was the situation not only in Canada-Quebec, but in many other jurisdictions, like in Sri Lanka[68]; and again recently, on many occasions, in Spain-Catalonia.[69]

For its part, WHICH highlights that the word "majority" may bring up (and might hide) issues relating to the options given to the population in the course of a sovereignty referendum. More often than not, the logic is binary: you vote "yes" or "no" to a question, that is that.[70] Sometimes the question put in a referendum gives two separate options, "a" or "b," but in explicit terms, such as in the

61 See Gadbin-George, Ringeisen-Biardeaud (eds), 2018.

62 See Łazowski, 2017a.

63 An example is the split of Czechoslovakia. See Luers, 1990.

64 An example is Ethiopia. See Bihonegn, 2015.

65 See Taillon, 2007. In Canada, based on the constitutional principle of parliamentary supremacy – from the Anglo-Saxon common law tradition of public law (confirmed in the legal challenge to Brexit case by the UK Supreme Court: see *R (Miller) v. Secretary of State for Exiting the European Union*, [2017] UKSC 5) – government cannot abdicate its responsibility to legislate; hence referendums cannot be binding, just advisory: see *Re Initiative and Referendum* Act [1919] A.C. 935 (Privy Council). Having said that, as it was recently suggested, "almost no difference exists in practice between consultative and legally binding referendums, since all consultative referendums have been considered as politically binding"; see Palermo, 2019, at 273.

66 *Agreement between the UK Government and the Scottish Government on a referendum on independence for Scotland* (2012). See MacIver, 2019.

67 See Morel, 2012, at 514 ff.

68 See Welikala, 2019.

69 See, in general, Xavier Cuadras Morató (ed.), *Catalonia: A New Independent State in Europe? – A Debate on Secession Within the European Union* (Abingdon: Routledge, 2016).

70 See Morel, 2018, at 160 ff.

2014 Crimean referendum: does the "majority" want to join a country (Russia) or remain in the current one (Ukraine)?[71] Now, WHICH implies too that there may be more than two options in a sovereignty referendum, with a possible outcome of winning with much less than 50%+1; actually 33.34% would suffice in a three-option case. This was indeed a scenario during the 2014 Scottish referendum – which in the end did not materialize – where it was considered to have a third option on the ballot, namely to obtain new devolution powers (Devo-Max) for the region.[72] In the several bills proposed for a sovereignty referendum in Puerto Rico, there were attempts too to move away from a binary (or dichotomous) choice by offering three options.[73] The question WHICH thus highlights how, sometimes, a "majority" may entail a much weaker popular support than one would think, intuitively.

WHEN is interested not so much in the timing of a referendum (early or during a negotiation; on mere propositions or on a new deal), but in the actual point in time, the occasion of the verification of popular support.[74] Put another way, should the required "majority" be determined once and that is all? Or, rather, could there be other times to test it again, at the end of the negotiation on a new political status, for instance? This was the case for the 1980 Quebec referendum,[75] where the very question referred to the need for a second consultation: "[...] any change in political status resulting from these negotiations will only be implemented with popular approval through another referendum [...]." In the situation where the "majority" says no in a sovereignty referendum, WHEN is also about the possible repeat of the consultation, what was coined in the Canada-Quebec context as the idea of "neverendum."[76] After the 2014 referendum in Scotland, rejected by quite a large "majority" (55–45%), the SNP leadership was on the record saying no new vote on independence for a while, a position that changed 180 degrees given that Brexit passed in spite of a strong Scottish "majority" against.[77] It is noteworthy that referendums in member states of the European Union, in recent history, have been repeated on many occasions

71 See the report by the European Commission for Democracy through Law (Venice Commission), entitled *Opinion on "Whether the Decision Taken by the Supreme Council of the Autonomous Republic of Crimea in Ukraine to Organise a Referendum on Becoming a Constituent Territory of the Russian Federation or Restoring Crimea's 1992 Constitution Is Compatible with Constitutional Principles"*, 21 March 2014, CDL-AD(2014)002.

72 See Mullen, 2016.

73 They were as follows: (1) Independence: Puerto Rico should become fully independent from the United States. (2) Sovereignty in association with the United States: Puerto Rico and the United States should form a political association between sovereign nations that will not be subject to the Territorial Clause of the United States Constitution. (3) Puerto Rico should be admitted as a State of the Union. See Gökhan Şen, 2015, at 263.

74 The whole process of having a referendum to test "majority" support would be flawed, some say, as it artificially freezes in time the will of the population; see Cohen, Grunberg and Manin, 2017.

75 See Lecours, 2018.

76 See Freed, 2017.

77 See McKenna, 2018.

in order to obtain popular support for different packages of reforms,[78] the most notorious cases out of the Republic of Ireland.[79] The question of WHEN a "majority" is ascertained, therefore, is crucial – the goal is to catch it once, some say like in a "lobster trap."[80]

Brexit also provides a vivid example of the question of WHERE the "majority" is assessed by means of a referendum.[81] Across the UK, the option to leave the European Union got the support of 52%, while the option to remain got 48%. However, the regional breakdown shows supports of 38–62% in Scotland, 44–56% in Northern Ireland; in Wales, the percentages were the same as countrywide. WHERE also raises the issue of whether a sovereignty referendum – e.g. on the secession of a region – should be assessing the support of the population of the whole parent state or whether the "majority" will is only concerned with the territory at stake.[82] This would be the situation in Spain, where Madrid says that the secession of Catalonia must be decided by the whole country, while of course Barcelona claims that the only "majority" that matters is that of the region alone.[83] From a Canada-Quebec perspective, in part because of the two-founding nations theory (different from the Spanish one-nation approach), the proposition of a countrywide referendum to decide on the secession of a province is borderline absurd and, in any case, does not correspond to the 1980 and 1995 experiences of testing "majority" support in a referendum. Having said that, the question of WHERE highlights another feature inherent to a referendum "majority," which may be put in terms of *uti possedetis*: indeed, can the various popular supports, region by region, justify a reconsideration of territorial borders of a secessionist region?[84] Let us recall, in that regard, an *obiter dictum* by the Supreme Court of Canada in the *Quebec Secession Reference* case: "Nobody seriously suggests that our national existence, seamless in so many aspects, could be effortlessly separated along what are now the provincial boundaries of Quebec."[85]

The ramifications of "majority" raised by WHO or WHOM – the latter being more grammatically correct – are interested in one simple thing: among those connected to the territory at stake, who gets the right to vote and decide the question put in a referendum? It really boils down to eligibility, a basic issue

78 See Özlem Atikcan, 2018.

79 Both the *Treaty of Nice* (2001, 2002) and the *Treaty of Lisbon* (2008, 2009) were submitted to the Irish population twice before it was approved by a "majority."

80 This was a most incredible image once used by a revered secessionist leader of the Parti Québécois, Jacques Parizeau, who suggested that obtaining a majority in a referendum on Quebec independence would be like catching a lobster in a trap, i.e. once you get it, there is no way out. See Beaulac, 2016.

81 Comparing Brexit and the Canada-Quebec experiences, including on this aspect of referendums, see Fitzgerald, 2018.

82 See Basta, 2017.

83 See Sanjaume-Calvet, 2018.

84 See Ratner, 1996.

85 *Reference re Secession of Quebec*, [1998] 2 S.C.R. 217, para. 96.

in democratic theory.[86] WHO concerns the requirements of citizenship and, in some instances, residence period in a territory – or at least not out of the jurisdiction – to be able to exercise the right to vote and thus be tallied in assessing a "majority."[87] The Brexit vote in June 2016 illustrates such requirements: the *Referendum Act 2015* restricted eligibility to citizens of the UK (no citizens of the EU residing in the UK) and even excluded those residing abroad for more than 15 years.[88] WHOM concerns also the age eligibility to vote and thus be counted towards a referendum "majority," which is generally 18 years old, the age of majority; for Brexit, it was 18 years. Of course, it may be brought down, which increases the pool of people consulted; such as in the case of the *Scottish Independence Referendum (Franchise) Act 2013*, which allowed persons aged 16 and up to vote.

(iii) "Majority": WHAT, HOW MUCH and HOW MANY

The last group of WH-questions will address several questions highly relevant to sovereignty referendums, from participation quorums and minimum vote requirements, to qualitative and quantitative popular supports, as well as the different possible numeric results, be it simple or qualified (a.k.a. super) majorities. All of those ramifications of the word "majority" will be illustrated with the help of the Canada-Quebec example which, accordingly, requires to be given some details. For the purposes of the discussion below, and although some of the figures are approximate, let us say that the whole population of Canada is 36 million people and that the province of Quebec is 8 million. In an election or a referendum, let us say there are 28 million and 6 million, respectively in Canada and in Quebec, who are citizens of 18 years of age or older, who are thus eligible to vote. We have already determined, pursuant to the question WHERE, that for the sake of assessing a "majority" in a sovereignty referendum on secession, the consensus in Canada-Quebec is to use the province only. Therefore, for the discussion that follows, the important initial number is 6 million, the number of eligible voters in Quebec.

a. The question of WHAT

The question WHAT is interested in the object of verification, the idea being that it is possible to explicate and actually impose conditions on the reference group in the context of a sovereignty referendum. Put another way, the word

86 See Oklopcic, 2012.

87 See Gökhan Şen, 2018, at 214 ff., identified four categories of voters: (i) resident natives, (ii) non-resident natives, (iii) non-native residents, and (iv) non-native non-residents.

88 See Shaw, 2017. Interestingly, a recent court case in Canada saw the Supreme Court strike down as unconstitutional the provision of the election legislation denying the right to vote in a federal election to Canadian citizens residing abroad for five consecutive years or more. See *Frank v. Canada (Attorney General)*, 2019 SCC 1, 11 January 2019.

"majority" ought to be seen as, potentially, involving minimum characteristics or requirements, all in the name of defining properly the object that popular support is meant to ascertain. Essentially, the features we are talking about here are quorums, which can be in relation to the turnout or with the approval. The former type are quorums of voters' participation which impose minimum turnouts in the sovereignty referendum, short of which, popular support will not be deemed demonstrated, no matter what is the final result of cast votes. The other type are quorums of registered voters' approval which require the support as determined not by a percentage of cast votes, but by a set portion of the whole electorate. Briefly, on each of them.

MINIMUM TURNOUTS

For quorums of participation, WHAT a "majority" is about in a referendum (the object of verification) requires to meet a preliminary condition. The process of assessing popular support must be true to its spirit and, therefore, be representative of the will of the population. By asking that, minimally, a good proportion of those eligible to vote do so in the referendum, the "majority" is validated as better reflecting what the population wants. Having said that, it was pointed out that, "while it can prevent the adoption of an ultra-minority measure, the quorum of participation is far from allowing it to reach the majority of the registered voters."[89] To take Quebec as an example, putting the minimum turnout at 50% means that a winning (simple) majority of cast votes would be 1.5 million plus one, out of a 6 million electorate. Although certainly better than nothing, a feature to define the object of "majority" allowing for a meagre 25%+1 of the registered voters to be sufficient support, theoretically, for one's sovereignty project is light, to say the least, if not complaisant. It can hardly be said to meet the objective of being truly representative of the will of the population, of WHAT a "majority" should be about in a referendum.

Often the minimum turnout threshold is set at 50% of the registered voters, such as in the 2006 sovereignty referendum in Montenegro.[90] The Venice Commission, in a study entitled "Referendums in Europe,"[91] identified the practice of a minimum turnout of 50% in referendums in a bunch of European countries: Bulgaria, Croatia, Italy, Latvia, Lithuania, Macedonia, Malta and Russia. Some make this threshold a condition for the referendum to be binding and not just advisory, like in Poland and Portugal. The Venice Commission notes that the minimum turnout may be set much lower, which is the case with Azerbaijan where the threshold is at 25% only; thus, if combined with a (simple) majority of cast votes, an extremely small 12.5%+1 of the population would be sufficient for a

89 Morel, 2018, at 152.

90 See Bérard and Beaulac, 2017, at 94.

91 European Commission for Democracy through Law (Venice Commission), *Referendums in Europe – An Analysis of the Legal Rules in European States*, 2 November 2005, CDL-AD(2005)034, at para. 112.

referendum to pass. WHAT is required in terms of the popular support in the latter case, in theory at least, would be ridiculously low. Indeed, the word "majority" generally brings up in people's mind a much high percentage of approval, intuitively.

Quorums, especially participatory ones, have been viewed as flawed however, the main reason being that it deems abstentions to be tantamount to no votes. This assertion is questionable, it is argued, because there may be a series of different reasons why voters abstain, ranging from a conscious decision to boycott the vote to contingencies like being stuck in traffic at the voting end. The next step, even more problematic, is to imagine that a camp in a referendum would actually promote abstention, with a view to preventing the results to prevail, that is to say, by hoping that the threshold of participation fails. This is a strategy that proved to be quite successful in Italy, as "most popular initiatives since the 1990s [were] invalidated because of a quorum not being met."[92] Here is how the Venice Commission illustrated the shortcomings of minimum turnout requirements:

> if 48% of electors are in favour of a proposal, 5% are against it and 47% intend to abstain, the 5% of opponents need only desert the ballot box in order to impose their viewpoint, even though they are very much in the minority.[93]

Having said that, the downside of quorums of participation is mitigated, or even perhaps cancelled out, in the context of sovereignty referendums, the main distinguishing fact being what is at stake, namely a fundamental change in political status. This is also based on the premise that the yes-side has *a priori* advantages, in a way, having set in motion the process of consultation and enjoying the lead on the debate and the actual question posed. Conversely, the no-side is forced to react, not having asked for a sovereignty referendum; the same could be said about the population on the territory, whose will (generally latent) is instrumentalized, like it or not. In this context, it might not be unreasonable to even out the playing field by having the no-side benefit, so to speak, from the abstention of the electorate because of a quorum of participation.

It is submitted that the question of WHAT is the "majority" about in a sovereignty referendum would, accordingly, be improved in terms of representativeness of popular support with minimum turnout requirements. Bottom line, the critique of these quorums should be given little weight because, as one author puts it, "the situation is different when it comes to existential issues such as secession and statehood."[94] Interestingly, it was the view expressed by the Venice Commission, it seems, in the case of Montenegro.[95] Noting that a participation quorum was a condition, among other precedents, in Slovenia's and Macedonia's

92 Morel, 2018, at 153.

93 European Commission for Democracy through Law (Venice Commission), *Code of Code Practice in Referendum*, 20 January 2009, CDL-AD(2007)008rev, para. 51.

94 Palermo, 2019, at 276.

95 See Cazala, 2006.

sovereignty referendums, it wrote the following: "Regarding international practice, a minimum turnout of 50% of the registered voters seems appropriate for a referendum on the change of state status."[96] WHAT the "majority" demonstrates, in such circumstances, is improved (slightly) as being more representative, for sure.

APPROVAL QUORUMS

Minimum thresholds may relate to the actual approval by a specific proportion of the whole electorate. The question WHAT is a "majority" focusing here not on the cast votes but rather on the percentage of votes within the reference group of the registered voters. To give an example: Slovenia, for its December 1990 referendum on sovereignty, where the required majority was set at 50%+1, calculated not on the basis of the number of votes in the ballot boxes but rather in proportion to the electorate as a whole. To use Quebec as an illustration, it would be like requiring that, out of the group of 6 million registered voters, the "majority" be at least 3 million plus one, i.e. 50%+1 of all people entitled to vote in the province. In previous writing, I have used the expression "absolute majority" to refer to this situation: a support in a referendum representing more than half of the population eligible to vote.[97]

In its opinion on the Montenegro referendum, the Venice Commission looked at not only the possibility of qualified majority – which we will examine below – but also this type of quorum. It was put as "a rule requiring that there must, in addition to simple majority of those voting, also be a specified number of Yes votes (e.g. 35%, 40%, 45%, 50%) of the total national electorate."[98] The European experience at large, where votes are taken on constitutional reforms for instance, shows several countries where the results are calculated based on specific proportions of the whole electorate: Albania, Armenia, Denmark, Hungary, Latvia. Interestingly, the Venice Commission acknowledged that a "majority" ought to be more stringent via an approval quorum when the consultation is on sovereignty issues.[99] The constitution of Macedonia, for example, calls for a majority of all registered voters if a referendum is held on the association or dissolution of a union or community with other states. For union or even secession in Slovakia, the constitutional requirement is also 50%+1 calculated on the basis of the whole electorate body. A vote in Lithuania on constitutional reforms that would affect

96 European Commission for Democracy through Law (Venice Commission), *Opinion on the Compatibility of the Existing Legislation in Montenegro Concerning the Organization of Referendums with Applicable International Standards*, 10 December 2005, CDL-AD(2005)041, para. 26.

97 Lussier, 2013.

98 European Commission for Democracy through Law (Venice Commission), *Opinion on the Compatibility of the Existing Legislation in Montenegro Concerning the Organization of Referendums with Applicable International Standards*, 10 December 2005, CDL-AD(2005)041, para. 27 [emphasis in original].

99 *Ibid.*, para. 33.

the fundamentals of the country (the independent democratic republic character of the state) must gather a support of 75% of the electorate as a whole.[100] That last hurdle is incredible, I am tempted to say, and goes a long way towards assuring that WHAT a "majority" is about in a sovereignty referendum will leave little (or no) doubt as to popular will.

When compared with the first type of requirements, minimum turnouts, quorums of approval are considered less problematic. Be it at 50% or (or even better) less of the electorate body, such a scenario would not allow a boycott on voting promoted by the no-side to have an impact on the result; so long as the yes-side gathers the number set in the approval quorum, calculated on the fixed reference group that is the electorate, there will be a "majority" support.[101] Of course, the closer to 50%+1 of the registered voters you get as a quorum, the stronger is the claim that it is a proper and full representation of popular will, that could indeed be called "absolute majority." A sort of compromise, that takes the best of both worlds, so to speak, can be a combination of minimum turnout and approval quorum requirements. This is the case in Lithuania, for a category of referendums that are mandatory, where the quorum of participation is 50% and the quorum of approval is set at 33.33% of registered voters.[102] The question WHAT in this last scenario – although not quite as much as that of absolute majority – brings out how quorum requirements may be excellent tools to boost support representativeness in a sovereignty referendum.

b. The question of HOW MUCH

Before addressing the key question of HOW MANY votes are actually required in a referendum (next), it is most useful to put the issue of popular support in terms of HOW MUCH. Indeed, one of the most interesting insights from the Supreme Court of Canada's decision in the *Quebec Secession Reference* case, seen above, was the distinction between the formal numeric aspect of popular support (the actual percentage, which was never set at any particular number), on the one hand, and what was referred to as the "qualitative evaluation"[103] of what is a "majority" support within the population, on the other hand. Right after, in the same paragraph of the reasons for judgment, the High Court adds this: "The referendum result, if it is to be taken as an expression of the democratic will, must be free of ambiguity both in terms of the question asked and in terms of the support it achieves."[104]

100 See European Commission for Democracy through Law (Venice Commission), *Referendums in Europe – An Analysis of the Legal Rules in European States*, 2 November 2005, CDL-AD(2005)034, at para. 114.

101 See Morel, 2018, at 153.

102 See European Commission for Democracy through Law (Venice Commission), *Referendums in Europe – An Analysis of the Legal Rules in European States*, 2 November 2005, CDL-AD(2005)034, at para. 115.

103 *Reference re Secession of Quebec*, [1998] 2 S.C.R. 217, para. 87.

104 *Ibid.*

This, semantically, is what should be understood by "clear majority," the opposite of "ambiguity"; the popular will "must be free of ambiguity," which speaks to both referendum question and the numeric results. Together, one presumes, is what the court meant by a "qualitative evaluation" of the "majority" – a "clear" "majority" – in a sovereignty referendum.[105]

Let me suggest that asking HOW MUCH is required of the "majority" is a way of assessing the support of the population that involves, as part and parcel of the debate, the referendum question. The qualitative evaluation of the "majority," therefore, is not solely numerical (referring to a percentage value), but also interested in the formulation of the actual question to be decided by means of a consultation. The question of the question, so to speak, has caused much ink to flow in the last 20 years, prompted in large part by the Canadian Supreme Court decision.[106] One also recalls that it was said in the most explicit terms that the particulars of what constitutes an intelligible question, among other things, will not be judicially determined, "not to usurp the prerogatives of the political forces that operate within that [constitutional] framework,"[107] identified by the Court. Indeed, "it will be for the political actors to determine what constitutes "a clear majority on a clear question" in the circumstances under which a future referendum vote may be taken"[108]; in other words, do not come back to us for judicial review, as to HOW MUCH a "majority" should be determined by means of an intelligible referendum question.[109]

It is in this context that, in 2000, the federal parliament in Canada adopted the so-called *Clarity Act*,[110] with a view *inter alia* to assuming the responsibility

105 Similarly, see Oklopcic, 2019, at 218, who writes that "the 'clarity' of a referendum majority may be seen as an evidence of three separate aspects of popular support: (1) its sufficient *magnitude*; (2) its sufficient *intensity*; and (3) its sufficient *constancy*" [emphasis in original].

106 See Rocher and Lecours, 2018; Rosůlek, 2016; Yale and Durand, 2011.

107 *Reference re Secession of Quebec*, [1998] 2 S.C.R. 217, para. 153.

108 *Ibid.* For another example where the evaluation of the majority support for a change in political status by means of a sovereignty referendum is left, explicitly, to the appreciation of political actors, see the Annex 1 of the *Belfast (Good Friday) Agreement* in Northern Ireland, struck in 1998.

109 Interestingly, the two recent experiences in sovereignty referendums in the United Kingdom – Scottish independence in 2014 and Brexit in 2016 – saw the evaluation of the question formulation given to an administrative body. See Electoral Commission (U.K.), *Referendum on Independence for Scotland Advice of the Electoral Commission on the Proposed Referendum Question* (2013); and Electoral Commission (U.K.), *Referendum on Membership of the European Union – Assessment of the Electoral Commission on the Proposed Referendum Question* (2015). See also Timothy William Waters, "For Freedom Alone: Secession After the Scottish Referendum" (2016) 44 *Nationalities Papers* 124.

110 *An Act to Give Effect to the Requirement for Clarity as Set Out in the Opinion of the Supreme Court of Canada in the Quebec Secession Reference*, S.C. 2000. In a tit-for-that reaction to the federal statutory initiative the Quebec legislature adopted *An Act Respecting the Exercise of the Fundamental Rights and Prerogatives of the Quebec People and the Quebec State*, C.Q.L.R. c. E-20.2, often referred to as Bill 99. The latter statute was challenged in court as constitutionally invalid, due to the alleged incompatibility with the decision of

to decide if, from the country's political perspective, the qualitative evaluation of the popular support is possible.[111] As the preamble of the *Act* states, "the House of Commons, as the only political institution elected to represent all Canadians, has an important role in identifying what constitutes a clear question and a clear majority." Section 1(3) of the *Act* provides for the following: "In considering the clarity of a referendum question, the House of Commons shall consider whether the question would result in a clear expression of the will of the population of a province on whether the province should cease to be part of Canada and become an independent state." In section 1(4), there are factors that would undermine the intelligibility of the question, essentially two scenarios:

(a) a referendum question that merely focuses on a mandate to negotiate without soliciting a direct expression of the will of the population of that province on whether the province should cease to be part of Canada; or
(b) a referendum question that envisages other possibilities in addition to the secession of the province from Canada, such as economic or political arrangements with Canada, that obscure a direct expression of the will of the population of that province on whether the province should cease to be part of Canada.

In its "Code of Good Practice on Referendums," adopted in 2009, the Venice Commission provides guidance as to the formulation of a question put in a sovereignty referendum. Using terminology that is reminiscent of the Supreme Court of Canada's, it suggests the following:

> The clarity of the question is a crucial aspect of voters' freedom to form an opinion. The question must not be misleading; it must not suggest an answer, particularly by mentioning the presumed consequences of approving or rejecting the proposal; voters must be able to answer the questions asked solely by yes, no or a blank vote; and it must not ask an open question necessitating a more detailed answer.[112]

It also recommends that the question be explicit as to the impact of the referendum, for instance if it is to be binding or advisory, final or part of negotiation

---

the Supreme Court in the *Quebec Secession Reference.* Using a technique of interpretation known as "reading down," the Superior Court of Quebec was able to construe the provisions of Bill 99 at stake as just establishing (and explicating) a framework for secession, not as a justification for a unilateral declaration of independence. See *Henderson v. Quebec (Procureur général)*, 2018 QCCS 1586, 19 April 2018; this judgment is under appeal before the Quebec Court of Appeal.

111 One must understand that in both previous referendums in Quebec, the provincial authorities drafted the question without any participation or input whatsoever from the Feds. See Gaudreault-DesBiens, 2019, at 44.

112 European Commission for Democracy through Law (Venice Commission), *Code of Code Practice in Referendum*, 20 January 2009, CDL-AD(2007)008rev, para. 15.

process. All of this shows that asking HOW MUCH is the "majority" to mean in terms of popular support is intrinsically linked to how intelligible the referendum question is; the Canadian Supreme Court called this feature the "qualitative evaluation" of what is a clear will to secede by the population.

c. *The question of HOW MANY*

Ironically in a sense, compared to many other features examined above, HOW MANY votes in the ballot boxes are required to succeed in a sovereignty referendum is (relatively) straightforward. It is indeed a quantitative question, which basically refers to the numeric dimension of the results following the holding of a consultation. The expression most often used for the purposes of crunching referendum numbers is simple "majority" – i.e. 50%+1 of the cast votes – which would correspond to the default position to decide, by means of a consultation, a binary question put to a popular vote. But to be crystal clear, this way of calculating a "majority" has a built-in assumption, a sort of implied feature: the reference group is not the registered voters, but the actual ones, those who expressed their right to vote. Here, HOW MANY is not interested in HOW MUCH, as the standpoint is that turnout does not matter, nor in fact broader issues about levels of participation or, importantly, the representativeness of the results.

Let us take a few examples to illustrate this numeric dimension, the first one from Canada-Quebec.[113] As suggested above, the electorate in the province being 6 million, the calculation of simple "majority" of cast vote needs first to adjust this number to take into account the turnout. Drawing from our last real experience with referendums, in 1995,[114] it is reasonable to set the participation at 90%. This means that the reference group is 5.4 million, with which to calculate the simple "majority" of 50%+1; the magic number is 2.7 million plus 1 then. Assessing the situation accountant-like, this outcome would not be too bad in terms of popular support and representativeness of the will of the population given that 2.7 million of cast votes represent 45% backing of the electorate and the favour of 33.75% of the entire population of Quebec (set at 8 million; see above). These numbers are not in the neighbourhood of absolute "majority," however.

Another recent example shows how using simple "majority" to ascertain the will of the population in a sovereignty referendum may prove much more problematic. This illustration draws from the latest experience in Spain-Catalonia,[115] specifically the vote on the region's independence taken in October 2017. Of course, there are many elements of context that are crucial to properly understand the circumstances of this sovereignty referendum;[116] but my analysis here is purely numerical: HOW MANY votes in the 2017 referendum?

113 See Langlois, 2018, at 65 ff.; and, generally, Gervais, Kirkey and Rudy (eds.), 2016.

114 The actual turnout in 1995 was in the low 90s%, in fact at 93.5%.

115 For a full historical context, as well as details about the 2014 referendum on Catalonia's independence, see Bérard and Beaulac, 2017, at 110 ff.

116 See López-Basaguren and Escajedo San-Epifanio (eds.), 2019.

Rounding up slightly the figures, the population of Catalonia is about 7.4 million people; the electorate body is roughly 5.3 million registered voters. Although there is no consensus on the exact number, the participation in the consultation was approximately 43%. This means that the reference group to calculate the results on the basis of a simple "majority" is about 2.28 million. In the end, the total yes-votes in the ballot boxes was a bit over 2 million, making it a "majority" near 90% of cast votes, quite an impressive support at first sight. However, when these figures are put in light of the electorate as a whole, 2 out of 5.3 million registered voters bring down the support at 37.7%; if the reference group is the population of Catalonia (7.4 million), then the number becomes a meagre 27%, barely more than a quarter of the people of that region. Thus, the question of HOW MANY is required to establish popular support, based on simple "majority," may bring in numbers that are pretty weak indeed as to the people's will to secede.

In numeric terms, a simple "majority" of cast votes is generally distinguished (or opposed) to a qualified "majority," what is also known as a super "majority." All of these standards are agnostic of the actual levels of participation in sovereignty referendums; the reference group remains generally the citizens, aged 18 years and above, that actually exercised their rights to vote. In its opinion on Montenegro in 2005, the Venice Commission wrote the following: "The required majority makes the validity of the results dependent on the approval (or perhaps rejection) of a certain percentage of the electorate."[117] Although the default standard would be simple "majority,"[118] it was acknowledged that this 50%+1 rule may be set aside in some cases and replaced by a qualified (or super) majority. It referred to, indeed, "a rule requiring a *qualified majority of those voting* (that could be e.g. 55%, 60% or 65%)."[119]

Actually, the referendum statute for the sovereignty referendum in Montenegro required such a qualified majority,[120] set out at 55%+1 of the cast votes (and a minimum turnout of 50%).[121] The population is about 620,000 and approximately 485,000 were registered voters in the 2006 referendum. In the end, the turnout was about 86.5% (thus no problem with this requirement) and the 230,711 yes-votes means that the qualified hurdle was met, at 55.5%, indeed a

117 European Commission for Democracy through Law (Venice Commission), *Opinion on the Compatibility of the Existing Legislation in Montenegro Concerning the Organization of Referendums with Applicable International Standards*, 10 December 2005, CDL-AD(2005)041, para. 29.

118 See also, in the context of Spain-Catalonia, the opinion of the Consell Assessor per a la Transició Nacional, *The Consultation on the Political Future of Catalonia*, 1st Report, Generalitat de Catalunya, Barcelona (2013), at 184.

119 *Ibid.* [emphasis in the original].

120 See Beaulac, 2016.

121 See *Law on the Referendum on State-Legal status of the Republic of Montenegro* (adopted on 1 March 2006), at art. 6: "The decision in favour of independence shall be considered as valid, if 55% of the valid votes are cast for the option 'yes', provided that the majority of the total number of registered voters have voted on the referendum."

very thin margin of 0.5%. It is interesting to see whether, with these numbers, there was an absolute majority in the Montenegro referendum, the reference group being the whole electorate. The answer is no: 47.6% of the registered voters (i.e. 230,711/485,000) voted in favour of independence. When put in terms of the country population, the proportion in support goes down to 37.2% (i.e. 230,711/620000), a little more than one-third. Again here, the question HOW MANY, even when considering the scenario of a qualified "majority," is very useful to have the full picture of the support in a sovereignty referendum, including how representative it is of the people's will.

This is mathematical, only. The question of HOW MANY votes are required for a consultation to pass, as simplistic as it may seem, must absolutely be apprehended in a comprehensive manner. The standard of a simple "majority" of cast votes is one option, sure, but it may certainly not be the best way to reduce the risk that a small proportion of the population highjacks the process. In theory, with no turnout or approval thresholds, a very tiny percentage of people can be enough to operate a transfer of sovereignty.[122] So long as the 50%+1 rule is satisfied, even if there was a general boycott that brought down the level of participation to very low, the referendum will be successful. Calculating the yes-votes against other reference groups, like the electorate body and the population as a whole, provides much-needed perspectives, those that feed into the "clarity" rhetoric often at the centre of the debate.[123] In any event, when all ramifications are considered (cast votes, electorate, population), pure numeric analysis contributes, along with other features, to having a true picture of the support and representativeness in a sovereignty referendum. When speaking of a "majority," HOW MANY votes does one actually need goes to the core of the will of the population, undoubtedly, but it is but one of the many facets that are at stake.[124]

V. Conclusion

What this chapter attempted to do is to show the numerous elements that the word "majority," used in the context of sovereignty referendums, dissimulates or hides within narratives addressing issues of the law of independence. Put another way, when an author or a political actor suggests that there is a consensus on the international standard with respect to what is required in terms of popular support to bring about the secession of a territory, for instance, and that "majority" actually sums it all up... well, he or she is not telling the whole story. To say that the whole question boils down to having a simple majority of 50%+1 to win a sovereignty referendum is misleading, borderline dishonest. The ascertainment of the support of a population is a multifaceted endeavour, as shown above,

122 See Morel, 2018, at 152, who speaks of not allowing the view of an "ultra-minority" to prevail.

123 See Rocher, 2018.

124 See Morel, 2018, at 152: "In practice, the combination of high participation and large victory is necessary to achieve a truly majority result."

involving a number of features that must be addressed head-on, in explicit terms. This is not simple, but more importantly, it is not simplistic.

The demonstration above relied on the WH-questions, borrowed from linguistics, with a view to showing the many content-information pertaining to the word "majority" used in referendum narratives. Thus why (reason), how (manner), which (choice), when (time), where (place), who or whom (person), what (object) as well as derivatives how much (amount, uncountable) and how many (quantity, countable), in connection with the idea of "majority," were examined. All of these interrogations – in addition to providing a structure for the chapter – are evidence that, instead of having this word beg numerous questions at the centre of referendum processes,[125] "majority" can and should be utilized to highlight and address the many facets of determining the people's will, the numeric standard of 50%+1 being but one of them, the easiest perhaps.

References

Andreas Auer, "National Referendums in the Process of European Integration: Time for Change", in Anneli Albi & Jacques Ziller (eds.), *The European Constitution and National Constitutions – Ratifications and Beyond* (Netherlands: Kluwer Law International, 2007), 267.

Ulrike Barten, *Minorities, Minority Rights and International Self-Determination* (Berlin: Springer, 2015).

Karlo Basta, "The State between Minority and Majority Nationalism: Decentralization, Symbolic Recognition, and Secessionist Crises in Spain and Canada" (2017) 48 *Publius: The Journal of Federalism* 51.

Stéphane Beaulac, "Turbulence en vue", *La Presse+*, 23 October 2016.

Frédéric Bérard & Stéphane Beaulac, *The Law of Independence – Quebec, Montenegro, Scotland, Catalonia* (Toronto, ON: LexisNexis, 2017).

Paloma Biglino Campos, "Cataluña, federalism y pluralism politico" (2016) 37 *Teoria y Realidad Constitucional* 449.

Tesfa Bihonegn, "Federalization with a Constitutional Guarantee to Secession: Controversies, Paradoxes and Imponderables in Ethiopia" (2015) 25 *Regional & Federal Studies* 45.

Ian Brownlie, *Principles of Public International Law*, 6th ed. (Oxford, UK: Oxford University Press, 2004).

Walter Bryce Gallie, "Essentially Contested Concepts" (1955–1956) 56 *Proceedings of the Aristotelian Society (New Series)* 167.

Allen Buchanan, "Self-Determination and the Right to Secede" (1992) 45 *Journal of International Affairs* 347.

Allen Buchanan, *Justice, Legitimacy, and Self-Determination – Moral Foundations for International Law* (Oxford, UK: Oxford University Press, 2007).

125 Indeed, on many issues concerning the law of independence, it is common to come across "mantra-like incantations" as part of the typical narratives used by some authors and political actors, which are in fact concealing more than revealing relevant features of the problems at stake. See Gaudreault-DesBiens, 2019, at 60.

Lee C. Buchheit, *Secession – The Legitimacy of Self-Determination* (New Haven, CT: Yale University Press, 1978).

David Butler & Austin Ranney (eds.), *Referendums around the World – The Growing Use of Direct Democracy* (Washington, DC: AEI Press, 1994).

Antonio Cassese, *Self-Determination of Peoples – A Legal Reappraisal (Hersch Lauterpacht Memorial Lectures)* (Cambridge & New York: Cambridge University Press, 1995).

Julien Cazala, "L'accession du Monténégro à l'indépendance" (2006) 52 *Annuaire français de droit international* 160.

Lisa Lai-Shen Cheng & Norbert Corver, *WH-Movement – Moving On* (Cambridge, MA: MIT Press, 2006).

Noam Chomsky, "On Wh-Movement", in Peter W. Culicover, Thomas Wasow & Adrian Akmajian (eds.), *Formal Syntax* (New York: Academic Press, 1977), 77.

Sujit Choudhry, "Referendum? What Referendm?" (2007) 15 *Literary Review of Canada* 7.

Sujit Choudhry & Robert Howse, "Secession: Constitutional Theory and the Quebec Secession Reference" (2000) 13 *Canadian Journal of Law & Jurisprudence* 143.

Harold D. Clarke, Matthew Goodwin & Paul Whiteley, *Brexit – Why Britain Voted to Leave the European Union* (Cambridge, MA: Cambridge University Press, 2017).

Carlos Closa, "Why Convene Referendums? Explaining Choices in EU Constitutional Politics" (2007) 14 *Journal of European Public Policy* 1311.

Carlos Closa, *The Politics of Ratification of EU Treaties* (London & New York: Routledge, 2013).

Élie Cohen, Gérard Grunberg & Bernard Manin, "Le référendum, un instrument défectueux" (2017) 193 *Le Débat* 137.

James Crawford, "State Practice and International Law in Relation to Secession" (1998) 69 *British Yearbook of International Law* 85.

James Crawford, *The Creation of States in International Law*, 2nd ed. (Oxford, UK: Clarendon Press, 2006).

Xavier Cuadras Morató (ed.), *Catalonia: A New Independent State in Europe? – A Debate on Secession Within the European Union* (Abingdon, UK: Routledge, 2016).

Giacomo Delledonne & Giuseppe Martinico (eds.), *The Canadian Contribution to a Comparative Law of Secession – Legacies of the Quebec Secession Reference* (New York: Palgrave Macmillan, 2019).

Giacomo Delledonne & Matteo Monti, "Secessionist Impulses and the Italian Legal System: The (Non) Influence of the Secession Reference", in Giacomo Delledonne & Giuseppe Martinico (eds.), *The Canadian Contribution to a Comparative Law of Secession – Legacies of the Quebec Secession Reference* (New York: Palgrave Macmillan, 2019), 185.

Pierre Derriennic, "Majorité claire: mode d'emploi" (1998) 26 *Cité libre* 33.

John Dugard, *The Secession of States and Their Recognition in the Wake of Kosovo* (The Hague: Pocketbooks of The Hague Academy of International Law, 2013).

Patrick Dumberry, "Lessons Learned from the Quebec Secession Reference Before the Supreme Court of Canada", in Marcelo G. Kohen (ed.), *Secession – International Law Perspectives* (Cambridge & New York: Cambridge University Press, 2006), 416.

Benjamin F. Elson & Velma B. Pickett, *Beginning Morphology and Syntax*, rev. ed. (Dallas, TX: Summer Institute of Linguistics, 1988).

Federico Fabbrini (ed.), *The Law & Politics of Brexit* (Oxford: Oxford University Press, 2017).

Oonagh E. Fitzgerald, "Lessons from Brexit: Reconciling International and Constitutional Aspirations", in Oonagh E. Fitzgerald & Eva Lein (eds.), *Complexity's Embrace – The International Law Implications of Brexit* (Waterloo, ON: Centre for International Governance Innovation & London: British Institute of International and Comparative Law, 2018), 281.

Oonagh E. Fitzgerald & Eva Lein (eds.), *Complexity's Embrace – The International Law Implications of Brexit* (Waterloo, ON: Centre for International Governance Innovation & London: British Institute of International and Comparative Law, 2018).

Josh Freed, "Coining 'Neverendum' as Conquered the Globe", *Montreal Gazette*, 22 April 2017.

Géraldine Gadbin-George & Juliette Ringeisen-Biardeaud (eds.), *Partir en solitaire – Conséquences du Brexit aujourd'hui et demain* (Paris, France: Éditions Panthéon-Assas, 2018).

Thierry Garcia (ed.), *La Reconnaissance du statut d'État à des entités contestées – Approches de droits international, régional et interne* (Paris, France: Pedone, 2018).

Jean-François Gaudreault-DesBiens, "The Quebec Secession Reference and the Judicial Arbitration of Conflicting Narratives about Law, Democracy, and Identity" (1999) 23 *Vermont Law Review* 793.

Jean-François Gaudreault-DesBiens, "Underlying Principles and the Migration of Reasoning Templates: A Trans-Systemic Reading of the Quebec Secession Reference", in Sujit Choudhry (ed.), *The Migration of Constitutional Ideas* (Cambridge, MA: Cambridge University Press, 2006), 178.

Jean-François Gaudreault-DesBiens, "The Law and Politics of Secession: From the Political Contingency of Secession to a 'Right to Decide'? Can Lessons Be Learned from the Quebec Case?", in Giacomo Delledonne & Giuseppe Martinico (eds.), *The Canadian Contribution to a Comparative Law of Secession – Legacies of the Quebec Secession Reference* (New York: Palgrave Macmillan, 2019), 33.

Stéphan Gervais, Christopher Kirkey & Jarrett Rudy (eds.), *Quebec Questions – Quebec Studies for the Twenty-First Century*, 2nd ed. (Don Mills, ON: Oxford University Press, 2016).

İlker Gökhan Şen, *Sovereignty Referendums in International and Constitutional Law* (Berlin: Springer, 2015).

İlker Gökhan Şen, "Sovereignty Referendums: People Concerned and People Entitled to Vote", in Laurence Morel & Matt Qvortrup (eds.), *The Routledge Handbook to Referendums and Direct Democracy* (Abington & New York: Routledge, 2018), 210.

Étienne Grisel, *Initiative et référendum populaires – Traité de la démocratie semi-directe en droit Suisse*, 3rd ed. (Berne: Stämpfli, 2004).

David Haljan, "A Constitutional Duty to Negotiate Amendments: Reference Re Secession of Quebec" (1999) 48 *International & Comparative Law Quarterly* 447.

Francis Hamon, *Le référendum – Étude comparative*, 2nd ed. (Paris, France: L.G.D.J., 2012).

Hurst Hannum, *Autonomy, Sovereignty, and Self-Determination – The Accommodation of Conflicting Rights* (Philadelphia, PA: University of Pennsylvania Press, 1990).

Chantal Hébert & Jean Lapierre, *Confessions post-référendaires – Les acteurs politiques de 1995 et le scénario d'un oui* (Montreal, QC: Éditions de l'Homme, 2014).

Christophe Hillon, "Accession and Withdrawal in the Law of the European Union", in Damian Chalmers & Anthony Arnull (eds.), *The Oxford Handbook of European Union Law* (Oxford, UK: Oxford University Press, 2015), 126.

Colin Kidd & Malcolm Petrie, "The Independence Referendum in Historical and Political Context", in Aileen McHarg, Tom Mullen, Allan Page & Neil Walker (eds.), *The Scottish Independence Referendum – Constitutional and Political Implications* (Oxford, UK: Oxford University Press, 2016), 29.

Suzanne Lalonde, *Determining Boundaries in a Conflicted World – The Role of Uti Possedetis* (Montreal, QC & Ithaca, NY: McGill-Queen's University Press, 2002).

Simon Langlois, "Évolution de l'appui à l'indépendance du Québec de 1995 à 2015", in Amélie Binette & Patrick Taillon (eds.), *La démocratie Référendaire dans les ensembles plurinationaux* (Quebec: Presses de l'Université Laval, 2018), 55.

Adam Łazowski, "Be Careful What You Wish for: Procedural Parameters of EU Withdrawal", in Carlos Closa (ed.), *Secession from a Member State and Withdrawal from the European Union – Troubled Membership* (Cambridge, MA: Cambridge University Press, 2017a), 234.

Adam Łazowski, *Withdrawal from the European Union – A Legal Appraisal* (London, UK: Edward Elgar Publishing, 2017b).

Jean Leclair, "Canada's Unfathomable Unwritten Constitutional Principles" (2002) 27 *Queen's Law Journal* 389.

André Lecours, "Référendums d'autodétermination: les experiences Québécoise et canadienne en perspective comparé", in Amélie Binette & Patrick Taillon (eds.), *La démocratie Référendaire dans les ensembles plurinationaux* (Quebec: Presses de l'Université Laval, 2018), 251.

Olivier Lecucq, *Secession et processus sécessioniste en droit international, européen et constitutionnel* (Bayonne, France: Institut Universitaire Varenne, 2017).

Alberto López-Basaguren & Leire Escajedo San-Epifanio (eds.), *Claims for Secession and Federalism – A Comparative Study with a Special Focus on Spain* (Berlin: Springer, 2019).

William H. Luers, "Czechoslovakia: Road to Revolution" (1990) 69 *Foreign Affairs* 77.

Jérôme Lussier, "Contestation de la loi 99: quelques questions pour Stéphane Beaulac", *Magazine L'Actualité*, 22 October 2013.

Alastair MacIver, "Metaconstitutionalising Secession: The Reference and Scotland (In Europe)", in Giacomo Delledonne & Giuseppe Martinico (eds.), *The Canadian Contribution to a Comparative Law of Secession – Legacies of the Quebec Secession Reference* (New York: Palgrave Macmillan, 2019), 111.

Susanna Mancini, "Secession and Self-Determination", in Michel Rosenfeld & András Sajó (eds.), *The Oxford Handbook of Comparative Constitutional Law* (Oxford, UK: Oxford University Press, 2012), 481.

Costanza Margiotta, *L'Ultimo Diritto – Profili Storici e Teorici sella Secessione* (Bologna, Italy: Il Mulino, 2005).

Kevin McKenna, "Sturgeon Is Preparing for a New Scottish Independence Battle", *The Guardian*, 1 July 2018.

Errol P. Mendes, "The Legacy of the Quebec Secession Reference Ruling in Canada and Internationally", in Giacomo Delledonne & Giuseppe Martinico (eds.), *The Canadian Contribution to a Comparative Law of Secession – Legacies of the Quebec Secession Reference* (New York: Palgrave Macmillan, 2019), 9.

Fernando Mendez & Micha Germann, "Contested Sovereignty: Mapping Referendums on Sovereignty Over Time and Space" (2018) 48 *British Journal of Political Science* 141.

Fernando Mendez, Mario Mendez & Vasilika Triga, *Referendums and the European Union: A Comparative Inquiry* (Cambridge, MA: Cambridge University Press, 2014).

Laurence Morel, "Referendum", in Michel Rosenfeld & András Sajó (eds.), *The Oxford Handbook of Comparative Constitutional Law* (Oxford, UK: Oxford University Press, 2012), 501.

Laurence Morel, "The Democratic Criticism of Referendums – The Majority and True Will of the People", in Laurence Morel & Matt Qvortrup (eds.), *The Routledge Handbook to Referendums and Direct Democracy* (Abington & New York: Routledge, 2018), 149.

Tom Mullen, "Introduction", in Aileen McHarg, Tom Mullen, Allan Page & Neil Walker (eds.), *The Scottish Independence Referendum – Constitutional and Political Implications* (Oxford, UK: Oxford University Press, 2016), 3.

Zoran Oklopcic, "Independence Referendums and Democratic Theory in Quebec and Montenegro" (2012) 18 *Nationalism & Ethnic Politics* 22.

Zoran Oklopcic, Secession Reference and Its Intellectual Legacy: Sceptical Notes from the European Peripheries", in Giacomo Delledonne & Giuseppe Martinico (eds.), *The Canadian Contribution to a Comparative Law of Secession – Legacies of the Quebec Secession Reference* (New York: Palgrave Macmillan, 2019), 209.

Ece Özlem Atikcan, "Les double référendums dans l'Union européenne", in Amélie Binette & Patrick Taillon (eds.), *La démocratie Référendaire dans les ensembles plurinationaux* (Quebec: Presses de l'Université Laval, 2018), 465.

Francesco Palermo, "Towards a Comparative Constitutional Law of Secession?", in Giacomo Delledonne & Giuseppe Martinico (eds.), *The Canadian Contribution to a Comparative Law of Secession – Legacies of the Quebec Secession Reference* (New York: Palgrave Macmillan, 2019), 265.

Randolph Quirk, Sidney Greenbaum, Geoffrey Leech & Jan Svartvik, *A Comprehensive Grammar of the English Language* (London, UK: Longman, 1985).

Matt Qvortrup, *A Comparative Study of Referendums – Government by the People*, 2nd ed. (Manchester, UK: Manchester University Press, 2005).

Matt Qvortrup, "Referendums on Independence, 1860–2011" (2014a) 85 *Political Quarterly* 57.

Matt Qvortrup, *Referendums and Ethnic Conflict* (Philadelphia, PA: University of Pennsylvania Press, 2014b).

Peter Radan, *Creating New States – Theory and Practice of Secession* (Aldershot, UK: Ashgate Publishing, 2007).

Peter Radan, "Secessionist Referenda in International and Domestic Law" (2012) 18 *Nationalism and Ethic Politics* 8.

Peter Radan, "Secession: A Word in Search of a Meaning", in Aleksandar Pavković & Peter Radan (eds.), *On the Way to Statehood – Secession and Globalization* (Abingdon & New York: Routledge, 2016), 17.

Steven R. Ratner, "Drawing a Better Line: Uti Possidetis and the Borders of New States" (1996) 90 *American Journal of International Law* 590.

François Rocher, "Self-Determination and the Use of Referendums – The Case of Quebec" (2014) 27 *International Journal of Politics, Culture, and Society* 25.

François Rocher, "Les incidences démocratiques de la nébuleuse obligation de clarté du Renvoi relatif à la sécession du Québec", in Amélie Binette & Patrick Taillon (eds.), *La démocratie Référendaire dans les ensembles plurinationaux* (Quebec: Presses de l'Université Laval, 2018), 205.

François Rocher & André Lecours, "The Correct Expression of Popular Will – Does the Wording of a Referendum Question Matter?", in Laurence Morel & Matt Qvortrup (eds.), *The Routledge Handbook to Referendums and Direct Democracy* (Abingdon & New York: Routledge, 2018), 227.

Přemysl Rosůlek, "Secession and Intelligibility of a Referendum Question (RQ) – from Québec to Scotland (1980–2014)" (2016) 10 *Annual of Language & Politics & Politics of Identity* 49.

Cedric Ryngaert, "Le référendum d'initiative populaire en Italie: une longue traverse du désert" (1982) 32 *Revue française de science politique* 1024.

Cedric Ryngaert & Sven Sobrie, "Recognition of States: International Law or Realpolitik? – The Practice of Recognition in the Wake of Kosovo, South Ossetia, and Abkhazia" (2011) 24 *Leiden Journal of International Law* 472.

Marc Sanjaume-Calvet, "Le débat catalan et l'éthique de la sécession", in Amélie Binette & Patrick Taillon (eds.), *La démocratie Référendaire dans les ensembles plurinationaux* (Quebec: Presses de l'Université Laval, 2018), 347.

Georges Scelle, *Précis du droit des gens – Principes et systématique*, vol. 2 (Paris, France: Sirey, 1934).

Michel Seymour, "Secession as a Remedial Right" (2007) 50 *Inquiry* 395.

Jo Shaw, "Unions and Citizens: Membership Status and Political Rights in Scotland, the UK and the EU", in Carlos Closa (ed.), *Secession from a Member State and Withdrawal from the European Union – Troubled Membership* (Cambridge, MA: Cambridge University Press, 2017), 153.

Min Shu, "Referendums and the Political Constitutionalisation of the EU" (2008) 14 *European Law Journal* 423.

Max Steinbeis, "Majority Is a Legal Concept" (2017) *Verfassungsblog*, available online: http://verfassungblog.de/majority-is-a-legal-concept.

Gary Sussman, "When the Demos Shapes the Polis – The Use of Referendums in Settling Sovereignty Issues" (2012) London School of Economics (unpublished paper), available online: http://www.iandrinstitute.org/docs/Sussman-When-the-Demos-Shapes-the-Polis-IRI.pdf.

Patrick Taillon, "Pour une redéfinition du référendum consultatif" (2007) 59 *Revue international de droit comparé* 143.

Patrick Taillon, *Le référendum expression directe de la souveraineté du people? Essai critique sur la rationalisation de l'expression référendaire en droit comparé* (Paris, France: Dalloz, 2012).

Stefan Talmon, "The Constitutive Versus the Declaratory Theory of Recognition: Tertium Non Datur?" (2004) 75 *British Yearbook of International Law* 101.

Antonello Tancredi, *Secessione nel Diritto Internazionale* (Padova, Italy: CEDAM, 2001).

Antonello Tancredi, "Neither Authorized nor Prohibited? – Secession and International Law after Kosovo, South Ossetia and Abkhazia" (2008) 18 *Italian Yearbook of International Law* 38.

Allan F. Tatham, "'Don't Mention Divorce at the Wedding, Darling!': EU Accession and Withdrawal after Lisbon", in Adrea Biondi, Piet Eeckhout & Stefanie Ripley (eds.), *EU Law after Lisbon* (Oxford, UK: Oxford University Press, 2012) 128.

Stephen J. Toope, "Right to Secede under Constitutional Law and Public International Law – Role of International Law in Canadian Courts" (1999) 93 *American Journal of International Law* 519.

Joe Verhoeven, *La reconnaissance internationale dans la pratique contemporaine – Les relations publiques internationales* (Paris, France: Pedone, 1975).

Mark D. Walters, "Nationalism and the Pathology of Legal Systems: Considering the Quebec Secession Reference and Its Lessons for the United Kingdom" (1999) 62 *Modern Law Review* 371.

Asanga Welikala, "Constitutional Migrations in the Commonwealth: The Quebec Secession Reference and Ski Lankan Constitutional Discourse", in Giocomo Delledonne & Giuseppe Martinico (eds.), *The Canadian Contribution to a Comparative Law of Secession – Legacies of the Quebec Secession Reference* (New York: Palgrave Macmillan, 2019), 135.

Christopher Heath Wellman, *A Theory of Secession – The Case for Political Self-Determination* (Cambridge, MA: Cambridge University Press, 2005).

Kenneth Wheare, *Federal Government* (Oxford, UK: Oxford University Press, 1963).

François Yale & Claire Durand, "What did Quebeckers Want? Impact of Question Wording, Constitutional Proposal and Context on Support for Sovereignty, 1976–2008" (2011) 41 *American Review of Canadian Studies* 242.

8 Independence referendums

History, legal status and voting behaviour

Matt Qvortrup

1. Introduction

There is something personal for me in writing a chapter about independence referendums. My political awakening in my earliest youth coincided with the rise in Quebecois nationalism – and then Canadian Prime Minister Pierre Trudeau's efforts to quell it. Indeed, my earliest political memory is the television pictures from 1980 of the dejected Quebecois nationalists wrapped in their blue and white *fleur-de-lis* flag, while separatist premier René Lévesque proclaimed that the result would only stand *"à la prochaine fois"* – "until next time"; until the next referendum. Fifteen years later, the "*la prochaine fois*" materialized, and – perhaps unsurprisingly – I chose this topic for Doctoral Dissertation. In a sense, therefore, this chapter is the product of nearly 40 years of reflections on the subject of independence referendums.

2. Referendums and nationalism

William Sumner Maine – a conservative writer from the end of the Victorian age – once mused,

> democracies are quite paralyzed by the plea of nationality. There is no more effective way of attacking them than by admitting the right of the majority to govern but denying that the majority so entitled is the particular majority which claims the right.
>
> (Maine 1897: 88)

This conundrum – and other problems associated with referendums on independence – has not affected their use.

Notwithstanding the constitutional illegality of most independence referendums, they have continued to proliferate since the 1990s, as "the symbolic political potential of the plebiscite as a road to national independence made it impossible to constrain" (Tierney 2012: 66).

Given this prominence of independence referendum several questions emerge; Has there been a historical increase in their number? What is their legal status? When have the referendums resulted in a yes vote; and; when have they led to the establishment of new independent states? This is theoretically an interesting question, not only as regards referendums on independence but also as this is related to the more general perception that there, "on the aggregate level, the number of referendums…has increased significantly" (Hollander 2019: 2). Each of these questions will be analyzed below. For this, I have identified a number of different hypotheses. I tested these hypotheses in relation to the factors conducive to a yes-vote and the factors conducive to the recognition of a new state following an affirmative vote in a referendum.

3. Concepts and definitions

Before addressing the substantial issues, it is necessary to define the concept of independence referendums. The subject under analysis consists of two words. In the following, the "independence" will be defined, per Pavkovic and Radan, as a "process of withdrawal of a territory and its population from an existing state and the creation of a new state on that territory" (Pavkovic and Radan 2007: 1). The referendum will be defined as a public vote on a policy issue.

There are a number of different categorizations of referendums. Some categorize referendums by initiation (controlled by the government or not) and their outcome (whether the outcome strengthens or weakens the government – so-called "hegemonic" or "non-hegemonic" outcomes) (Qvortrup 2000) (Smith 1976).

Others, above all David Altman distinguishes between different types of, what he calls, *Mechanisms of Direct Democracy* (MMD), which he subcategorizes as those "Required by Constitution or Law," "Top-Down (or From Above)" and "Citizen-Initiated (Through collection of Signatures)" (Altman 2010: 11). This categorization is similar to the one adopted by Morel (2012), though she uses a simpler terminology. Overall, according to Morel (2012) and Altman (2010) there are three types of referendums:

- Ad hoc (top-down) referendums (questions to solve a perceived political issue – such as David Cameron's decision to hold a referendum on UK membership of the European Union 2016);
- Initiatives (votes initiated by a specified number of electors on a) already enacted legislation (as in Switzerland) or b) on new laws (as in Hungary), and:
- Constitutional Referendums (see next paragraph).

By convention, there are three types of Constitutional Referendums. According to Morel, "the Constitutional doctrine normally distinguishes between three types of constitutional referendums: on the approval of the constitution, on its revision, and on sovereignty issues (like the foundation of a new state)" (See Morel 2012 for an overview of the literature).

Some scholars have challenged this categorization. For example, Mendez and Germann, find that sovereignty issues are a kind of blanket category that covers virtually anything pertaining to sovereignty, such as federalization, devolution and border disputes (Mendez and Germann 2018). The problem with this categorization is that it becomes so broad that it gets conceptually meaningless.

Hence Morel's categorization has been chosen as it is more parsimonious. In her categorization, sovereignty referendums are only the ones that deal with the issue of whether a particular territory votes to become (or not) "a new state."

While there has been considerable debate on independence referendums and scholarly writings about them (Laponce 2010), (Leduc 2003) (Qvortrup 2014), the number of them is comparatively small, if we apply Morel's categorization. Thus, out of the 1200 nation-wide only 61 have pertained to independence (of which only four have returned a "no" vote (Quebec, in respectively, 1980 and 1995, Scotland in 2014 and New Caledonia in 2018) – though other referendums have failed because they did not satisfy super-majority requirements (e.g. in Nevis in 1998 and in several referendums in Palau in the 1980s)

4. The short history of independence referendums

Historically, the independence referendums have come in waves, a few in the early 1860, when the US states of Arkansas, Tennessee, Texas and Virginia – held referendums on independence following the election of Abraham Lincoln to the US presidency. All the referendums were won but no country recognized the results (Mattern 1921).

After the American Civil War, the US Supreme Court established in *Texas v White* that unilateral declarations of independence are unconstitutional, a case that was most recently used by the Alaskan Supreme Court in 2006 in *Kohlhaas v Alaska* to ban a constitutional initiative for independence for this state.

After the American secession-votes, there was a gap of a few decades before the Norwegian referendum in 1905. Then a hiatus opened again until the mid-1930 when the number of independence referendums began to pick up. The unrecognized, but successful, independence referendum in Western Australia in 1933 and the vote for independence for the Philippines in 1935 marked a turning point. In Australia, 68% voted in favour, but the vote was ignored as the secessionist party lost the state election on the same day (Qvortrup 2014: 29).

Especially after the Second World War, the referendum was occasionally used to show popular approval for decolonization, such as in Cambodia (1945), Algeria (1961) and Western Samoa (1961). But, overall, "the use of [the independence] referendum in the decolonization era was again rare" (Tierney 2012: 65).

After a drop in the 1970s, there was an explosion of independence votes in the years immediately following the fall of the Berlin Wall and the collapse of Soviet Communism. Until that time, the international community was sceptical regarding the legality of independence referendums (We shall return to this in the next section). But overall, their number increased and was like an incoming tide after the fall of the Berlin Wall.

These referendums have differed considerably, in a number of respects, such as the size of the entity, the level of economic development and the consolidation of democratic norms. However, one thing has been consistent, turnout has been

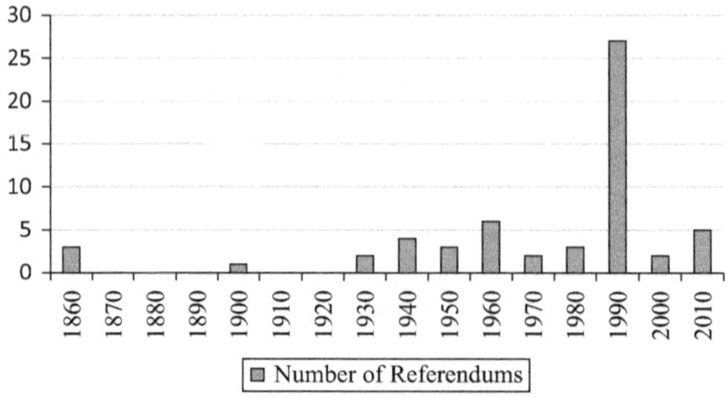

Figure 8.1 Referendums on independence 1860–2010.[1]

high. The average turnout in the 40 independence referendums held since 1980, has been 86%. Similarly, support for independence, notwithstanding the legality of the referendum (See Section 3), has been high. On average, 78% of those voting have supported independence.[2]

Before we go on to analyze the factors that lead to "yes" results and the ones that result in the establishment of independent states, we need to consider when entities are allowed to hold these votes at all.

5. The legality of independence referendums

Independence referendums come in different forms. To understand this, we need a further subdivision from that suggested by Morel (2012). Following Sen, we can distinguish between three forms (Sen 2018: 213), namely,

1) Postcolonial (e.g. Philippines 1935);
2) By agreement (Montenegro 2006 and a fortiori Bougainville 2019);
3) Unilateral: Catalonia 2017, Quebec 1980 and 1995 and Estonia 1991.

Unilateral independence referendums – the ones that are *stricto sensu* illegal – are nevertheless the most common ones. These constitute 36 out of the total. By

1 Based on Qvortrup (2014) (2017). Note: This figure does not include the four multi-option referendums in Puerto Rico (1968, 1993, 1998 and 2012), which formally included "independence" as one of the options. However, the table includes the two-round multi-option referendum in Newfoundland in 1948 as independence was one of the choices in the run-off. The independence options lost to "statehood" and the former British territory became a Canadian Province (See Qvortrup 2014: 69).

2 Source: C2D, Zentrum fur Demokratie, Aarau (http://www.c2d.ch, Accessed 1 October 2018).

contrast, here there were only four postcolonial referendums and two were held by agreement.

But when are referendums on independence "legal"? Notwithstanding the rhetoric about "Self-Determination," – a doctrine codified in the UN Charter (Art. 2.1), "no principle [has] emerged in international law that considered a demonstration of popular support by a discrete sub-state national group to be, by itself, a legally consequential step towards independent statehood" (Tierney 2012: 64).

So, what then, is the legal position? While the late legal theorist Neil MacCormick, in the case of the United Kingdom, believed one could answer the question "Is there a constitutional path to Scottish independence?" affirmatively (MacCormick 2000), this is very much a minority view among constitutional lawyers (see Margiotta, Chapter 2, this volume). In the words of another Scottish lawyer, "there was certainly no right to statehood, whether sub-state peoples could mobilize massive support for such a claim by a referendum or not" (Tierney 2012: 66).

Thus, while one may philosophically disagree with the ethical and moral tenants of legal positivism, this doctrine holds sway in practical politics. Hence, the following is based on a reading of the "black letter law" pertaining to independence referendums (see Margiotta's arguments in this volume on legal positivism and legal relevance of secession).

The black letter law of the "right" to self-determination referendums is, in a sense, very simple. In the words of James Crawford, "there is no unilateral right to secede based merely on a majority vote of the population of a given subdivision or territory" (Crawford 2006: 417). Those who espouse a similar legal positivist approach will further stress that this is consistent with the jurisprudence of international courts. Thus, in an *obiter dicta* in the Kosovo Case Judge Yusuf, opined,

> A radically or ethnically distinct group within a state, even if it qualifies as a people for the purposes of self-determination, does not have the right to unilateral self-determination simply because it wishes to create its own separate state.
>
> (Re Kosovo, 2010: 1410)

This view regarding the legality of independence referendums is near identical to the doctrine followed by domestic courts. In the Canadian case of *Bertrand v. Québec,* it was held *per* Justice Robert Lessage that a referendum on a unilateral declaration would be, "manifestly illegal." This is still the legal position notwithstanding the reasoning in the much-cited (and often misunderstood) *Re Quebec* (See Martinico, Chapter 6, this volume).

Thus, the general rule is that referendums have to be held either in accordance with existing constitutions (such a provision exists in Art 39(3) of the Ethiopian constitution but in few other states), or following an agreement between the area that seeks secession and the larger state of which it is part (this is what happened in the very different cases of East Timor 1999, South Sudan 2011, Scotland 2014 and a fortiori Bougainville) (Radan 2012: 14).

Following this logic, it would seem that the referendums in both Catalonia and Kurdistan, to take two recent examples, were both illegal and unconstitutional.

Based on this reasoning, the Soviet leader Mikhail Gorbachev was well within his right to claim that the Latvian, Estonian and Lithuanian referendums on independence in the spring of 1991 were illegal and that he was the guarantor of *Pravovoe gosudarstvo* – the equivalent of the rule of law in Soviet jurisprudence. Of course, some would say, previously, under the so-called *Stalin Constitution 1936*, individual Soviet states did indeed have the right to self-determination referendums under Art 48. But this provision had been dropped in *Khrushchev Constitution* of 1956. Consequently, the Baltic republics were in breach in the early 1990s. (Though some claim their annexation by the Soviet Union in 1939 was illegal and hence their declaration of independence was merely a statement of a reassertion of sovereignty.)

Does this change the legality of the Catalan and Kurdish cases? Not really, as, respectively, the Iraqi and the Spanish constitutions do not allow for independence referendums, the respective votes held in these two entities were, it would seem, *ipso facto*, unconstitutional.

Yet matters are not that simple. Admittedly, all other things being equal, a country only has a right if it follows the rules. However, when a region is part of an undemocratic constitutional order, matters are a bit more complex. Antonio Cassese has argued,

> When the central authorities of a sovereign State persistently refuse to grant participatory rights to a religious or racial group, grossly and systematically trample upon their fundamental rights, and deny them the possibility of reaching a peaceful settlement within the framework of the State structure…a group may secede – thus exercising the most radical form of external self-determination – once it is clear that all attempts to achieve internal self-determination have failed or are destined to fail.
>
> (Cassese 1995: 119–120)

As Iraq is not a well-functioning democratic state, it could be argued that Kurdistan meets these criteria. Again, the comparison with the Soviet Union is illustrative. Notwithstanding Gorbachev's reforms, the USSR was not a democratic regime, which consequently, provided the Baltic States with a legal justification for holding referendums on independence.

But, given that Spain is a democratic state, this rule hardly covers Catalonia. While the Spanish government, arguably acted in a way that appeared grossly disproportionate (to wit police violence and arrest of democratically elected politicians which appears disproportional notwithstanding the letter of the law), the legal argument remains the same. Catalonia is not currently part of a non-democratic state.

Based on the situation, as it stands now, the Catalan referendum in 2017 was from a purely legal perspective extra constitutional. In a legal system under the rule of law, the powers of state institutions have to be enumerated in law. The basic principle of *État de droit* is that citizens can do anything unless it is expressly prohibited. Public bodies or "emanations of the state" can only do things that are expressly allowed. Thus, the latter cannot *legally* speaking take actions that are not prescribed in enabling legislation. To pass legislation outside the boundaries of the constitution or enabling legislation is the very definition of being *ultra vires*; in plain English, illegal.

But does the law have to be that inflexible? Not necessarily. In Canada, the two referendums held in Quebec in, respectively, 1980 and 1995, were not strictly speaking within the powers granted to the Provinces by the Canadian Constitution (Sen 2015).

Technically speaking, the referendums were *ultra vires*. Yet, the Canadian judges, realizing that legality ultimately rests on a modicum of legitimacy followed a more pragmatic logic. In the celebrated case, *Re Quebec*, the court was asked the question, "Under the *Constitution* of Canada, can the National Assembly, legislature or Government of Quebec effect the secession of Quebec from Canada unilaterally?"

The court held that while the "secession of Quebec from Canada cannot be accomplished…unilaterally," a referendum itself was not unconstitutional but a mechanism of gauging the will of the francophone province. Consequently, a referendum, provided it resulted in a "clear majority," "would confer legitimacy on the efforts of the Quebec government" (*Re Secession of Quebec*, 1998: 385).

In other words, a result in favour of secession would require the rest of Canada to negotiate with Quebec. Needless to say, this ruling does not apply in Spain, although even in Spain the Spanish Constitutional Court opened to this possibility if exercised within the limits of constitutional reform process (Spanish Constitutional Court, judgment 42/2014). But the Canadian example suggests that other countries' courts have shown a flexibility and appreciation of nuances that is conducive to compromises.

Thus, referendums on independence are often illegal. But does that really matter? Doesn't democracy override legalistic concerns? There is – on the face of it something persuasive about Stephen Tierney's suggestion that,

> Although international law and its institutions have…attempted to emasculate the application of the principle of self-determination in claims to independent statehood by nationalist movements, the referendum, infused as it is with the purported legitimacy of a self-determining people, constantly re-emerges as a political trump card to challenge the legal formalism of the settled order of states.
>
> (Tierney 2012: 62)

But if the referendum is such a "trump card," is this reflected in their outcomes? Or, what generally determines the outcome of them?

6. What determines the outcome of independence referendums?

There is relatively sparse literature on the determinants of independence referendums. Most of this is country specific and focuses on idiosyncratic factors behind a unique event (See e.g. Conley 1997). While there are some studies that contrast independence referendums, for example Quebec 1995 and Montenegro 2006 (Oklopcic 2012), there are relatively few studies devoted to the comparative study of independence referendums (though see: Dion 1996) (Qvortrup 2014).

Moreover, only a subset of the former literature deals with the determinants of the vote (e.g. Clarke and Kornberg 1996; Leduc 2002). The aim of this part of the chapter is first to contribute to the comparative psephology of independence referendums and to determine whether these votes follow a recurrent pattern?

In line with conventional social science methodology, it is *de rigueur* to test specific hypotheses. Hence, we have developed five hypotheses based on previous literature.

Some of the previous studies make generalized claims, for example, that secession is difficult in developed societies (Dion 1996). There is, on the face of it, something to be said for this. Hence, we hypothesize that *Referendums are less likely to succeed in developed countries* (H1).

Independence and secession contribute to the establishment of a collective entity; a new nation. In order to succeed it is to be expected that the elites (irrespective of political ideology) share a commitment to independence. Hence, our second hypothesis is, *Support for independence (a yes vote) is correlated with elite consensus* (H2).

Democracy is about legitimacy. A low turnout will not confer legitimacy on a momentous and irreversible decision such as independence. For this reason, we hypothesize that *Support for independence will be correlated with higher turnouts* (H3).

Sometimes – for example in the post-Soviet states – autocratic leaders desire independence in order not to be governed by a larger entity (See e.g. the case of Belarus). These referendums fall far short of the standards for free and fair elections, and generally do not, therefore, reflect the will of the voters. More generally, it is reasonable to hypothesize that *the support of independence yes-vote is correlated with the level of democratization* (H4).

In the wake of the collapse of Soviet Communism several independence referendums were held (Tierney 2012 for an overview). Hitherto oppressed national groups were able to appeal to ethnic sentiments. These referendums constitute a unique set of votes, and led to a spike in the number of independence referendums (see Figure 8.1).

Consequently, one could hypothesize that *Referendums held in post-communist societies are likely to be correlated with high-yes votes* (H5).

In addition to these hypotheses we are also testing a number of factors that could be deemed to have an influence on the outcome of an independence referendum. For example, given the importance of self-determination in French jurisprudence and constitutional history (See Mattern 1921), one might expect that voters in Francophone countries would be more prone to vote affirmatively in referendum. And, given that many referendums were held in the aftermath of armed conflict (for example Algeria 1961), one might hypothesize that voters, eager to put conflict behind them, would be more likely to vote "yes" in an independence referendum.

7. Statistical findings[3]

Statistical analysis does not support all of these hypotheses. To start with, French colonial legacy and armed conflict are not statistically significant. Nor, for that matter are H1 (level of economic development) or H5 (the vote takes place in a post-Soviet state). Similarly, there is little support for the proposition that the support for independence correlates with a higher turnout (H3). You can win independence on a low turnout. Often, it would seem, because the opposition boycotts the vote (as in the cases of Bosnia and Catalonia).

Yet it is not all doom and gloom. As Table 8.1 shows, there are certain patterns in how referendums on independence are decided.

There is similarly support for the hypothesis that referendums on independence tend to be more successful in countries, which have low levels of democratization (as measured by a high Polity IV Scores). Though this too is limited to one of the models. This is an interesting finding that needs to be explored in greater depth. Given that referendums on independence tend to occur in countries with low levels of democratization we can, perhaps, question whether the official result is, in fact, a true representation of the "will of the people." Four out of the six referendums held in countries categorized as "democratic" under Polity IV, namely Quebec (1980, 1995), Scotland (2014) and New Caledonia (2018), failed to yield a "yes" majority. Conversely, referendums in polities with suboptimal levels of democratization, such as Kurdistan, South Sudan and Eritrea

3 A note on data: As noted above, there is disagreement as to what constitute independence referendums (See discussion of Mendez and Germann 2018). In this chapter, referendums are included if an entity (a smaller part of a recognized state) held a referendum on the establishment of a potentially new international law subject. In most cases, the votes have been on whether the entity in question wished to become independent. However, in some cases Philippines (1935), Malta (1964), Abkhazia (1999), Somaliland (2001) and South Ossetia (2001) the votes were formally on a new constitution for an independent country. While these referendums were not *strictu sensu* independence referendums they were *de facto* plebiscites pertaining to independence as a rejection of the proposition would have meant the continuation of the status quo ante. Democracies figures are based on *Polity IV* as this database covers all years back to 1800. The alternative measure *Freedom House* was deemed unsuitable, as it did not cover the period prior to 1973. Data for the individual referendums were based on Qvortrup (2014b), which in turn is based on specialist assessment by country experts and data from *C2D, Zentrum fur Demokratie, Aarau* (http://www.c2d.ch).

Table 8.1 Statistical determinants of yes-votes in independence referendums (dependent variable yes-vote)

Variables	*Model 1*	*Model 2*
Turnout	0.323	0.350
	(0.192)	(0.201)
Polity IV	–0.401**	–0.321
	(0.190)	(0.197)
Elite Consensus	18.363***	18.190***
	(4.935)	(5.312)
Post-Communist	6.791	–1.628
	(4.912)	(7.181)
French	–3.359	
	(7.866)	
Armed Conflict	6.930	
	(6.375)	
First World	–8.88	
		(7.81)
Constant	39.051**	40.043**
	(16.25)	(16.798)
	R;Squared: 37 N: 60	R-Squared: 41 N: 60

*: p< 0.1, **: p<0.05, *** p< 0.01

succeeded. This suggests that independence referendums are likely to have been rigged, and that we – at a minimum – need to closely monitor them if we are to recognize the results as true representations of the majority of the voters' preferences. The examples of this are legion, but Belarus is an illustrative case. Elgie and Zielonka commented: "The procedures, form and substance of the referendum were imposed by the president, who also enjoyed total monopoly over the mass media" (Elgie and Zielonka 2001: 41). Short of these tactics, it is difficult to win support in an independence referendum.

The only consistent statistical finding is that referendums are more successful if there is an elite consensus. This finding is consistent across both models.

One of objections against the use of referendums to decide the issue of independence is that it is likely to result in an entrenchment of the conflict and the bullying of a small majority. A referendum can serve "to explode the myth of national unity in plurinational states… and can in fact be highly dangerous in deeply fractured societies" (Tierney 2012: 61). The statistical evidence does not rule this danger out, but it suggests that high-level support for independence is correlated with elite consensus, i.e. cases where all the major players support independence (as was the case in Norway 1905, Eritrea 1993, East Timor 1999 and South Sudan 2011).

8. When are referendums on independence recognized?

Not all of these different types of independence referendums have been equally conducive to the establishment of a new independent state. As Figure 8.2 shows, all the referendums in postcolonial territories (such as the Philippines in 1935, Micronesia 1983 and most recently in East Timor in 1999) have been recognized. The same is true for referendums held following an agreement, such as in the cases of the Montenegro referendum in 2006 and the referendum in South Sudan in 2011.

It seems that the international community – which oversees these two types of referendums – have been keen to ensure that their endeavours have not gone to waste.[4]

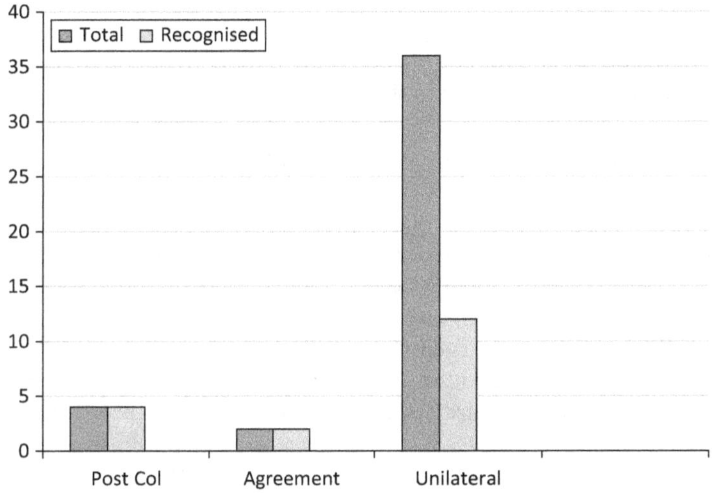

Figure 8.2 Types of referendums and international recognition.

Based on Sen (2018) and Qvortrup (2017).

4 It should be noted that some international agreement on referendums have not resulted in actual referendums, such as the referendum on the future of Kashmir and Western Sahara. These two latter referendums deserve to be mentioned although – or perhaps because – no referendum has taken place in either of the jurisdictions. Thus, despite being condemned by the UN Security Council for its illegal annexation of Western Sahara, Morocco has delayed holding a referendum on the future status of annexed area in flagrant contravention of international law due to uncertainties over the electorate. Similar delaying tactics have been deployed by India over the disputed territory of Kashmir. The UN Security Council called for a referendum in Resolution 47, which stated that "A plebiscite will be held when it shall be found by the Commission that the cease-fire and truce arrangements set forth in Parts I and II of the Commission's resolution of 13 August 1948." That was 70 years ago at the time of writing. To date no referendum has been held.

However, when referendums are held, the outcome has been accepted by the international community and by the parent states. Indeed, even when the result of the referendum was not legally binding (due to the doctrine of parliamentary sovereignty) the outcome of the referendum has been ratified by parliaments. Thus, the parliament of Indonesia – after considerable pressure from the international community – recognized the outcome of the 1999 East Timorese independence referendum.

The situation is markedly different for unilateral independence referendums. This type of independence referendum constitutes the majority of the 42 independence referendums held since 1980. Thirty-six or 85% were in this category. Only one in 12 cases was the referendum followed by international recognition of the new state (see below).

Why is it that some referendums – even unilateral ones – result in the establishment of a new state (such as in the case of Bosnia, Estonia and the Ukraine) but not in other cases such as in Catalonia, Tartarstan and Somaliland? To answer this, we need to look at the legal aspects pertaining to – what misleadingly – is called the "right to self-determination" (Dobelle 1996).

Of course, as (Beulac argues elsewhere in this collection), the establishment of a new state is not the same as recognition by the whole of the international community. Some states, such as Somaliland, Northern Cyprus, Nagorno-Karabakh and to an extent South Ossetia, have become relatively enduring entities, and have used the "mandate" from "the people" to legitimize this claim. In most cases, however, these established but unrecognized states survive thanks to the benevolence of a larger state. But much as these entities are "phantom states" (Scheindlin 2012), with no rights, the votes have often bolstered support internally notwithstanding the rejection by the international community.

So far, we have found that referendums are mostly held in contravention of constitutional law, though not necessarily in contravention of international law. We have also found that they yield a yes-vote when there is elite consensus about the outcome (e.g. as in the cases of Iceland 1944 and Estonia 1991), and that they tend to be associated with low levels of democratization. But a "yes" in a referendum does not mean that the entity will be recognized as an independent state.

What are the factors conducive to this? While governments may confidently cite lofty principles, the practice of independence referendums seemingly owe more to national interest than to adherence to principles of jurisprudence. For example, the states of Western Europe readily recognized the secessions of several former Yugoslav republics in the early 1990s – although these new states did not adhere to the legal principles outlined above.

And yet, in other cases, international recognition has been less forthcoming even if the countries have seemingly followed the established norms. To wit, no state has to date recognized the outcome of Nagorno-Karabakh's referendum in 1991, although Azerbaijan is very far from being a democratic state (the country has a Freedom House Score of 7 – the same as North Korea!) and despite the greater freedoms for the citizens/inhabitants of the break-away republic.

Similarly, no state recognized the referendum in Somaliland although this enclave is considerably more democratic, peaceful and respecting of the rule of law than Somalia, which at the time of the referendum was an arch-typical failed state.

All the legal arguments notwithstanding, acceptance of referendum results seem to be a political rather than a legal decision. One might thus be tempted to see these recognitions as examples of what IR scholar Stephen Krasner (1999) with an apt phrase called "organised hypocrisy." Others may simply call it *Realpolitik!* Lawyers are interested in what is – or is not – legal and in accordance with more or less rigid rules. Political scientists, by contrast, are interested in what actually happens and what the causes are. Are there from a political science (or international relations) point of view causes and tendencies associated with recognition of referendum results? Or, are independence referendums simply recognized when the rules are followed? Alternatively, do we now live in a democratic age in which the gold standard of legitimacy is popular support? And, if the answer is in the affirmative, do independence referendums tend to be recognized when secession is supported by a large majority of the new *demos* on a large turnout? Or is it all down to power politics?

Politicians who are sure of the backing of the people often point to the legitimizing effects of referendums. This, indeed, has been characteristic of independence referendums since the earliest days. In the nineteenth century, referendums began to be used by movements espousing independence or, in the case of Italy, the unification of the territory. As Tierney wrote in an authoritative account,

> Following the upheavals of 1848, as demand for increased participation in politics grew, the plebiscite became a tool in the independence and reunification struggles of the latter part of the century...By 1860 they were ...deployed more systematically in several Italian provinces on the question of unification, culminating with a vote in Rome following the fall of the city to the army of unification in 1870.
>
> (Tierney 2012: 62)

Camillo Benso di Cavour (1810–1861), the Italian statesman, who was responsible for this use of the referendum summed up the general view when he wrote,

> I await with anxiety the result of the count, which is taking place in Central Italy. If, as I hope, this last proof is decisive (*questa ultima prova)*, we have written a marvellous page in the history of Italy. Even should Prussia and Russia contest the legal value of universal suffrage, they cannot place in doubt (*non potranno mettere in dubbio*) the immense importance of the event today brought to pass. Dukes, archdukes and grand-dukes will be buried forever beneath the heap of votes deposited in urns of voting places of Tuscany and Emilia.
>
> (Cavour 1883: 211)

Back then, legal principle was of little importance. Rather, the will of the people trumped jurisprudence in the early 1870s. This perception was even stronger a couple of generations later when the American political scientist Sarah Wambaugh observed, "There was not one of the great powers, not even Austria or Russia, which did not participate in those years [1848–1870] in some form of appeal to national self-determination to settle Europe's numerous territorial questions" (Wambaugh 1933: xxxiii).

In the light of the latter, it would seem reasonable and plausible that outcomes of referendums on independence would have an even stronger legitimizing force in an age where "democracy" – to use a term from analytical philosophy – is an illocutionary speech-act, a term that demands unconditional observance.

Yet, based on recent referendums – such as the one in Kurdistan in 2017 – it seems that independence referendums, despite this near-universal acceptance of the rhetoric of democracy, only tend to lead to independence and recognition when this is in the national interest of major powers. Despite relying on support from Kurdish forces in Syria, neither Britain, America nor France, found it in their national interest to support the creation of a new state in the volatile region. But can this hunch be supported by empirical facts or even statistical data? While a quantitative analysis can never finally settle a matter, it can render a conclusion more plausible.

Since 1990, a total of 44 referendums on independence have yielded a "yes" outcome. The question is, what are the factors associated with the establishment of these new states? Causes associated with recognition include the legal ones, such as "the seceding entity was part of a non-democratic state." But there are also more political ones, for example a high turnout and a massive yes-vote. And then, there is the power politics factor, namely, whether the new state has the support of the international community – or, more specifically, the three "democratic" permanent members of the UN Security Council.

In the analysis below, we have measured some of the factors that statistically could be conducive for when states are recognized using what is known as a multiple logistic regression analysis. Without going into technical details, this analysis measures the strength of the different given factors behind a phenomenon. The dependent variable is whether the state was recognized and took up a seat in the UN.

The independent variables are the official yes vote, the turnout, the Freedom House Score of the country from which the entity sought to secede and lastly a dummy variable for whether there was support for secession among the five permanent members of the Security Council (in practice the USA, Britain and France).[5]

These countries seem important for several reasons. Britain and France have considerable "soft power" over former colonies and are often able to influence decisions in a way that is seemingly out of proportion with their relatively

5 We have used Freedom House Scores as all cases occurred after 1973.

limited economic and military power. Crucial to this is their role in, respectively, *The Commonwealth* and *La Francophonie* (*Organisation Internationale de la Francophonie*), organizations which newly established states often seek to join.

The USA, by contrast has both considerable "soft" and "hard" power. These factors seem to account for the three democratic powers' influence over a majority of the UN member states, which are either members of the Commonwealth or La Francophonie, or which all aspire to be on good terms with the USA.

As Table 8.2 shows Security Council Support from the three permanent Western powers is the key determining factor (statistically significant at $p<0.01$). All the other variables were not statistically significant.

Whether the country is part of a democracy or not (i.e. if the vote was held under the rules prescribed by the legal norms) statistically speaking is irrelevant. While the direction of the statistical correlation is negative as expected (a high Freedom House score indicated less democracy), the level of margin of error – is several times above the conventionally accepted levels.

Likewise, whether the turnout was high or low did not matter when it came to recognizing states. Some countries with low turnout became independent, e.g. Bosnia, others did not, e.g. Tartarstan. Whether the support (the yes-vote) was high or low was equally academic. Indeed, the yes-vote in Somaliland (1999) and Krajina (1992) both had very high yes-votes and both countries remain unrecognized. As another scholar has written, using a different methodology, "international politics ultimately determine which aspiring system members will succeed in becoming new states" (Coggins 2011: 433).

Table 8.2 Logistic regression: determinants of recognition of successful independence referendums

Variables	*Model 1*
Security Council Dummy	4.258***
	(1.778)
Freedom House Score	–0.298
	(0.742)
Turnout	0.100
	(0.90)
Yes-Vote	0.055
	(0.065)
Negotiation/Constitutional Provision	1.054
	(2.35)
Constant	–15.134
	(9.709)

R;Squared: .72 (Nagelkerte): .52 N: 38

*: p< 0.1, **: p< 0.05, *** p< 0.01

9. Conclusion

"As long as our world is made up of national groups which aspire to self-governance and to territorial sovereignty, ours will be a world of sovereign states and secessions from them" (Pavkovic and Radan 2007: 256). The question is when do groups have a legal right to do so? When do referendums yield a "yes-vote"? And when are the entities recognized by the international community?

Historically, referendums of independence first emerged in the 1860s, but they only became commonly used in from the mid-1960s and their use reached an all-time high in the 1990s.

This chapter has presented a *tour d'horizon* of the history, theory and practice of referendums on independence or secession. Having narrowed down the category of independence referendums (as distinct from other referendums), the history of their use was outlined. This was followed by a relatively detailed exposition of their legal status. This showed that the majority of referendums are unilateral. As a general rule, referendums on independence are, what lawyers call *ultra vires*, in plain English, illegal. However, there are – as is always the case in constitutional law – an exception to the rule. Hence, independence referendums are permissible *if* there is no democratic redress (if the entity is part of a non-democratic state, as in Estonia in 1991, for example).

Having established the legal position, the chapter went on to look at the factors conducive to winning an independence referendum. Using, statistical methods it was shown that it was easier to win support for independence if the government controlled the process. Thus, independence referendums are very often proof of Stalin's (perhaps apocryphal) adage, "it doesn't matter who votes. What matters is who counts the votes."

This might explain why the independence referendums in Quebec failed. Canada is a very democratic society – one with transparency and due process. Unlike in South Sudan, Somaliland and South Ossetia, where it is easy for the incumbent to rig the poll, the Quebecois nationalists had to play by the rules. And, much as nationalists liked to claim to speak for the "people," the brute fact – in Quebec and elsewhere – was that there was very little appetite for independence! As the subsequent cases of New Caledonia and Scotland showed, independence referendums in polyarchies are notoriously difficult to win. No fully developed democratic society has voted for independence for the past 50 years!

One factor above all is conducive for winning independence; an elite consensus. Referendums on independence tend to succeed – or yield a majority for secession – when there is an elite consensus. This is the common denominator for Norway in 1905, Iceland in 1944, Estonia in 1991 and Bougainville in 2019.

But winning the referendum is only part of winning independence. Indeed, less than half of the countries that vote for independence were recognized. So, what determines this low success rate? The answer is that the factors, which determine success – or otherwise – of an independence referendum are neither whether the entity is part of a non-democratic regime (as legal theory would have us believe) nor the turnout and the yes-vote (as democratic norms would suggest). The decisive factor is whether secession is supported by (and in the interest of) Britain, France or the USA.

To put it crudely, it was not in the interest of these democratic countries to recognize Kurdistan, Tartarstan, South Ossetia, or Catalonia. The great democratic powers' arguments for not doing so might be legalistic or even philosophical but the statistical evidence suggest that these factors rarely are adhered to in practice; ultimately, what matters is the elusive and yet very real "national interest." Recognizing new states and their "right" to hold referendums on independence is statistically and empirically unrelated to high theory and owes a lot to power politics and *Realpolitik.* This is neither a comfortable conclusion in an age of democracy, nor is it one that may appeal to those who espouse theories of natural rights in the sphere of democracy. But as political scientists we are bound to describe the world as it is not as we would like it to be. Only a "realistic" appreciation of the existing practices will enable us to challenge these – if we so wish. But overall it is imperative that we acknowledge how difficult it is not just to hold a referendum on independence but also to ensure that the result is implemented.

In 1995, a few months before the referendum on independence, the Quebecois premier Jacques Parizeau made a visit to Paris to convince Jacques Chirac, the Gaullist President, to recognize a future independent state of Quebec. He also reached out to US President Bill Clinton. Some criticized him for going abroad when there were battles to fight at home. With the benefit of hindsight, he probably made the right decision. Winning the support of the international community is key to achieving independence but it is not the only factor. First you need to win a referendum. And Parizeau, narrowly lost the vote, he didn't manage to convince enough of his compatriots of the merits of – what he would have called – a *Québec libre.*

And, perhaps, this is the major lesson for those aspiring statehood; voters in democracies very rarely vote for secession or independence. In the words of Neil Sedaka, "Breaking up *is* hard to do!"

References

Altman, D. (2010). *Direct Democracy Worldwide.* New York: Cambridge University Press.

Cassese, Antonio (1995). *Self-Determination of the Peoples: A Legal Reappraisal.* Cambridge, MA: Cambridge University Press.

Cavour, Camillo (1883). *Lettere edite ed inedite di Camillo Cavour.* Rome: Roux.

Clarke, H. D., & Kornberg, A. (1996). Choosing Canada? The 1995 Quebec sovereignty referendum. *PS: Political Science & Politics, 29,* 676–682.

Crawford, James (2006). *The Creation of States in International Law,* 2nd edition. Cambridge, MA: Cambridge University Press.

Coggins, B. (2011). Friends in high places: International politics and the emergence of states from secessionism. *International Organization, 65*(3), 433–467.

Conley, R. S. (1997). Sovereignty or the status quo? The 1995 pre-referendum debate in Quebec. *Journal of Commonwealth & Comparative Politics, 35*(1), 67–92.

Dion, S. (1996). Why is secession difficult in well-established democracies? Lessons from Quebec. *British Journal of Political Science, 26,* 269–283.

Dobelle, J.-F. (1996). Référendum et droit à l'autodétermination. *Pouvoirs*, *77*(1), 41–60.

Elgie, Robert, & Zielonka, Jan (2001). Constitutions and constitution building: A comparative perspective, in Jan Zielonka (Editor), *Democratic Consolidation in Easter Europe*. Oxford, UK: Oxford University Press, pp. 25–47.

Hollander, Saskia (2019). *The Politics of Referendum Use in European Democracies*. London, UK: Palgrave Macmillan.

Krasner, Stephen D. (1999). *Sovereignty: Organised Hypocrisy*. Princeton, NJ: Princeton University Press.

Laponce, J. (2010). *Le référendum de souveraineté: comparaisons, critiques et commentaires*. Quebec City: Les Presses de l'Université Laval.

Leduc, L. (2002). *The Politics of Direct Democracy: Referendums in Global Perspective*. Toronto, ON: Broadview Press.

Leduc, L. (2003). *The Politics of Direct Democracy: Referendums in Global Perspective*. Toronto, ON: Toronto Broadview Press.

MacCormick, N. (2000). Is there a constitutional path to Scottish independence? *Parliamentary Affairs*, *53*, 725–726.

Maine, Henry Sumner (1897). *Popular Government*. Indianapolis, IN: Liberty Fund.

Mattern, J. (1921). *The Employment of the Plebiscite in the Determination of Sovereignty*. Baltimore, MD: Johns Hopkins University Press.

Mendez, Fernando, & Germann, Micha (2018). Contested sovereignty: Mapping referendums on sovereignty over time and space. *British Journal of Political Science*, *48*(1), 141–165.

Morel, Laurence (2012). Referendum, in M. Rosenfeld and A. Sajo (Editors), *The Oxford Handbook of Comparative Constitutional Law*. Oxford, UK: Oxford University Press, pp. 501–528.

Oklopcic, Z. (2012). Independence referendums and democratic theory in Quebec and Montenegro. *Nationalism and Ethnic Politics*, *18*(1), 22–42.

Pavkovic, Aleksander, & Radan, Peter (2007). *Creating New States: Theory and Practice of Secession*. Aldershot, UK: Ashgate.

Qvortrup, M. (2000). Research note: Are referendums controlled and pro-hegemonic? *Political Studies*, *48*(4), 821–826.

Qvortrup, M. (2014). *M. Referendums and Ethnic Conflict*. Philadelphia, PA: University of Pennsylvania Press.

Qvortrup, M. (2017). Demystifying direct democracy. *Journal of Democracy*, *28*(3), 141–152.

Radan, P. (2012). Secessionist referenda in international and domestic law. *Nationalism and Ethnic Politics*, *18*(1), 8–21.

Scheindlin, Dahlia (2012). Phantom referendums in phantom states: Meaningless farce or a bridge to reality? *Nationalism and Ethnic Politics*, *18*(1), 65–87.

Sen, Ilker Gökhan (2015). *Sovereignty Referendums in International and Constitutional Law*. Heidelberg, Germany: Springer.

Sen, Ilker Gökhan (2018). Sovereignty referendums: People concerned and people entitled to vote, in Laurence Morel and M. Qvortrup (Editors), *The Routledge Handbook of Referendums and Direct Democracy*. Abingdon, UK: Routledge, pp. 210–226.

Smith, G. (1976). The functional properties of the referendum. *European Journal of Political Research*, *4*(1), 1–23.

Tierney, Stephen (2012). *Constitutional Referendums: The Theory and Practice of Republican Deliberation*. Oxford, UK: Oxford University Press.
Wambaugh, Sarah (1933). *Plebiscites Since the World War*. New York: Carnegie.

Cases cited

Bertrand v. Québec (Procureur général); 1995 Carswell Que 131, 127 D.L.R. (4th) 408.
Kohlhaas v Alaska 147 P 3d 714 (2006).
Re Kosovo (2010), ICJ Advisory Opinion, International Law Materials, 1410.
Re Secession of Quebec (1998) 161 DLR (4th) 385.
Texas v White 74 US 700 (1868).

Part III

Non-institutional actors

9 The framing of secessionism in the neo-liberal crisis

The Scottish and Catalan cases

Donatella della Porta, Francis O'Connor and Martín Portos

Introduction

The topics of secessionism and "right to choose" are particularly relevant in times of economic and political crisis. The *Great Recession* that hit the world in 2008 functioned as a critical juncture, generating socioeconomic but also political transformations. Some of the political developments during the crisis have challenged civil, political and social rights, triggering a *Great Regression* in terms of democratic rights and both individual and collective liberties. In the geographical areas that have been hit the hardest by the financial crisis, particularly in the European periphery, waves of protest have challenged the austerity policies adopted by national governments under heavy pressure from international institutions including the European Central Bank, the European Union and the International Monetary Fund. As the financial crisis degenerated into a crisis of political legitimacy, with declining trust in representative institutions, old political cleavages re-emerged. This was visible, first and foremost in a revived attention to social justice within a class cleavage, but was also visible in a reactivation, in various forms, of a centre–periphery cleavage. This has in particular regained momentum as sub-state entities have been pushing for their secession within the European Union. On the one hand, the Scottish National Party (SNP) in government in the Scottish parliament in Edinburgh called for a referendum on independence from the United Kingdom, which took place in September 2014. The unionist side ultimately prevailed, nevertheless, a sizable proportion of voters (44.7%) supported Scottish secession in a huge turnout of 84.59% (Álvarez Pereira, Portos and Vourdas 2018). In order to achieve such a level of mobilization, the grassroots and canvassing efforts of social movement organizations that tried to promote their vision of a more socially just and democratic society was critical. In Catalonia, preceded by more than 500 municipal-level non-binding consultations on independence in 2009–2011 (Muñoz and Guinjoan 2013), about 2.3 million people symbolically cast their votes in a massive unofficial voting performance led by extra-institutional actors – with the collaboration of the Catalan Government – on 9 November 2014. Notwithstanding strong opposition from the Spanish government and courts, on 1 October 2017, 2.2 million Catalans turned out to vote (della Porta, O'Connor and Portos 2019).

The level of Catalan popular unrest and Scottish mobilization largely has resulted from a combination of three root contextual causes, as three intertwined socioeconomic, political, and territorial crises spiralled. The key argument we develop throughout this chapter is that the implementation of austerity policies along with a crisis of political legitimacy (and self-government) have facilitated the emergence of democratic-emancipatory and social justice frames for mobilization. These frames have a high potential for resonance across audiences and therefore, for mobilization. As a matter of strategic and deliberate choice, Catalan and Scottish movements have tried to broaden their constituencies by emphasizing democratic and redistributive axes over traditional nationalist and identity components.

This chapter builds on empirical materials collected for our book "Social Movements and Referendums from Below: Direct Democracy in the Neoliberal Crisis," which combined fieldwork as well as desktop research on the Scottish and Catalan secessionist movements (della Porta, O'Connor, Portos and Subirats Ribas 2017a). Specifically, research for the book included secondary analysis of the existing literature, analysis of relevant primary source documents related to the referendum campaigns (e.g. movement declarations and writings, regional government documents and party manifestoes), as well as in-depth interviews with key informants, politicians and activists. In the next section, we introduce concepts and literature relevant to the concept of referendums from below and framing theories in social movement studies. We interpret this chapter's contribution as a chance to have a further look at frames for mobilization in light of more recent developments in both cases, which occurred after the period covered in the book (up to the referendums in 2014). We conclude by summarizing some key findings and implications on the role of framing theories for nationalist movements and the re-intensification of the territorial cleavage amidst the neoliberal crisis.

Referendums from below and framing in social movements

New states proliferated following historical landmarks such as the aftermath of the First World War, the de-colonization period and the breakdown of the Soviet Union, before declining in intensity in recent times (Haklai 2015: 462). However, a steady trickle of non-state nations or ethnic groups continues to assert demands for collective self-determination in vastly differing political contexts, from Scotland and Catalonia to New Caledonia, Kurdistan and Bougainville. Within this trend, referendums have been increasingly used to put forward and validate claims to self-determination. This specific utilization of referendums accompanies a more general increment in the adaptation of direct democratic forms, once considered as a residual vestige of older conceptions of democracy. Social science literature on referendums and other mechanisms of direct democracy has identified their increasing use as a way to address the malfunctioning of representative democracy (Qvortrup 2014a, b). Referendums can serve as laboratories for democracy, as

> Endowed with the possibility and responsibility of direct law-making, citizens internalize the civic duty to participate in politics. In that process,

> they experience their efficacy and become active citizens. Besides, citizens in direct democracies are frequently and immediately exposed to political information since politics is constantly (and not only during election season) on the agenda.
>
> (Fatke 2015: 103)

Under some conditions – importantly not all, as the fallout from the Brexit vote demonstrates – referendums can be considered as instruments for a more participatory and, even deliberative form of mass political engagement resonate with the modus operandi of a range of progressive movements (della Porta et al. 2017a). Both popular initiatives, oriented to promote new policies, and abrogative referendums give citizens some policy-controlling capacity. They can contribute to a transparent and deliberative political process (Schiller 2009). In light of the challenge of declining trust in the political system, referendums have been considered as a "synchronization mechanism between politicians and citizens" (Altman 2011: 197), thus helping to fill the gap between the increasing interest in politics and the decline of conventional forms of participation (Tierney 2012: 302) and putting pressure on decision-makers (Fatke 2015). There is indeed a "tendency of intense campaigns to draw attention to the arguments of the oppositional minority" (Kriesi 2005: 177), which are traditionally marginalized in the public sphere.

Referendums are of course still used as a tool by institutional political actors, especially in constitutional and facultative referendums or in cases of political gridlock (Closa 2007; della Porta et al. 2017a: 3–4), However, recent research has demonstrated that referendums are not simply an elite designed, technical procedure but increasingly involve mass engagement and mobilization beyond the vote itself (della Porta et al. 2017a). Referendums have been induced and/ or appropriated by social movements in many contexts, well beyond the states with constitutionally enshrined rights for citizen-initiated referendums like Italy or states with deep-rooted traditions of direct democracy such as Switzerland. Irrespective of their legal status (institutionally endorsed, legally binding or symbolic) referendums have become epicentres of contestation in broader cycles of contention. Instead of mere devices that institutional actors use to retrospectively legitimize technocratic decisions, the term "referendums from below" has been coined to emphasize the participatory and grassroots processes that foster – and conversely, are fostered by – years of civil society agitation that pre-date the actual vote (della Porta et al. 2017a, 2017b).

Notwithstanding some risks of direct democracy conflicting with deliberative conceptions defended by progressive social movements, referendums "from below" are particularly conducive to broadening participation and enhancing political engagement. In particular, citizen-initiated referendums or those with wide-scale appropriation of institutionally promoted referendums might in fact improve the quality of direct democracy (della Porta et al. 2017). Referendums from below are characterized by number of normative commitments, including encouraging mass participation and an emphasis on prefigurative practices and deliberation. The involvement of social movements increases participation, as movements create new public arenas and utilize subaltern public spheres. They increase the discursive quality of referendum campaigns by introducing new arguments and multiplying the points of view which are expressed. Valuing horizontal communication, social movements can therefore counterbalance the potential domination of referendum campaigns by political elites, and by bringing specific knowledge and viewpoints absent in macro-level institutional politics. The campaigns for independence referendums in Scotland and Catalonia confirm that referendums do offer social movements the chance to make a decisive contribution to issues of substantial political importance. Through resource mobilization, appropriation and forging of opportunities, and capacity to develop resonant frames, movements have successfully changed political debates.

Even when (as it is often the case) referendums do not succeed in obtaining a majority for secession, the promoters of referendums on issues of independence often achieve public attention, opening arenas of debate, increasing the salience of, and knowledge about, their claims. This seems to be in particular the case with nationalist frames, as nationalist identities are shaped during intense moments, before then becoming more enduring and broadly accepted. As Mark Beissinger noted,

> Not all historical eras are alike. There are times when change occurs so slowly that time seems almost frozen, though beneath the surface considerable turbulence and evolution may be silently at work. There are other times when change is so compressed, blaring, and fundamental that it is almost impossible to take its measure.
>
> (2002: 47)

Collective identities sometimes crystallize suddenly rather than developing gradually (Brubaker 1996), and are to be seen not only as "a cause of action, but also as the product of action" (Beissinger 2002: 11). Interactions during mobilization influence frames that emerge from the protest events as, "Thickened history had provided the context for a fundamental transformation of identities which, in "quieter' times, were once believed to be fixed and immutable" (Beissinger 2002: 148). While in quiet times political entrepreneurs indeed aim at building some structural advantages, these advantages are then put to work in noisy times, when "the constraining parameters of politics undergo fundamental challenges, leading to rapidly shifting assumptions about the limits of the possible" (Beissinger 2002: 151). Referendums on independence can trigger this thickened moment, producing an acceleration of time (della Porta 2018).

Social movement studies have emphasized the relevance of framing processes for understanding mobilization dynamics (see Lindekilde 2014). In order to recruit new members and keep on motivating individuals who are already mobilized, social movement organizations build rationales for action and engagement. In social movement research, framing efforts refer to

> the signifying work or meaning construction engaged in by movement adherents (e.g., leaders, activists, and rank-and-file participants) and other actors

> (e.g., adversaries, institutional elites, media, social control agents, countermovements) relevant to the interests of movements and the challenges they mount in pursuit of those interests.
>
> (Snow 2013)

In other words, frames are the dominant worldviews that guide and coordinate the behaviour of social movement organizations.

The concept of frame was coined by Erving Goffman in his seminal work *Frame Analysis* (1974). Framing theories are rooted in the symbolic interactionist and constructionist principle that meanings are not naturally attached to the objects, events or experiences. Instead, cultural interpretive processes mediate the attribution of meanings. Frames thus refer to the symbolic construction of external reality by performing three main functions (Snow and Benford 1988a; Snow 2013). First, frames focus attention by determining what, in relation to the object of orientation, is relevant (i.e. what is "in-frame") and what is irrelevant (i.e. what is "out-of-frame") in our sensorial field. Second, they help to articulate narratives by tying together different aspects so that one set of meanings is conveyed to the detriment of others. Third, frames transform how objects of attention are seen or conceived and their relationships between one another or to the actors. There are two different approaches to framing within social movement scholarship (Johnston and Noakes 2005). On the one hand, a body of literature emphasizing cognitive processes looks at the ways in which individuals frame events into familiar categories in order to make sense of social dynamics (Gamson 1988). Looking instead at the meso level, some contributions have shed light on the symbolic construction of reality by collective entrepreneurs and organizations (Snow and Benford 1988a). Normally, these processes of meaning attribution consist of three different stages. First, certain occurrences, which might previously have been attributed to individual responsibility or to natural factors and phenomena, are recognized as and converted into problems; second, potential strategies to address them are identified and developed; and third, motivations to act upon this knowledge are put forward. In the words of Snow and Benford (1988b), these three steps correspond to the diagnostic, prognostic and motivational dimensions of framing.

In what follows, focusing on the Catalan and Scottish cases, we will show how similar framing mechanisms operated. In particular, in a situation of dramatic socioeconomic crisis, the issue of social justice come to the fore. Even in cases of relatively rich regions (such as Catalonia), the call for independence is for a large part, justified as a way to ensure social protection within inclusively defined national communities. Especially, as the constituency of secessionist campaigns reaches beyond the traditional supporters, with the spread of left-wing narratives resonant with progressive and leftist movements' frames. Social movement organizations act as promoters of these frames, becoming brokers between independentism and other social movements on the Left. Through the participation of social movements, a participatory democratic frame is consolidated. The right to decide is advocated for, in the name of the people living in these would-be states: Central state elites are accused of depriving these composite nations of their democratic rights, relying on prevailing institutional power rather than any form of ongoing democratic legitimacy. Resonant with these visions, horizontal organizational forms and the opening of inclusive public spheres are developed. In sum, the collective identities that emerge in this process tend to be inclusive and horizontal, as movements act as constituent powers.

Beyond these relevant similarities, the following analysis also points at the different historical experience in the relationship between the centre and the periphery as well as in the more contingent context in which struggles for independence have been embedded. In particular, the disruptive effects of the economic crisis have been more visible in Catalonia, making the issue of economic justice more central, especially as independentism frames spread within existing social movements that had mobilized against austerity measures. However, this might be in part, balanced by the historical leaning of Scottish nationalism, more rooted in the prefiguration and fulfilment of social justice in an independent Scotland. An additional difference lies in the degree and forms of policing of national minorities (della Porta, O'Connor and Portos 2019). In this sense, strong repression in Catalonia of an unrecognized referendum can be expected to bring about more radical claims for democracy, resonant also with the normative concerns of a massive campaign of anti-austerity protests mobilized in the streets. The United Kingdom's institutionalist framework which, recognizes Scotland as a nation with a right to decide its ongoing relationship with the rest of the United Kingdom, would be expected instead to have channelled a strong ethnonationalist identity in a more institutionalized narrative. In Catalonia, given the institutional closure on the side of state authorities, frames around democratic emancipation facilitated – and in turn were facilitated by – the evolution of the initial "right to decide" master frame into outright independence. By contrast, in line with traditional Scottish nationalist rhetoric, socioeconomic issues prevailed over identity aspects in the debates around the referendum.

Framing the Catalan *procés*

With the social-democratic PSOE in power at the national level since 2004 (although it had rejected a Basque proposal for greater autonomy), the Catalan government exploited a window of opportunity to enhance the region's autonomy, launching a public debate on institutional reforms. Approved by the Catalan Parliament in 2005, the proposed statute (which defined Catalonia as a "nation") was however rejected by the conservative Partido Popular and also triggered internal tensions within the PSOE. New negotiations brought about a revamped agreement between the PSOE and the centre-liberal nationalist Covergència i Uniò coalition. Adopted by the Catalan Parliament (with the opposition of the pro-independence Esquerra Republicana de Catalunya that viewed it as insufficient in scope) and ratified by referendum in June 2006 (73% voted "yes," with less than 50% participation), the new statute was not enacted, due to appeals on the grounds of unconstitutionality by the PP and several autonomous communities.

Between 2006 and 2010, the pending decision of the Constitutional Court on the new statute of autonomy was constructed "from below" as a prospectively framed event that shows the impossibility of a negotiated solution, thus demanding an urgent reaction (Basta 2017). The Constitutional Court's decision of 28 June 2010 (STC 31/2010) invalidated several provisions with reference to the Catalonia's status and language as well as the devolution of some economic and political competencies (see Ferreres Comella 2014; Burg 2015). Popular outrage at this decision led to massive street demonstrations calling for the recognition of the Catalan nation and triggered a major boost in support for independence, which theretofore had been rather marginal and marginalized in Catalonia (Dowling 2014), as were the openly secessionist parties before 2010–2012 (Basta 2017).

Besides the 2010 march, there was a wave of pro-independence mobilization in Catalonia throughout the 2009–2015 period. Importantly, pressure from the streets through mass mobilizations was present— especially in the form of street protests during the 2012–2015 *diadas* (National Day of Catalonia) launched by civil society organizations such as Òmnium Cultural and Assemblea Nacional Catalana (della Porta et al. 2017a). Apart from these grand-scale events, the collective performances of pro-independence activism have also included international publicity campaigns, performances and local grassroots and dissemination activities (Crameri 2015: 104–105). Importantly, consultations over independence were held in 552 municipalities across Catalonia between 2009 and 2011 (Muñoz and Guinjoan 2013). Thus, 58% of the Catalan municipalities organized a referendum, potentially encompassing 77.5% of the total population (Muñoz and Guinjoan 2013). Pressure mounted on the Catalan authorities to hold a binding referendum, as exemplified by civil society organizations organizing a mass unofficial and non-binding voting performance in November 2014, with over 2.3 million votes cast. A total of 80.8% of participants ticked the "yes–yes" option – "yes" for a state for Catalonia; "yes" for an independent state (Álvarez Pereira, Portos and Vourdas 2018).

The increase in support for and mobilization around independence goes together with the repositioning of the moderate nationalist forces (Rico and Liñeira 2014: 258). The shift between accommodation and contestation is related to electoral competition and parties' outbidding on the independentist positions (Barrio and Rodríguez-Teruel 2016), as well as the opportunities and incentives offered by a loose institutional framework (Colomer 2017). Yet, the social mobilization contributed to triggering "a process of polarisation that pushed the traditionally moderate Catalan nationalist parties to an increasingly radical stance, as claims moved from autonomy to independence" (della Porta et al. 2017a: 160). Specifically, CiU abandoned its once nationalist pragmatic positions (note it supported the PP government in power 2000–2004) and embraced more openly pro-independence stances. Unlike the Scottish movement, Catalan actors did not merely mobilize for a specific positioning in a referendum campaign but actually to hold a referendum in the first place. Moreover, while the Catalan procés gathered a large consensus around the idea of "the right to decide," nationalist milieus increasingly embraced secessionist stances.

In line with Montserrat Guibernau (2004: 10), we argue that relevant actors of minority nationalist movements tend to put forward two main arguments in order to legitimize their discourse: a political argument prioritizing popular sovereignty and democracy, and cultural argument that stressed differential identities, language, traditions and traits. Catalan nationalists have historically been no exception to this trend. Yet, Catalonian nationalism has traditionally asserted itself as a form of "civic nationalism," where common and inclusive values and culture are emphasized to the detriment of ethnic features (Balcells 1996; Conversi 1997). For instance, Jordi Pujol, President of Catalonia between 1980 and 2003 and historic leader of CiU, famously defined a Catalan as "anyone who lives and works in Catalonia and who wants to be Catalan" (Pujol 1976). Similarly, Carod Rovira, leader of the pro-independence ERC from 1996 until 2008 declared that

> We [the Catalans] are not a race, we are a culture with values, referents, shared emotions, and a language. The good thing about the language is that you can learn it! Our project [independence of Catalonia], in contrast to the Spanish state's enterprise, is not ethnic-essentialist but inclusive and democratic. An identity cannot be inherited; an identity cannot be imposed; you choose your identity.
>
> (in Crític 2015)

Consistent with these inclusive views put forward by the historical nationalist vanguard, there was a deliberate attempt to downplay national-identity narratives and appeals to differential cultural aspects. This was mostly due to strategic reasons, as it allowed the expansion of the movement's constituency beyond its traditional core, and incorporating second-generation immigrants coming from other regions of Spain. Also, amidst a changing global context, this move distanced the Catalan procés away from ethno-nationalist discourses put forward by other secessionist forces such as the New Flemish Alliance (see dalle Mulle 2016).

Nevertheless, not only are people socialized in a Catalan-centric cultural frame of reference more permeable to nationalist claims (Fernández-i-Marín and López 2010): they are also keener to support and mobilize for independence (Serrano 2013). This is consistent with findings for other cases: while identity factors are key to the understanding of the pro-independence movement in the Basque Country, both political and economic conjunctural factors are likewise important (Alkorta and Leonisio 2019). In fact, Catalan nationalists have traditionally embraced claims that stressed a common heritage, in which the promotion of the vernacular language is fundamental (Balcells 2013). Additionally, during the recent independentist upsurge, cultural aspects have been emphasized. For instance, the campaign for the 2014 referendum made often symbolic reference to the 1714 Siege of Barcelona. Furthermore,

> one of the ideas drawn from traditional nationalism frame was the narrative of a nation dominated by Spain, which worked as a motivational frame and led to emotional claims and statements associated with a self-understanding

> of accomplishing a historical mission. Claims such as "we need to recover the right course of history", and demands for "acting responsibly" with regard to "our legacy and ancestors' struggle."
>
> (della Porta et al. 2017a: 117)

Having said that, national identity and culture-related discourses were actively downplayed in favour of socioeconomic narratives and frames around democracy, political regeneration and collective dignity. On the one hand, socioeconomic frames relate to material conditions, social justice and redistribution. The socio-economic frame in Catalonia has often been articulated in terms of institutional unfairness caused by the redistributive policies of the Spanish government (resonant slogans included e.g. "Spain is stealing from us, the Catalans"). Exacerbated by a context of recession, some narratives stress that Catalonia has disproportionally contributed to central state budgets, and received low public investment in return, which adds to long-term feelings of economic mistreatment, and under-funding for autonomy (Guibernau 2004: 92). However, the left-wing milieus in particular, have put forward the image of an alternative, socially just independent Catalonia. In fact, many saw in an eventually independent Catalonia the possibility to build a progressive polity more egalitarian, dignified, just and inclusive, taking advantage of the frames of reference built during the broader wave of mobilization against austerity in the whole of Spain. For instance, since 2012, the civil society organization Assemblea Nacional Catalana participated in the 1st May demonstrations under the slogan "Catalonia New European State, more just, prosperous and solidary" (della Porta et al. 2017a: 120).

On the other hand, political frames focused on popular sovereignty and citizen involvement developed during the procés. Not in vain, "terms such as 'deliberative democracy', 'inclusiveness', 'civil society', 'progress', 'empowerment', 'social state' and 'redistribution' played a central role in the Catalan campaign" (della Porta et al. 2017a: 121). This frame tries to bridge nationalism and democratic-emancipatory discourses, representing an emergent pro-secessionist approach based on democratic rights and renewal that seeks to link state independence and democratic enhancement. As della Porta et al. conclude, the Catalan movement

> deliberately avoided the historical national-identity frame and instead addressed the socioeconomic frame, presenting the general idea that... Catalonia would be wealthier, more egalitarian, less corrupt and, generally speaking, better places to live once they had achieved independence. For many actors in both places, independence was not seen as an end in itself, but a democratic means to the realisation of greater social equality, which was claimed to be unobtainable within existing institutional structures.
>
> (2017a: 127)

The cycle brought about a considerable degree of radicalization and polarization of claims, frames and justifications for independence (and anti-secessionism) but a relatively limited amount of actual violence, which mainly came in the form of some clashes with police. Although there has not been much change in the political balance of support between the pro- and anti-independence sides, there has been a hardening of frames: positions polarized (among both civil society and elites) and conflict escalated as disruptive tactics on the side of challengers interacted with growing repression by the authorities. As the policing strategies toughened, the organizers of 2017 referendum were targeted by harsh policing of the various protest events and juridical action that led to the arrest of various Catalan pro-independence politicians and prominent figures (della Porta, O'Connor and Portos 2019; della Porta et al. 2017b). This repressive turn reinforces the democratic-emancipatory frames the *procés* actors had been developing in the preceding years. For instance, the president of the civil society organization Òmnium Cultural, Jordi Cuixart, is held in preventive detention since 16 October 2017, without bail, on charges of sedition against the state, carrying a maximum sentence of 15 years. He frames his imprisonment as a way to circumvent democratic rights of the Catalan peoples:

> We are deprived of our freedom for having made use of our right to free expression and demonstration, for the simple act of publicly and democratically defending the right of Catalonia to decide its future as a people at the poll.
>
> (Cuixart 2017)

Framing the Scottish campaign for independence

The principle pro-independence frames in Scotland were democratic and instrumental (dalle Mulle and Serrano 2019: 637): democratic in the sense that in an independent Scotland "the most important decisions about our economy and society will be taken by the people who care most about Scotland, that is by the people of Scotland" (Scottish Government 2013: i). The instrumental aspect being that the current institutional status quo, guarantees permanent Scottish minitorization leaving it at the whims of a Tory government imposing economic policies inimical to the reputed progressive political orientation of Scotland (dalle Mulle and Serrano 2019: 638). However, Scottish independence did in the past rely on more conventional national-identity frames. Although the SNP resolutely advances an inclusive form of nationalism today, historically elements of the party were hostile towards the country's mostly ethnically Irish, Catholic community and many Catholics viewed independence as a Protestant project (Clayton 2005, 111). Catholic wariness and distance towards the SNP were also shaped by the Labour party's strong embedding in the community (Dodd's and Seawright 2014: 112). The SNP has worked assiduously on the lingering memory of its sectarianism and has successfully won over Catholics both as voters (Clements 2017) and as members (Mitchell et al. 1998). Beyond the Catholic-Protestant cleavage, there have been some accusations of anti-English prejudice in actions in 2013 and 2014, but these protests were directed against the UKIP party and its immigration policies and can certainly not be conflated with a broader hostility to

English society in general (Mason 2013; RIC 2014). Although some pro-independence activists have attempted to draw on more traditional nationalist frames, these "identitarian flag-waving" factions were rigorously marginalized and dismissed by the broader movement (Della Porta et al. 2017a, 79). Accordingly, the SNP and broader pro-independence actors have actively policed and excluded identitarian elements, prioritizing the socioeconomic and democratic frames. Indeed, since the 1970s, the SNP has drawn exclusively on these frames (Dalle Mulle 2016: 4, 6).

The campaign was framed entirely on socioeconomic arguments reiterating that an independent Scotland would be a fairer and more prosperous society. In 2012, the SNP government released a document which stated: "Scotland is not oppressed and we have no need to be liberated. Independence matters because we do not have the powers to reach our potential. We are limited in what we can do to create jobs, grow the economy and help the vulnerable. We shouldn't have a constitution which constrains us, but one which frees us to build a better society" (Scottish Government 2012: 2). The inclusivity of the narrative was evidenced in its extension of the franchise to all UK and EU residents over 16 years of age in Scotland and the exclusion of Scots resident elsewhere in the UK or further afield (Electoral Commission 2014). Accordingly, there were no ethnic essentialist connotations to Scottishness; rather that Scotland comprised its residents instead of any cultural or genetic criteria. As Mooney and Scott explained, "in the language deployed by SNP politicians, Scotland is open to all and each and every person migrating to Scotland can be a fully Scottish citizen" (2016: 249). The SNP has also strongly strived for the inclusion of its more recent immigrant communities: former SNP leader Alex Salmond declared that "our Asian community are amongst the most patriotic Scots in the country", alleging that a "clear majority" of them support independence (in Mycock 2012: 57). Indeed, the SNP has been so committed to the territorialized non-essentialist vision of Scottishness that it comprehensively distanced itself from any other nationalist movements which had culturally defined elements in their identity, including, controversially, the movement in Catalonia (Della Porta et al. 2017a: 116).

The SNP's projected vision of a more democratic and socially just, independent Scotland, resonated with the masses struggling under the austerity policies of the UK's Tory governments since 2010, as well as the lingering effects of the structural vandalism committed by Thatcher and successive Tory governments in the 1980s. Scotland is neither a particularly under- or over-privileged country, in fact its "GDP per capita [is] nearer to the mean than any other nation or region of the UK (96 per cent)" (Keating 2010: 371). Nevertheless, it has concentrations of inter-generational poverty and disadvantage, the country boasts western Europe's lowest life expectancy for males (Hassan and Ilett 2011: 18–19). In certain Glasgow neighbourhoods such as Shettleston and Calton, males can expect to live 14 and 24 years less than the UK national average, respectively (Gillan 2006; Davidson 2014a, 24). By framing independence as a means to resolve enduring socioeconomic ailments it tapped into popular frustration as well as firmly aligning independence with a diffuse Scottish self-perception as being more left-wing than its neighbours south of the border (Dalle Mulle 2016: 5; Salmond 2013). The truth of Scotland's left-wing credentials is a bit more ambiguous. YouGov surveys show that Scots are more left-oriented on a range of social issues than the rest of Britain (Jordan 2015), while others have argued that ideological differences "are modest at best" (Curtice and Ormston 2011). The Tory resurgence in Scotland in the 2017 general election, also suggests that the country might not be as left-wing as believed (Curtice 2018). Nevertheless, this sense of a distinct political identity and the perceived impossibility of realizing politics coherent with it due to Scotland's marginal leverage vis-à-vis Westminster rendered the SNP's campaign on independence vision an alluring prospect. As Keating has remarked, "the entrenchment of neo-liberal economic policies and the Thatcherite doctrine of the small state at UK government level has undermined the functional basis of the union" (Keating 2009: 103).

The official SNP dominated Yes Scotland campaign outlined the rationale of independence as such:

> ... to put Scotland's future in Scotland's hands [...] to gain the ability to make our own decisions [...] to have the opportunity to make our nation a better place to live, [and] to build a greener, fairer and more prosperous society that is stronger and more successful that it is today.
>
> (Yes Declaration 2014)[1]

Such an inclusive and hopeful vision was sufficiently vague to incorporate support from across the political spectrum, from disgruntled ex-Labour voters to the far-left and beyond. However, it concealed as much as it displayed about the practical understandings of how an independent Scotland would actually function. There was a clear division between those who viewed independence as clean slate upon which to start anew and others which viewed independence as a chance to slightly tweak and improve the existing status quo: in short, radical change or slight improved continuity. The SNP viewed "independence as an evolution of devolution" (Foley and Ramand 2014: 80). A pro-independence activist and well-regarded folk singer Kate Polwart pithily summed up the SNP's vision, "Scotland won't be that different post-independence, just a mite more prosperous, and self-determinedly. 'Scottish" (Polwart 2013: 118). Arguably the most substantial points of divergence were the strong neo-liberal wing within the SNP which envisioned itself governing an open economy with low tax rates similar to the Irish economic model, albeit with an additional layer of ameliorative re-distribution (Cuthbert and Cuthbert 2009: 107; Keating 2009: 103). Other points were Scotland's membership in NATO, the role of the monarchy and potential membership of a currency union with the rest of the UK.

In an interview, a key figure in the Scottish Socialist party (SSP) remarked that "the SNP does not favour mass mobilisations on the street. The SNP is

1 http: //www.yesscotland.net/join-in/sign-the-declaration

a bourgeois neoliberal party" (in della Porta et al. 2017a: 94). This is perhaps a very blunt assessment, but it encapsulates two aspects relevant to the framing of the independence campaign. First, it exemplifies the different visions of a future Scotland but second, it also addresses the means of communicating these frames. The official Yes Scotland campaign was heavily dominated by the SNP and made use of a conventional repertoire, running the campaign almost as if it were an election, which failed to capture the attention of the masses of voters. As a prominent activist explained "They [SNP/Yes Scotland] didn't want a movement and when a movement emerged that they didn't really want, quite quickly, they tried to pretend that they were the movement, that this was all a subset of them" (in della Porta et al. 2017a: 94). Accordingly, pro-independence frames were consistent with the existing electoral habitus which had in the preceding decades done little more than reduce the Scottish electorate to a de-politicized slumber. Yet, when the same frames were embraced by movements and grassroots initiatives it captured the attention of the masses and was certainly crucial in increasing participation. Indeed, remarkably 97% of the Scottish electorate was registered to vote. The intensity of this process was such that in the month of August immediately preceding the vote, 119,000 voters were registered (Brooks 2014). The grassroots initiatives bridged the national and the local and were key to thickening the mobilization. And as we argued in our book, along with our colleague Anna Subirats, although the

> social movements were not initiators of the campaign, but they have masterfully seized on the institutional opening forged by the SNP. Scottish movements diffused the campaign into what had been hitherto political wastelands, characterised by local apathy and institutional neglect.
>
> (della Porta et al. 2017a, 98)

And a key aspect of this strengthening of the campaign was the role movements played in frame-diffusion, by bringing the hopeful template of independence to the local level and facilitate voters in projecting their visions of a more equitable Scotland into it. Although it was still insufficient to bring about independence it certainly ensured the concept of an independent Scotland became embedded into the popular imagination, potentially a key victory in the "war of position" in the long campaign which remains far from over.

Conclusion

In *Nations and Nationalism*, paraphrasing a 1940s film, Ernest Gellner remarked that "every girl ought to have a husband, preferably her own; and every high culture now wants a state, and preferably its own" (2008: 49).[2] However, the two cases addressed here show that this telos of a state for every nation is not

2 See dalle Mulle's (2016) for the original use of the same metaphor.

necessarily a sufficiently convincing frame for more inclusive forms of nationalism. Independence is framed as a practical solution to specific problems with the added benefit of enhancing democratic participation and fairness for the people within the boundaries of Scotland and Catalonia rather than being reserved from some *jus sanguinis* defined visions of Scots and Catalans. Notwithstanding, such laudable aspirations, all nationalism by definition has to draw a difference between and an “us” and a “them,” albeit here the cleavage is between those who live in Scotland and Catalonia and those who live beyond the territorial confines of their would-be states. Understandably, the us/them division is less salient in the Scottish case as the English–Scottish divide is found along a cultural and political spectrum rather than one with a strong linguistic divide as in Catalonia, tensions between settler and indigenous populations in New Caledonia and Bougainville, or a multi-faceted distinctions in secessionist conflicts such as South Sudan and West Papua.

In the cases examined in this chapter, the campaigns did not simply focus on the question of secession as the ultimate objective. While, of course, that was the *prima facie* preferred outcome, closer analysis of the campaigns shows that independence was framed as the best strategy to obtain a whole range of other political goals. Accordingly, the putative independent states of Scotland and Catalonia were framed by many secessionist milieus as a chance for greater democracy and enhanced political participation, and a socioeconomic re-configuration that would protect the vulnerable and result in greater equality. Yet, it would be reasonable to suspect that many of the more neo-liberal elements of the CiU and even within the SNP, were strategic in their deployment of such frames, viewing them as campaign slogans rather than future policies. Nevertheless, as we have outlined in this chapter, many mobilizing frames used throughout were inclusive and heavily oriented towards the reduction of inequalities and strengthening of democracy. We argue that the dominance of this framing is largely a result of the incessant pressure and mobilization “from below,” which shifted the emphasis away from independence as an end in itself but rather as a means to re-configure society in a more equitable fashion. Naturally, other factors also played a role, such as the differing constitutional frameworks, which rendered the frame of the denial of democracy much more salient in Catalonia than in Scotland. And while the impact of movements and grassroots mobilization on established political actors is clear, an interesting avenue of future research would be an assessment of the contrary dynamics, how movements and smaller parties such as the CUP and SSP, have been in turn shaped by engaging and supporting institutional political actors.

Bibliography

Alkorta, Eider, and Leonisio, Rafael. 2019. ‘Not Just Identity: Key Factors Involved in the Basque Pro-independence Movement’, *Revista Española de Investigaciones Sociológicas*, 165: 25–42.

Altman, David. 2011. *Direct Democracy Worldwide*, Cambridge, MA: Cambridge University Press.

Álvarez Pereira, Brais, Portos, Martín, and Vourdas, John. 2018. 'Waving Goodbye? The Determinants of Autonomism and Secessionism in Western Europe', *Regional Studies*, 52(2): 197–211.

Balcells, Albert. 1996. *Catalan Nationalism. Past and Present*, London, UK: Macmillan Press.

Balcells, Laia. 2013. 'Mass Schooling and Catalan Nationalism', *Nationalism and Ethnic Politics*, 19(4): 467–486.

Barrio, Astrid, and Rodríguez-Teruel, Juan. 2016. 'Reducing the Gap Between Leaders and Voters? Elite Polarization, Outbidding Competition, and the Rise of Secessionism in Catalonia', *Ethnic and Racial Studies*, 40: 1776–1794. doi: 10.1080/01419870.2016.1213400.

Basta, Karlo. 2017. 'The Social Construction of Transformative Political Events', *Comparative Political Studies*, 51: 1243–1278. doi: 10.1177/0010414017740601.

Beissinger, Mark R. 2002. *Nationalist Mobilization and the Collapse of the Soviet State*, Cambridge, UK: Cambridge University Press.

Brooks, Libby. 2014. 'Scottish Independence: 97% Register to Vote in Referendum', *The Guardian*, September 11, 2014.

Brubaker, Rogers. 1996. *Nationalism Reframed: Nationhood and the National Question in the New Europe*, Cambridge, MA: Cambridge University Press.

Burg, Steven L. 2015. 'Identity, Grievances, and Popular Mobilization for Independence in Catalonia', *Nationalism and Ethnic Politics*, 21(3): 289–312.

Colomer, Josep M. 2017. 'The Venturous Bid for the Independence of Catalonia', *Nationalities Papers*, 45(5): 950–967.

Conversi, Daniele. 1997. *The Basques, the Catalans, and Spain: Alternative Routes to Nationalist Mobilisation*, Reno: University of Nevada Press.

Crameri, Kathryn. 2015. 'Political Power and Civil Counterpower: The Complex Dynamics of the Catalan Independence Movement', *Nationalism and Ethnic Politics*, 21(1): 104–120.

Crític. 2015. 'Josep-Lluís Carod-Rovira: "El país ha estat en mans de gent de classe alta, barcelonina i de cognoms Catalans. Ara ho estem invertint"', December 10, http: //www.elcritic.cat/entrevistes/josepllluis-carod-rovira-el-pais-ha-estat-en-mans-de-gent-de-classe-altabarcelonina-i-de-cognoms-catalans-ara-ho-estem-i nvertint-7147.

Clayton, Tristan. 2005. "'Diasporic Otherness': Racism, Sectarianism and 'National Exteriority' in Modern Scotland", *Social & Cultural Geography*, 6(1): 99–116. doi: 10.1080/14649360520003359991.

Clements, Ben. 2017. 'Catholic Voters in Britain: What Are Their Political Preferences?', *British Politics and Policy at LSE (Blog)*, May 15, 2017, http:// blogs.lse.ac.uk/politicsandpolicy/catholic-voters-in-britain-what-are-their-politic al-preferences/.

Closa, Carlos. 2007. 'Why Convene Referendums? Explaining Choices in EU Constitutional Politics', *Journal of European Public Policy*, 14(8): 1311–1332.

Cuixart, Jordi. 2017. 'I'm in Prison for Defending Catalonia's Rights. Spain Must Free us Immediately', *The Guardian*, December 5, 2017, https://www.theguard ian.com/commentisfree/2017/dec/05/jordi-cuixart-prison-catalonia-rights-cat alan-spain-eu.

Curtice, John. 2018. 'The 2017 Election: Scotland Re-Enters British Politics?', *Scottish Geographical Journal*, 134(1–2): 39–44. doi: 10.1080/14702541.2018.1475856.

Curtice, John, and Ormston, Rachel. 2011. 'Is Scotland More Left-Wing than England?', *British Social Attitudes*, 28. Edinburgh, UK: ScotCen Social Research.

Cuthbert, Jim, and Cuthbert, Margaret. 2009. 'SNP Economic Strategy: Neo-Liberalism with a Heart'. In *The Modern SNP: From Protest to Power,* edited by Gerry Hassan, 105–119. Edinburgh, UK: Edinburgh University Press.

Dalle Mulle, Emmanuel. 2016. 'New Trends in Justifications for National Self-Determination: Evidence from Scotland and Flanders', *Ethnopolitics*, 15(2): 211–229.

Dalle Mulle, Emmanuel, and Serrano, Iván. 2019. 'Between a Principled and a Consequentialist Logic: Theory and Practice of Secession in Catalonia and Scotland', *Nations and Nationalism*, 25(2): 630–651. doi: 10.1111/nana.12412.

Davidson, Neil. 2014a. 'A Scottish Watershed', *New Left Review*, 89(September-October): 5–26.

Davidson, Neil. 2014b. "'Yes'", *Radical Philosophy (Blog)*. 2014.

della Porta, Donatella. 2018. 'Protests as Critical Junctures: Some Reflections Towards a Momentous Approach to Social Movements', *Social Movement Studies.* doi: 10.1080/14742837.2018.1555458.

della Porta, Donatella, O'Connor, Francis, and Portos, Martin. 2019. 'Protest cycles and referendums for independence: closed opportunities and the radicalization path in Catalonia', forthcoming.

della Porta, Donatella, O'Connor, Francis, Portos, Martín, and Subirats Ribas, Anna. 2017a. *Social Movements and Referendums from Below: Direct Democracy in the Neoliberal Crisis*, Bristol, UK: Policy Press/Bristol University Press.

della Porta, Donatella, O'Connor, Francis, Portos, Martín, and Subirats Ribas, Anna. 2017b. '"The Streets Will always Be Ours"—Catalonia, a Referendum from below', *Open Democracy*, 5 October 2017, https://www.opendemocracy.net/can-europe-make-it/donatella-della-porta-francis-oconnor-martin-portos-anna-subirats-ribas/streets-w.

della Porta, Donatella, and Portos, Martín. 2018. A bourgeois story? The class basis of Catalan independentism, paper presented at 'The Political Consequences of Inequality: II. Inequalities, territorial politics, nationalism' seminar, 22nd–23rd November 2018, Scuola Normale Superiore, Florence.

Dodds, Antonia, and Seawright, David. 2014. 'The Politics of Identity: Scottish Nationalism'. In *Devolution and British Politics*, edited by Michael O'Neill, 90–112. Abingdon, UK: Routledge.

Dowling, Andrew. 2014. 'Accounting for the Turn Towards Secession in Catalonia', *International Journal of Iberian Studies*, 27(2–3): 219–234.

Electoral Commission. 2014. 'Scottish Independence Referendum Report on the Referendum Held on 18 September 2014'. ELC/2014/02. The Electoral Commission.

Fatke, Mathias. 2015. 'Participation and Political Equality in Direct Democracy: Educative Effect or Social Bias?', *Swiss Political Science Review*, 21(1): 99–118.

Fernández-i-Marín, Xavier, and López, Jaume. 2010. 'Marco cultural de referencia y participación electoral en Cataluña', *Revista Española de Ciencia Política*, 23: 31–57.

Ferreres Comella, Víctor. 2014. 'The Spanish Constitutional Court Confronts Catalonia's "Right to Decide" (Comment on Judgment 42/2014)', *European Constitutional Law Review*, 10(3): 571–590.

Finlay, Richard J. 2005. 'The Turbulent Century: Scotland since 1900'. In *Scotland: A History*, edited by J. Wormald, 201–224. Oxford, UK: Oxford University Press.

Foley, James, and Ramand, Pete. 2014. *Yes: The Radical Case for Scottish Independence*, London, UK: Pluto Press.

Gamson, William. 1988. 'Political Discourse and Collective Action'. In *From Structure to Action*, edited by B. Klandermans, H. Kriesi, and S. Tarrow, 219–246. Greenwich, CT: JAI Press.

Gellner, Ernest. 2008. *Nations and Nationalism*, Ithaca, NY: Cornell University Press.

Gillan, Audrey. 2006. 'In Iraq, Life Expectancy Is 67. Minutes from Glasgow City Centre, It's 54', *The Guardian*, January 21, 2006.

Goffman, Erving. 1974. *Frame Analysis: An Essay on the Organization of Experience*, New York: Harper Colophon Books.

Guibernau, Montserrat. 2004. *Catalan Nationalism: Francoism, Transition and Democracy*, London, UK: Routledge.

Haklai, Oded. 2015. 'From Independent Statehood to Minority Rights: The Evolution of National Self-Determination as an International Order Principle in the Post-State Formation Era', *Ethnopolitics*, 14(5): 461–469.

Hassan, Gerry, and Rosie Ilett, eds. 2011. *Radical Scotland: Arguments for Self-Determination. Viewpoints*, Edinburgh, UK: Luath Press.

Johnston, Hank, and John A. Noakes (eds.). 2005. *Frames of Protest: Social Movements and the Framing Perspective*, Lanham: Rowman & Littlefield.

Jordan, William. 2015. 'Scots Are to the Left of the Rest of Britain on Almost Every Issue', *YouGov*.

Keating, Michael. 2009. 'Scottish Independence', *Scottish Affairs*, 68(First Series) (1): 100–118.

Keating, Michael. 2010. 'The Strange Death of Unionist Scotland', *Government and Opposition*, 45(Special Issue 03): 365–385.

Kriesi, Hanspeter. 2005. *Direct Democratic Choices: The Swiss Experience*, Lanham, MD: Lexington Books.

Lindekilde, Lasse. 2014. 'Discourse and Frame Analysis'. In *Methodological Practices in Social Movement Research*, edited by D. della Porta, 195–227. Oxford, UK: Oxford University Press.

Mason, Chris. 2013. 'Nigel Farage Blasts 'Fascist' Protesters after Edinburgh Confrontation', *BBC News*, May 17, 2013, http://www.bbc.com/news/uk-scotland-22566183.

Mitchell, James, Denver, David, Pattie, Charles, and Bochel, Hugh. 1998. 'The 1997 Devolution Referendum in Scotland', *Parliamentary Affairs*, 51(2): 166–168.

Mooney, Gerry, and Scott, Gill. 2016. 'Welfare, Equality and Social Justice: Scottish Independence and the Dominant Imaginings of the 'New' Scotland', *Ethics and Social Welfare*, 10(3): 239–251. https://doi.org/10.1080/17496535.2016.1194445.

Muñoz, Jordi, and Guinjoan, Marc. 2013. 'Accounting for Internal Variation in Nationalist Mobilization: Unofficial Referendums for Independence in Catalonia (2009–11)', *Nations and Nationalism*, 19(1): 44–67.

Mycock, Andrew. 2012. 'SNP, Identity and Citizenship: Re-Imagining State and Nation', *National Identities*, 14(1): 53–69. doi: 10.1080/14608944.2012.657078.

Polwart, Karine. 2013. 'Karine Polwart: Imagination Vital to Telling the Yes Story', *The Scotsman*, February 17, 2013, http://www.scotsman.com/news/opinion/karine-polwart-imagination-vital-to-telling-the-yes-story-1-2795982.

Pujol, Jordi. 1976. *La immigració, problema i esperança de Cataluña*, Barcelona, Spain: Nova Terra.

Qvortrup, Matt. 2014a. 'Conclusion'. In *Referendums around the World*, edited by M. Qvortrup, 246–251. London: Palgrave.

Qvortrup, Matt. 2014b. 'Introduction: Theory, Practice and History'. In *Referendums around the World*, edited by M. Qvortrup, 1–16. London: Palgrave.

RIC. 2014. "Press Release: Hundreds Rally against Farage in Edinburgh: 'Anti-UKIP, Not Anti-English'", *Radical Independence Campaign (Blog)*, May 9, 2014.

Rico, Guillem, and Liñeira, Robert. 2014. 'Bringing Secessionism into the Mainstream: The 2012 Regional Election in Catalonia', *South European Society and Politics*, 19: 257–280.

Salmond, Alex. 2013. 'Alex Salmond's Speech to the 2013 SNP Conference', Eden Court, Inverness.

Schiller, Theo. 2009. 'Conclusions'. In *Referendums and Representative Democracy*, edited by M. Setälä and T. Schiller, 207–219. London, UK: Routledge.

Scottish Government. 2012. *'Your Scotland, Your Referendum'*, Edinburgh, UK: Scottish Government.

Scottish Government. 2013. *'Scotland's Future. Your Guide to an Independent Scotland'*, Edinburgh, UK: Scottish Government.

Serrano, Ivan. 2013. 'Just a Matter of Identity?: Support for Independence in Catalonia', *Regional & Federal Studies*, 23(5): 523–545.

Snow, David A. 2013. 'Grievances, Individual and Mobilizing'. In *The Wiley-Blackwell Encyclopedia of Social and Political Movements*, edited by D.A. Snow, D. della Porta, B. Klandermans, and D. McAdam, 1–6. Oxford, UK: Wiley-Blackwell. doi: 10.1002/9781405198431.wbespm434

Snow, David A., and Benford, Robert D. 1988a. 'Ideology, Frame Resonance, and Participant Mobilization', *International Social Movement Research*, 1: 197–217.

Snow, David A., and Benford, Robert D. 1988b. 'Ideology, Frame Resonance, and Participant Mobilization'. In *From Structure to Action*, edited by B. Klandermans, H. Kriesi, and S. Tarrow, 197–218. Greenwich, CT: JAI Press.

Tierney, Stephen. 2012. *Constitutional Referendums: The Theory and Practice of Republican Deliberation*, Oxford, UK: Oxford University Press.

10 The Europeanization of the Catalan debate

A "war of attrition"?

Mattia Guidi and Mattia Casula

Introduction

It is not surprising that secession demands in advanced democracies receive a lot of attention. They are usually dismissed, at both national and international level, with the argument that liberal democracies already guarantee civil and political rights, as well as self-government, and therefore there is no justification for breaking their legal order.[1] So, the exercise of a particular right (the right of self-determination) is denied to certain groups of voters on the basis of the democratic nature of the regime they live in – which is to some extent paradoxical. On the one hand, the existence of a democratic regime allows the political actors of a certain region to promote secessionist projects and to legitimately use policy-making tools to advance their ideas within the region. On the other, pro-independence political actors have a very hard time convincing voters and elites in other countries that their demands are well founded. For these reasons, we may end up in situations of high conflict that neither the national government nor the international community is able to easily accommodate.[2]

This chapter focuses on the case of Catalonia. Besides belonging to the category of secessionist movements in advanced democracies, the Catalan case is particularly interesting for its relationship with the supranational political system in which both Spain and Catalonia are embedded: the European Union (EU). The destiny of regions that would gain independence from an EU member state remains a hotly debated topic, for three main reasons. First, the EU being a community of (mostly) advanced democracies, it is very likely that what happens in one of its members will become a precedent. Hence, we can expect that EU institutions and member states will handle such demands with caution.

1 See for instance the famous judgment of the Canadian Supreme Court on the Québec case (Reference re Secession of Quebec, [1998] 2 S.C.R. 217, available at: https://scc-csc.lexum.com/scc-csc/scc-csc/en/item/1643/index.do), in which the court argued, first, that a right of unilateral secession exists only under "exceptional circumstances," for instance "the exceptional situation of an oppressed or colonial people" (para. 112), and, second, that these "exceptional circumstances are manifestly inapplicable to Quebec under existing conditions" (para. 138).

2 For a summary of legal arguments in favour or against secession, see Hannum (1998).

Second, EU membership translates into a series of rights that affect all economic actors in a territory. If one territory ceases to belong to the EU, what happens to these rights? The answer to this question is one of the many battlefields on which secessionists and unionists confront each other. Third, Catalonia is the European region that has gone furthest in claiming its right to independence, making it impossible for Spain to just ignore its demands. The acts and decisions that Catalan policy-makers have carried out have inevitably prompted the Spanish government to react and repress the region's "rebellion." But repression may ultimately bring into question the democratic nature of the regime that a region seeks to become independent from – if it is no longer democratic, does secession become legitimate?

The confrontation between the governments of Catalonia and Spain has been going on for more than a decade (see Cuadras-Morató 2016). In 2005, a very large majority (89% of the regional parliament) passed a new statute (*Estatut d'autonomia*), which was then confirmed by a referendum in 2006. As a response, the centre-right *Partido Popular* (PP) took a very strong stance against the new statute and asked the Constitutional Court to rule if parts of it were in conflict with the Spanish constitution. In 2010, the Constitutional Court ruled that some articles of the statute were unconstitutional, and others had to be interpreted restrictively. As a reaction, pro-independence parties have radicalized and put the realization of a binding referendum on independence on top of their agendas. After the 2012 election, with rising support for secession among voters (see Guinjoan and Rodon 2016), a pro-independence majority (composed by centrist *Convergencia i Unió*, CiU and the centre-left *Esquerra Republicana de Catalunya*) was formed with the goal of holding a referendum. However, given the opposition of the Spanish government, the Catalan government could organize only an informal consultation, which was held on 9 November 2014. The government coalition then decided to call a snap election in 2015, claiming that this would be equivalent to a referendum on independence. The government coalition parties formed an alliance to run under the same platform (*Junts pel Sí*, United for the yes), but they failed to reach a majority in terms of both votes and seats. To form a new government, which (as promised) set as its primary goal the independence referendum, they had to ally with the pro-independence far-left party *Candidatura d'Unitat Popular* (CUP). Among the compromises necessary to form this unprecedented government coalition, the most problematic proved to be the choice of the president, who is elected by the regional parliament. CUP opposed the election of Artur Mas, long-time leader of CiU, who was nevertheless the only candidate proposed by *Junts pel Sí*. When a snap election appeared the most likely scenario, due to the inability of the parliament to invest a president, *Junts pel Sí* and CUP struck a last-minute deal, on 10 January 2016, on the choice of Carles Puigdemont as President of Catalonia.

Our chapter analyses the events going from the end of 2015, when the Catalan election took place, and the imposition of direct rule by the Spanish government, at the end of October 2017. These two years have been marked by the Catalan attempts to build support (both internally and internationally) for the referendum. Given the resistance opposed by the Spanish government, the Catalan executive has pursued a strategy of *internationalization* of the independence issue, which was seen as the only possibility to maximize its chances of success. This internationalization has been, to a large extent, a *Europeanization* of the Catalan issue. Members of the Catalan government, and most notably President Puigdemont and his Minister for External and Institutional Relations Raül Romeva, have repeatedly appealed to other EU member states and EU institutions with the objective of obtaining their support, or at least their neutrality, in the struggle with the Spanish government. The latter, however, did not simply observe this attempt. Instead, it successfully reacted to prevent the formation of this external support.

While it is self-evident that, at the time of writing, the strategy of the former Catalan government has not borne fruits, it is nonetheless interesting to analyze why it was chosen and how it was carried out. This chapter, therefore, aims to answer the following questions: why did the Catalan government embark on such a risky strategy, knowing that it had a lot to lose and little chances of winning? Was it a bluff or a miscalculation? How did the Catalan government try to create international support for Catalan independence? How did the Spanish government react to these efforts? How did EU institutions react? In doing so, the chapter will model the choices of the main actors involved (the Catalan and the Spanish governments) as a "war of attrition" game – a game in which each actor aims at resisting (i.e. delaying the moment in which it will abandon the game, accepting the defeat) as long as possible. In our empirical analysis, we show how each actor has played the game and how the model helps explain the choices made.

The remainder of this chapter proceeds as follows. The next section briefly reviews the literature on secession, with a focus on its application to advanced democracies. Subsequently, we will illustrate the model that we use to interpret the events that occurred between the end of 2015 and the end of 2017 in Catalonia. Then, the chapter turns to present a narrative of the events, focusing on the strategy played by both actors and the results they have obtained. The final section draws some concluding remarks.

The right of secession and its practical application

Demands for secession, or for the split or separation of established states, continue to characterize national and international politics worldwide. While the fastest growing rate of states' establishment was reached in the decades after the end of Second World War (in the 1960s and 1970s in particular), a decisive impulse to the creation of new states was also represented by the collapse of the Soviet Union. The latter influenced not only the formation of new independent states from the former republics of the USSR (among which there were three current members of the EU like Estonia, Latvia and Lithuania), but also the disgregation of Yugoslavia and the separation between the Czech Republic and Slovakia.

In more recent decades, secessionist demands have for the first time involved democratic polities. These demands have been particularly relevant in Canada (with Québec, see Mendelsohn 2003), Great Britain (with Scotland, see Pattie and Johnston 2017) and Spain (with Catalonia, see Muñoz and Tormos 2015), in which requests for greater decentralization have overlapped with secessionist grievances (Guibernau 2006). However, also Italy (with the grievances of the northern part of the country against the central state) and Belgium (with the secessionist movement in the Flemish region) have experienced this phenomenon.

Economists explain this growth of secessionist demands with the increased economic interdependence between nations. Alesina and Spolaore (1997: 1041) argue that this is the case because "the benefits of [being part of] large countries are less important if small countries can freely trade with each other," while "a breakup of nations is costlier if it implies more trade barriers and smaller markets." A similar argument is developed by Casella and Feinstein (2002) who distinguish between markets (groups of actors who exchange private goods) and jurisdictions (groups of actors who cooperate in the provision of public goods), concluding that the two must not necessarily coincide. More specifically, when markets are large, multiple jurisdictions (i.e. multiple states) are "both possible and desirable" (Casella and Feinstein 2002: 437).

While in theory these distinctions are reasonable, in practice it is not easy to argue that one political community (like a region) can leave the jurisdiction it belonged to while retaining the same status within the market in which it participated. This observation is particularly appropriate for countries and regions within the EU, whose ability to take advantage of the single market and the euro as a common currency clearly depends on being part of the EU jurisdiction. Although no clear rules exist in the EU treaties for dealing with secessions within member states, the interpretation that has prevailed in Brussels since 2004 has been that territories gaining independence from a member state would become *de facto* third countries: EU law would cease to apply to their territory, and they should apply to become member states if they wanted to restore the conditions predating their independence.

This interpretation has been labelled as "Prodi doctrine," from the name of President of the Commission Prodi, who, in a response given to the member of the European Parliament Eluned Morgan on 1 March 2004, stated that

> [w]hen a part of the territory of a Member State ceases to be a part of that state, e.g. because that territory becomes an independent state, the treaties will no longer apply to that territory. In other words, a newly independent region would, by the fact of its independence, become a third country with respect to the Union and the treaties would, from the day of its independence, not apply anymore on its territory.
>
> (Prodi 2004)

This interpretation is particularly discouraging for regions aspiring to independence. Not only do they risk losing all the benefits related to their EU membership, but they also risk having to wait a long time before regaining them. As the accession procedure requires a unanimous consensus among all the existing members on the entry of a new state, the veto of a member state (the one from which the region seceded, for instance) would be sufficient to stall the procedure indefinitely. Ultimately, the member states retain the lion's share when it comes to recognizing a new state: the EU as such can only acknowledge what national governments decide (see Closa 2016, 2017 for an overview of the issue; see also Coppieters 2017: 38). However, the lack of a clear EU legal framework for dealing with secessions (be they unilateral or "legal") remains a potential source of uncertainty. This uncertainty allows actors to hold different (and often conflicting) interpretations of what could be done in response to secession, and it could, as a matter of fact, make secession look less costly (and thus more appealing) to a region aspiring to independence (Closa 2016: 243).

Against this backdrop, the political science literature on secession has provided evidence for the fact that democratic countries are very reluctant to support secessionist movements in other democratic countries (Bélanger et al. 2005). On the one hand, the legitimacy of secessionist movements in democratic states is questioned, both in practical and in legal terms.[3] On the other, democratic countries will not want to establish a precedent that could be applied to themselves too. This behaviour of democratic countries makes secessions in established democracies very unlikely, because it inhibits one of the most important factors determining the success of an independence movement – international support. Looking at the EU, it is easy to observe that, while secessionist demands *inside* the union have so far been disregarded as unviable, the attitude towards secessionist demands *outside* the union has been more flexible (Coppieters 2017).

As the support offered by Germany to Croatia shows (Crawford 1996), international recognition is crucial for the success of a secession (Young 1994). However, for the reasons mentioned above, because "the existing international regime favors the territorial integrity of states at any cost," and because of the "fear of a domino effect" (Heraclides 1990: 377), the explicit endorsements of independence in situations of this kind are rare. This is confirmed by the states' reluctance to legally accept the possibility of secession: as argued by Coggins (2017: 27), "[t]oday, only around a dozen countries (out of approximately 194) have a potential legal means to secession." In other words, secession almost always entails breaking up the existing legal order, with all the costs and consequences that this implies.

Catalonia's secession bid: preferences, constraints, strategies

This section seeks to formulate a sketched representation of the game played by the government of Catalonia and the government of Spain in the period we

3 See also footnote 1.

analyze in this chapter. Although we know that in democracies different political actors (with different preferences) can affect the course of action of a political system, we will assume, for simplicity's sake, that Catalonia and Spain are *unitary actors.* Both at regional (in Catalonia) and state level (for the Spanish national government) there is a parliamentary system. Since the majority that is formed in the assembly after the election (which can be composed by one party or multiple parties) controls the government, it does not make sense to consider legislature and executive as separate actors (see Moe and Caldwell 1994). Therefore, the parliamentary majority in Barcelona's *Parlament* and the parliamentary majority in Madrid's *Congreso de los Diputados* will be the two unitary actors that we will consider. If a position is taken or a decision is adopted by one of the two governments, we assume, it is because the coalition has reached an internal agreement on it. In the remainder of this chapter, whenever we identify the two actors as "Catalonia" or "Spain," we refer to the political actors that, in the period of analysis, had the power to take binding decisions for the whole polity, and not to all citizens and/or parties in the two systems.[4]

A second methodological comment regards the period we analyze. Although the confrontation between the Catalan government and the Spanish one has developed across many years (see Introduction), we choose to focus on a shorter period, going from the end of 2015 to the end of 2017, for two reasons. First, in this period the main political actors did not change: Mariano Rajoy was the prime minister of Spain (even though he led a caretaker government from the beginning of the year until 4 November 2016) with a minority government,[5] and the coalition governing Catalonia was the one resulting from the election of September 2015.[6] In this way, we can claim that we analyze a clearly defined event, that is "the motion and action occurring between an initial situation and a terminal situation such that all and only the movers and actors of the initial situation [...] are included in the terminal situation" (Riker 1957: 61). Second, throughout all this period the Catalan government in office had as its main goal, holding a binding referendum. This allows us to examine to what extent this strategy was viable in the presence of a firm commitment, on both sides, to not appease the opponent.

4 It is a known fact that, in Catalonia, the percentage of the population in favour of independence has hardly reached 50% in these years. Therefore, when we use the expressions "Catalonia" or "Catalan government," we by no means imply that the position represented by the Catalan government is shared by a large majority of the Catalan population.

5 The members of the two Rajoy cabinets were either from the prime minister's party (the *Partido Popular*, PP) or independents. The first Rajoy government acted as caretaker from the December 2015 general election (in which the PP lost the majority in the *Congreso* to November 2016, when the second Rajoy government was sworn in. The second Rajoy government was supported by the centrist *Ciudadanos*, but could enter into office with a formal vote only thanks to the abstention of the *Partido Socialista Obrero Español.*

6 The coalition included Puigdemont's party, the *Partit Demòcrata Europeu Català* (PDECat, a centre-right party), the centre-left *Esquerra Republicana de Catalunya* and the far-left *Candidatura d'Unitat Popular.*

With this premise in mind, we can now illustrate the main features of the game played by the two actors. First of all, as concerns the relationship between Catalonia and (the rest of) Spain, both actors have a preferred outcome: for the Catalan government, this is being allowed to hold a *legal and binding* referendum for declaring independence from (the rest of) Spain; for the Spanish government, it is the *status quo*. The period we analyze can be interpreted as a series of decisions (as summarized in Figure 10.1) in which the two actors face, at any stage, a choice between accepting the other actor's most-preferred outcome or sticking to their initial position.[7] When an actor must move, it will calculate whether (in the language of game theory) it is preferable to "go straight" or "swerve," based on the costs and benefits of each option (see Griffiths 2017).

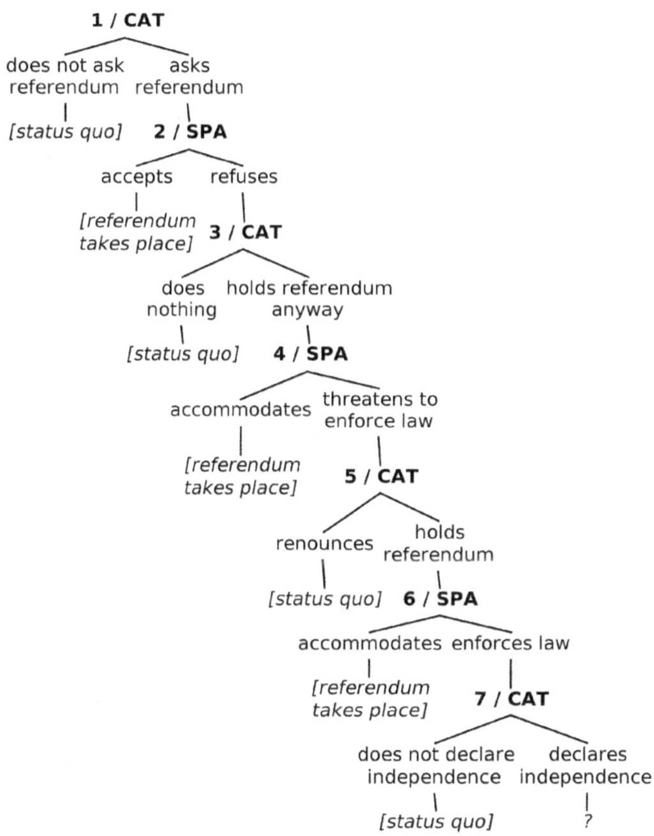

Figure 10.1 The sequence of decisions.

7 This representation is obviously a simplification of real-world decisions. In the real world, it would be possible at any moment for the two actors to find a compromise that is halfway between the two most preferred outcomes. For simplicity's sake, however, and also because this has not happened in the period of interest, we do not consider this possibility.

What are the expected costs and benefits of going straight or swerving at each stage? Let us see them in detail. A reasonable assumption of the game is that the costs of playing the game increase as an actor goes on. In other words, the cost c_1 of abandoning the game at t_1 is lower than the cost c_2 of abandoning the game at t_2: $c_1 < c_2 <_{\dots} < c_n$. Therefore, what makes an actor go straight is the expectation that, by continuing the game, the benefit (which is represented by the probability of winning and the value an actor attaches to it) will be higher than the cost. For each actor, we can assume that there is a "baseline cost," which is given by its strength and position of advantage or disadvantage, and a "value of victory" that is attributed independently of the baseline cost.

So, for each actor we can define the following variables:

k, that is the baseline cost, which must not necessarily be the same for both actors;

v, that is the value of victory for each actor attributes.

The "net" value of victory V is thus given by $V = v - k$. Following the notation first proposed by Maynard Smith (1974) for the game that he defined as "war of attrition," we can write the probability that actor i will abandon the struggle at a certain stage t as:

$$p_i(t) = \frac{1}{V_i} e^{(-t/V_i)}$$

This simple model can help us visualize the probability of abandoning the game that two actors with different baseline costs have. In relation to the case we analyze in this chapter, we believe it is reasonable to assume that the baseline cost of Spain is considerably lower than the baseline cost for Catalonia ($k_s < k_c$), for a number of reasons. First, the Catalan government's goal of achieving independence represents a big change with respect to the status quo; Spain's goal, instead, is just maintaining the status quo. This gives Spain an advantage known as "status quo bias" (Samuelson and Zeckhauser 1988). Second, Spain is a state that can legitimately use the force to preserve the existing legal order, while Catalonia cannot do that. Third, Spain already has international recognition in the international community, while Catalonia has to struggle to gain this recognition. Fourth, Spain is bigger and economically more powerful than Catalonia.

Given this asymmetry in costs, the role played by the value of victory that actors signal is crucial. In other words, if the Catalan government wants to have a fair chance of winning the game, it must declare that its value of victory is very high, and at least higher than Spain's value of victory. At the same time, the Catalan government must seek to increase Spain's costs of playing the game. However, we can expect that Spain will attempt to do the same, for instance underlying how secession would damage Catalonia economically (Woertz 2017: 105). It goes without saying that the credibility of both actors in undermining the other's efforts does not depend much on what is *declared* (it is very easy and not costly to state that one is ready to go on forever), but rather on what is *done*. Put differently, actions signal an actor's commitment to continue the struggle.

As Figure 10.2 summarizes, if both actors attribute a high value to victory, the cost of continuing the game is clearly higher for Catalonia than for Spain. Therefore, the probability of abandoning will be lower for the latter than for the former. Differently, if Catalonia (the weaker actor) manages to push Spain (the stronger actor) to attach a low value to victory, the situation would change, and Spain would become more likely than Catalonia to abandon the game.

This game, in its simplicity, already allows us to derive some basic predictions regarding the behaviour of the Catalan and Spanish governments. In particular, we can expect the following:

- all else equal, the Catalan government, being less powerful, is more likely than the Spanish one to swerve;
- both actors will try to undermine the opponent's value of victory;
- even if the Catalan government cannot significantly reduce Spain's value of victory, it might still have an incentive to resist (to not abandon the game), because this improves its position vis-à-vis Spain;

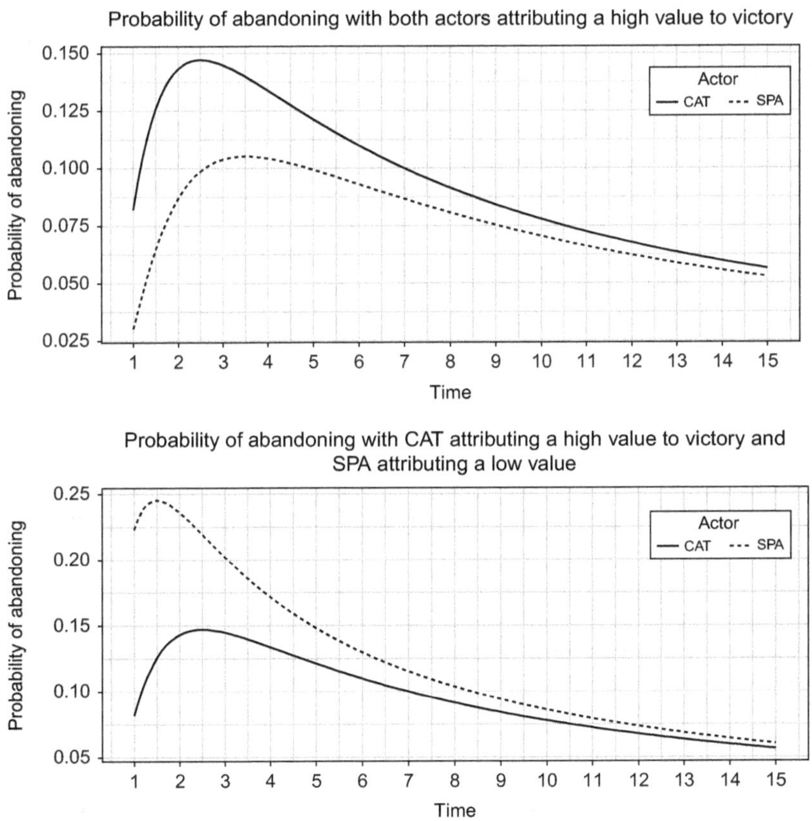

Figure 10.2 Probability of abandoning the game with different values of victory.

- as the difference between p_c and p_s tends to reduce as time passes, the stronger actor has an incentive to win the game (i.e. force the other to abandon) as early as possible.

In the next section, we will examine to what extent these predictions are in line with the events observed between the end of 2015 and the end of 2017.

A narrative of the Catalan crisis (2015–2017)

In this section, the events between the end of 2015 and the end of 2017 will be interpreted in light of the theoretical framework introduced above. The findings presented below are based on a qualitative analysis of documentary data. This collection has started from the consultation of the Twitter accounts of the main Spanish, Catalan and European political figures involved in the Catalan independence debate.[8] In particular, we have analyzed the tweets published in the period between September 2015 and December 2017 which referred to the referendum debate or to Catalan independence more broadly. These data have been used to identify the most salient junctures in the period considered. Once these junctures had been identified, the search has proceeded with a triangulation of multiple journalistic sources. We divide our narrative in three periods: the first covers the events preceding the choice of holding the referendum; the second covers the organization of the referendum and the vote; the third covers the period going from the vote to the declaration of independence and the imposition of direct rule by the Spanish government.

First period: to hold or not to hold the referendum?

During the first stage, which begins with the Catalan government's request to hold a binding referendum on independence (see first step in Figure 10.1), the strategy of the Catalan government has been constantly oriented towards obtaining support from European institutions, emphasizing the democratic nature of its independence demands. At the same time, the attitude towards the central government has been characterized by signalling the Catalan government's willingness to hold the referendum in any case. In the language of our game, the

8 The Twitter accounts of the following Spanish and European political figures had been consulted: Mariano Rajoy (@marianorajoy), Pedro Sánchez (@sanchezcastejon), Albert Rivera (@Albert_Rivera), Carles Puigdemont (@KRLS), Raül Romeva (@raulromeva), Oriol Junqueras (@junqueras), Gianni Pittella (@giannipittella), Jean-Claude Juncker (@JunckerEU), Martin Schulz (@MartinSchulz), Antonio Tajani (@Antonio_Tajani), Donald Tusk (@donaldtusk) and the Twitter accounts of the President of the European Council (@eucopresident) and of the European Parliament (@EP_President). The tweets published between September 2015 and December 2017 related to the Catalan debate were first selected, then examined one to one.

Catalan government has repeatedly signalled that it would not abandon the game even if confronted with an outright Spanish refusal.[9]

This strategy was exposed in a public event, entitled "The Catalan Referendum," that the Catalan government organized, on 24 January 2017, in the headquarters of the European Parliament, and to whom members of the European Parliament from 14 European countries and all political groups took part.[10] In this event, Catalan President Puigdemont emphasized that their project had to be considered as a European issue, given Calatonia's commitment to remaining part of the EU. For this purpose, he stressed that their proposal for a referendum was "Europeanist since it [was] rooted in one of [Europe's] fundamental principles, that is, democracy." Puigdemont continued saying that "in recent decades Europe has seen how new states arise. Unlike other cases not too distant in time, Catalonia aims at achieving independence peacefully, in a civic way, and armed exclusively with democracy."

Puigdemont urged the EU "to be part of the solution to the Catalan situation,"[11] and to act as a mediator between Catalonia and the Spanish government to reach an agreement on a binding referendum. Since the beginning of 2017, in fact, the Catalan government has declared its will to organize a referendum agreed upon with the Spanish government (*referèndum pactat*), identifying this as the solution "most acceptable [...] for everyone."[12] Nevertheless, Puigdemont stressed that if the Spanish government had denied the referendum, they would "hold it anyway."[13]

Together with these signals of determination, attempts to "Europeanize" the Catalan debate and to involve European institutions as mediators have been confirmed during all the first period. Raül Romeva i Rueda, former member of the European Parliament and minister for external affairs in the Puigdemont government, for instance, declared, in March 2017, that "7.5 million citizens in Catalonia [...] will not cease to be citizens of the European Union, regardless of the political decision which the country is taking. The question [for the EU] is how are you going to manage that?"[14] These positions have been accompanied by

9 See for instance the language used by Puigdemont in his investiture speech: "Puigdemont es investido president de la Generalitat y promete que se 'dejará la piel' por la independencia", Público, 10.01.2016, available at: https://www.publico.es/politica/puigdemont-investido-president-generalitat-y.html.

10 "MEPs from fourteen countries and all political groups attend hearing with Puigdemont, Junqueras and Romeva in Brussels," Vilaweb, 25.01.2017, available at: https://www.vilaweb.cat/noticies/meps-from-fourteen-countries-and-all-political-groups-attend-hearing-with-puigdemont-junqueras-and-romeva-in-brussels/.

11 "Puigdemont: "Europe cannot look the other way", CatalanNews, 25.01.2017, available at: http://www.catalannews.com/politics/item/puigdemont-europe-cannot-look-the-other-way.

12 *Ibidem.*

13 *Ibidem.*

14 "Catalans prepare vote for independence from Spain," TodayOnline, 02.03.2017, available at: https://www.todayonline.com/world/catalans-prepare-vote-independence-spain

appeals to shared European values of democracy, self-determination and respect for human rights. In this respect, Romeva claimed that the referendum could be a "model" for Europe.[15]

During all the first stage, the Spanish government maintained the approach adopted since 2014, arguing that a legal referendum would have never been granted (see second step in Figure 10.1). Like Catalan political leaders, Rajoy too appealed to European institutions and leaders, in view of obtaining their support.[16] Moreover, he implicitly formulated the threat to not allow an independent Catalonia to join the EU (since the Spanish government would have, like all other member states' governments, the power to veto the accession of any new member). In a speech given on 25 September 2015, two days before the Catalan elections, Rajoy asked, "what would happen [in case of a Catalan independence] with the European Union? [...] What would happen with your rights as a Spanish and a European? Where would they export to?"[17] This position has been reiterated in 2016, and the Catalan referendum has consistently been labelled as "illegal."

The Catalan government's reaction to these arguments has been to downplay the risk of an exit of Catalonia from the EU legal space. In an interview given to the *Financial Times* in March 2016, Puigdemont stated that "the EU has a healthy capacity to adapt and solve conflicts on the basis of realpolitik," claiming that "the attitude of the EU to unforeseen situations [like a new Catalan state]" would have been to adapt to it.[18] Hence, with such positions held by the Catalan and Spanish governments, the two players headed for a collision course in 2017. Both refused to swerve and, as a result, the crisis escalated with the Catalan government's decision to hold the referendum anyway.

Second period: preparing the referendum

The first period, as we have seen, ended with the central government' refusal to "legalize" Catalan demands. In spite of this refusal, the Catalan government continued to resist and to avoid abandoning the game, in the hope to improve

15 Raül Romeva i Rueda (@raulromeva), tweet of 22.05.2017, 7:38PM: https://twitter.com/raulromeva/status/866709883642576897.

16 See for instance the meeting with German Chancellor Merkel, in which the latter endorsed Rajoy's position of keeping Spain united. See "Merkel recuerda a Catalunya que hay que respetar la legalidad de España y Europa", La Vanguardia, 01.09.2015, available at: https://www.lavanguardia.com/politica/20150901/54436152419/merkel-catalunya-respetar-legalidad-espana-europa.html.

17 "Spain: Rajoy warns against Catalan independence," Express, 25.09.2015, available at: https://www.express.co.uk/videos/4509953201001/Spain-Rajoy-warns-against-Catalan-independence.

18 "Catalonia can secede without Madrid's backing, says new leader", Financial Times, 17.03.2016, available at: https://www.ft.com/content/f37ef1a4-ec4b-11e5-bb79-2303682345c8.

its position vis-à-vis Spain. The main events and actions that characterized this period are illustrated below.

> On 9 June 2017, Carles Puigdemont announced that the referendum would be held on 1 October, and that its result would have been binding regardless of the number of voters participating (see the third step in Figure 10.1). The question on the ballots would have been the following: "Do you want Catalonia to become an independent state in the form of a republic?"[19] This announcement inevitably contributed to exacerbating the crisis with the Spanish government: Rajoy immediately declared the independentist referendum as "unconstitutional," reiterating that the central government would oppose it at any cost (see step four in Figure 10.1).[20] It is worth noting that the two other main Spanish parties were not fully aligned on this issue. While the Spanish socialists, led by Pedro Sánchez, opposed the referendum but invited Rajoy to dialogue with the Catalan government, accusing his confrontational strategy of putting the Spanish national unity at risk,[21] *Ciudadanos*, was more on Rajoy's side.[22]

The escalation yielded tensions within the Catalan government as well. On 3 July, Puigdemont sacked the Catalan minister for enterprise, Jordi Baidget, for expressing his doubts on holding a referendum with Spain's opposition.[23] A few days later, three other ministers of the cabinet were replaced for the same reason.[24] These events indicate how the cost of continuing the game for the Catalan government was increasing, up to a point where some members of the government were not willing to pay the price of explicitly violating the law. At the same time, by sacking members of the government who were reluctant to accept the consequences of a "collision" with Spain, Puigdemont reaffirmed its government's willingness to continue the game at any cost.

19 Carles Puigdemont (@KRLS), tweet of 09.06.2017, 02:08PM: https://twitter.com/krls/status/873104476248211458Raül Romeva i Rueda (@raulromeva), tweet of 22.05.2017, 7:38PM: https://twitter.com/raulromeva/status/866709883642576897

20 "Damage to Catalonia," *The New York Times*, 03.10.2017, available at: https://www.nytimes.com/2017/10/03/opinion/catalonia-spain-referendum.html.

21 Pedro Sánchez (@sanchezcastejon), tweet of 7.02.2017, 09:30PM: https://twitter.com/sanchezcastejon/status/829064905458335746.

22 "Inés Arrimadas: 'Sr. Puigdemont, deje de mentir a los catalanes: usted sabe que no habrá ni referéndum, ni independencia'", 05.04.2017, available at: http://parlament-catalunya.ciudadanos-cs.org/es/2017/04/05/ines-arrimadas-sr-puigdemont-deje-de-mentir-a-los-catalanes-usted-sabe-que-no-habra-ni-referendum-ni-independencia/.

23 See "Catalan Minister fired by president Puigdemont after voicing doubts about referendum", Catalan News, 03.07.2017, available at: http://www.catalannews.com/politics/item/catalan-minister-fired-by-president-puigdemont-after-voicing-doubts-about-referendum.

24 Minister for internal affairs Jordi Jané, Minister for education Meritxell Ruiz, and the government's spokesperson Neus Munté left the government on 14 July 2017. They were replaced respectively by Joaquim Forn, Clara Ponsatí and Jordi Turull.

Despite these tensions, on 6 September the Catalan parliament approved the law establishing the referendum, with 72 favourable votes. The 11 representatives of left-wing *Catalunya Sí que es Pot* abstained, while the other parties opposing the referendum (*Partido Popular*, *Partit dels Socialistes de Catalunya* and *Ciudadanos*) did not take part in the vote. Their aim was indeed to avoid giving any support to an act they considered illegal. With the same numbers, the parliament passed on 8 September the so-called "*Llei de transitorietat jurídica i fundacional de la República,*" which aimed to regulate the transition to independence in case of a positive outcome of the referendum. These acts triggered the central government's reaction. On 7 September, the Spanish Constitutional Court suspended the referendum and its related rules, accepting an urgent appeal presented by the Spanish government. In addition to that, the General Prosecutor initiated a proceeding against the Catalan leaders for the crimes of disobedience and prevarication.[25]

European institutions, which had initially kept a low profile on the issue, could no longer avoid taking a position – which was that of substantially backing the Spanish government. The President of the European Parliament, Antonio Tajani, stated on 7 September that "any act contrary to the Constitution of a Member State [of the Union] is an act contrary to the European Union."[26] Tajani also stressed that an independent Catalonia would have had to leave the EU. A few days later, on 15 September, President of the European Commission Jean Claude Juncker confirmed that the referendum result would have been recognized only if approved by the Spanish Parliament and the Constitutional Court.[27]

Rajoy, at the same time, affirmed that there would be no referendum, and that he would do whatever was necessary to prevent it, to respect the law and preserve national unity.[28] Even the language used in the weeks' preceding the referendum signals Rajoy's willingness to send a message of intransigence. On the one hand, he openly defined the referendum "crime and disobedience" that "will not be tolerated."[29] On the other, he aimed at denying legitimacy to the vote by calling

25 "La Fiscalía se querellará contra los miembros de la Mesa del Parlament que han admitido a trámite la Ley del Referéndum", El Mundo, 6.09.2017, available at: https://www.elmundo.es/cataluna/2017/09/06/59afe894e5fdea84708b4598.html.

26 "Tajani: "Cualquier acción contra la Constitución de un estado miembro es una acción contra la UE," Lavanguardia, 07.09.2017, available at: https://www.lavanguardia.com/internacional/20170907/431106175242/tajani-cualquier-accion-contra-constitucion-estado-miembro-accioncontra-ue.html.

27 "Jean-Claude Juncker clears the confusion over Catalonia", EuroNews, 15.09.2017, available at: https://www.euronews.com/2017/09/15/jean-claude-juncker-clears-the-confusion-over-catalonia.

28 Mariano Rajoy (@marianorajoy), tweet of 09.09.2017, 1:27PM: https://twitter.com/marianorajoy/status/906479078664011777.

29 Mariano Rajoy (@marianorajoy), tweet of 23.09.2017, 2:03PM: https://twitter.com/marianorajoy/status/911561773198782464.

it a "staging"[30] and a "screenplay."[31] Spain did not only legally challenge the referendum, but also promoted actions to prevent the vote from taking place. On 20 September, an estimated 10 million ballot papers were seized by the *Guardia Civil.*[32] On the same day, 14 public officials, including the Catalan Economy and Finance Secretary General Josep Maria Jové, were arrested.[33] Moreover, in the days preceding the referendum, the Spanish National Police deployed around 16,000 police and military officers in Catalonia.[34]

Despite the resolute law enforcement carried out by the Spanish police on the day of the referendum, the vote actually took place (steps five and six in Figure 10.1). Catalan leaders appeared further motivated to go on, as they aimed at highlighting the contrast between the peaceful exercise of the right to vote on the one hand, and the forceful reaction of the Spanish police on the other. Raül Romeva, on the day of the referendum, tweeted that voting was a "democratic and peaceful act" made "against state violence."[35] In another tweet, he stated:

> "The Spanish government has shown their arguments: repression and violence. We will continue to show ours: ballot boxes, votes, democracy and peace."[36]

Third period: to declare or not to declare independence?

According to the Catalan government, more than 2.2 million people voted in the referendum. Among those who participated (around 43% of the registered voters), 90.18% voted "Yes," 7.83% voted "No" and 1.98% cast a blank vote.[37] As we have already seen in the previous section, the Spanish government refused to recognize the vote of 1 October 2017, and it reinforced the strategy adopted until that point, thus denying any kind of validity to the public consultation.

30 Mariano Rajoy (@marianorajoy), tweet of 01.10.2017, 8:47PM: https://twitter.com/marianorajoy/status/914562451223523329.
31 Mariano Rajoy (@marianorajoy), tweet of 01.10.2017, 9:20PM: https://twitter.com/marianorajoy/status/914570628493127681.
32 "La Guardia Civil incauta nueve millones de papeletas del referéndum en Bigues i Riells," ElPeriodico, 21.09.2017, available at: https://www.elperiodico.com/es/politica/20170920/12-detenidos-en-una-operacion-de-la-guardia-civil-contra-el-referendum-6297933.
33 *Ibidem.*
34 "Spain Hires Cruise Liner to House Police in Rebel Catalonia," Bloomberg, 21.09.2017, available at: https://www.bloomberg.com/news/articles/2017-09-21/spain-hires-cruise-liner-to-house-police-in-rebel-catalonia.
35 Raül Romeva i Rueda (@raulromeva), tweet of 01.10.2017, 10:15AM: https://twitter.com/raulromeva/status/914403368860254209.
36 Raül Romeva i Rueda (@raulromeva), tweet of 01.10.2017, 12:07PM: https://twitter.com/raulromeva/status/914431588825526273.
37 "El Govern trasllada els resultats definitius del referéndum de l'1 d'octubre al Parlament de Catalunya," Generalitat de Catalunya, 06.10.2017, available at: https://web.archive.org/web/20171006212613/http://www.govern.cat/pres_gov/govern/ca/monografics/303541/govern-trasllada-resultats-definitius-referendum-11-doctubre-parlament-catalunya.html.

The King of Spain, Felipe VI, immediately declared the illegality of the referendum, warning that "it is the responsibility of the legitimate state powers to ensure constitutional order" and that Catalan leaders' "irresponsible conduct could put at risk the economic and social stability of Catalonia and all of Spain."[38]

Even after the referendum, Rajoy continued to further "Europeanize" the debate on Catalonia. In an interview to *El País* on 8 October, for example, he argued that he encouraged "Europe to continue with what it's doing which is defending the unity of its nations, the enforcement of the law and the Constitutions of its member states." Rajoy also compared the Catalan government's attempts to subvert the Spanish legal order to those of populists like Farage and Le Pen "that challenges the supremacy of the law and respect for people's rights."[39] In other words, Rajoy re-framed the Catalan leaders' appeals to the "values of Europe," by which they meant democracy and self-determination, claiming that the real European value at stake was the rule of law. The socialist leader Pedro Sánchez too did not recognize the referendum, even though he invited Rajoy to resume dialogue with the Catalan government.[40] The leader of *Ciudadanos*, Albert Rivera, urged Rajoy to apply Article 155 of the Spanish Constitution, which allows the central government to impose direct rule in one of the regions if this "does not fulfil the obligations imposed upon it by the Constitution or other laws, or acts in a way that is seriously prejudicial to the general interest of Spain," to dissolve the Catalan parliament and call a snap election.[41]

Despite the central government's attitude, in the days immediately following the referendum Catalan leaders showed their intention to resist and to do not abandon the game, taking it to the "next level" – represented by a formal declaration of independence. On 3 October, Puigdemont announced that a declaration of independence would be presented during the parliamentary session that had to take place seven days later. On 10 October, the majority of the Catalan Regional Parliament approved a document that declared the constitution of the Catalan Republic as an independent state.[42] The declaration, however, was immediately suspended in view of facilitating the dialogue with the Spanish government. The ambiguous choice of declaring independence but suspending its effects was a

38 "Spain rejects mediation as Catalans plan to declare independence," NewStraitsTime, 05.10.2017, available at: https://www.nst.com.my/world/2017/10/287692/spain-rejects-mediation-catalans-plan-declare-independence.

39 "Spanish PM: 'Catalonia is Europe's battle'," El País, 08.10.2017, available at: https://elpais.com/elpais/2017/10/07/inenglish/1507389735_673588.html.

40 "COMUNICADO TRAS EL ENCUENTRO MANTENIDO ESTA TARDE ENTRE PEDRO SÁNCHEZ Y MARIANO RAJOY", 02.10.2017, available at: http://www.psoe.es/actualidad/noticias-actualidad/comunicado-tras-el-encuentro-mantenido-esta-tarde-entre-pedro-sanchez-y-mariano-rajoy/.

41 "Albert Rivera pide a Rajoy aplicar el artículo 155 en Cataluña para convocar elecciones," El Mundo, 02.10.2017, available at: https://www.elmundo.es/espana/2017/10/02/59d1f439468aeb860c8b458b.html.

42 "Catalan leader signs declaration document", EuroNews, 10.10.2017, available at: https://www.euronews.com/2017/10/10/catalan-leader-signs-declaration-document.

compromise reached within the Catalan government coalition, most notably between the hardcore independentists (the radical left CUP, which wanted a unilateral declaration) and the more moderate members (mostly from the PDECat, who still hoped to reach an agreement with Madrid and were uncertain about the consequence of openly breaking the rule of law). This move, however, showed the sharp contrasts emerging within the Catalan government, and further pushed the Spanish government to avoid any compromise.

On 27 October, in the absence of any sign of dialogue established between the two actors, a final resolution that declared the Catalan independence from Spain was officially passed by the Catalan parliament. A total of 70 of 135 MPs voted in favour of this resolution, 10 voted against and 2 cast a blank vote.[43] Fifty-three MPs from the opposition were not present during the vote, as a signal of protest after the declaration of unconstitutionality of the regional law establishing the referendum by the Tribunal Constitutional (Spanish Constitutional Court), on 17 October.[44] The European reaction is neatly summarized by the tweet of President of the European Council Tusk: "For EU nothing changes. Spain remains our only interlocutor. I hope the Spanish government favours force of argument, not argument of force."[45]

A few hours after the vote, the Spanish government obtained from the Senate the authorization to apply Article 155 of the Constitution. By means of this act, Spain's deputy prime minister Soraya Sáenz de Santamaría was appointed as acting president of Catalonia.[46] The Spanish government immediately dissolved the Catalan parliament and called a snap regional election for 21 December.[47] The imposition of the direct rule by the Spanish government was accepted peacefully by the Catalan parties and society, with no violent resistance or opposition. Puigdemont and some other ministers left Catalonia to escape from the charges issued against them by the Spanish judges.[48] As far as the game theorized in this chapter is concerned (see Figure 10.1), the declaration of independence was proclaimed but not enforced, either by the Catalan authorities or by the Catalan people. By accepting the imposition of direct rule by the Spanish government,

43 "Spain dissolves Catalan parliament and calls fresh elections," The Guardian, 28.10.2017, available at: https://www.theguardian.com/world/2017/oct/27/spanish-pm-mariano-rajoy-asks-senate-powers-dismiss-catalonia-president.

44 "El Parlament de Cataluña aprueba la resolución para declarar la independencia", ElPaìs, 27.10.2017, available at: https://elpais.com/ccaa/2017/10/27/catalunya/1509105810_557081.html.

45 Donald Tusk (@eucopresident), tweet of 27.10.2017, 4:10PM: https://twitter.com/eucopresident/status/923914819631271936.

46 *Ibidem.*

47 "Spain dissolves Catalan parliament and calls fresh elections", The Guardian, 28.10.2017, available at: https://www.theguardian.com/world/2017/oct/27/spanish-pm-mariano-rajoy-asks-senate-powers-dismiss-catalonia-president.

48 "Catalan leaders facing rebellion charges flee to Belgium", The Guardian, 30.10.2017, available at: https://www.theguardian.com/world/2017/oct/30/spanish-prosecutor-calls-for-rebellion-charges-against-catalan-leaders.

the pro independence coalition confirmed that no independence had *de facto* taken place.

Discussion and conclusions

In this chapter, we have argued that actions carried out in the period of interest by the Catalan and the Spanish governments could be modelled as "war of attrition" game. As the empirical section has shown, the model proposed was able to represent coherently the set of moves put in place. The Catalan government, being the weakest actor, has since the beginning signalled its willingness to not abandon the game. In this way, it hoped not only to motivate supporters of the Catalan cause, but to let the Spanish government know that the price of not allowing the referendum would have been very high. At the same time, the Catalan leaders' have tried to mobilize external support for the referendum. These efforts have been mainly directed towards other European countries and the EU institutions.

The Spanish government, however, has not remained passive, and it has used any weapon in its arsenal to offset the Catalan executive's actions. Rajoy has always been careful not to legitimize, under any conditions, a unilateral referendum. At the same time, he has never made proposals that could favour dialogue between the two parties. Taking advantage of its position, the Spanish government has secured support for Spain from virtually all EU member states and EU bodies as well, leaving Catalonia completely isolated. The resolute law enforcement carried out on the day of the referendum and the imposition of direct rule have certainly exacerbated the anti-Spanish feelings of pro-independence voters in Catalonia, but Rajoy has considered them necessary for showing that Catalan independence was not going to happen, and that, regardless of what they declared, secessionists were not willing to take the struggle to the extremes. From Rajoy's point of view, the reputational cost of the police actions has been worth paying.

More in general, the lack of external support for Catalan secession can be identified as the main cause of its failure. Once that threat had been neutralized, the Spanish government has felt itself legitimized to fight the referendum and its political consequences within the Spanish legal system. From this point of view, the game played in the 2015–2017 period has concluded with a clear winner, and a clear loser. The last move of the Catalan parliament, the declaration of independence, has been little more than a symbolic statement. No one in the Catalan society and public administration has enforced it. The supremacy of the Spanish law has been ultimately accepted. It is also worth noting that, since independence has never been embraced by a truly large majority of the Catalan voters, the Catalan government also lacked the *internal* support to further continue the game.

At the time of writing, it is difficult to say if this outcome is definite or not. The December 2017 election, which followed the imposition of direct rule, assigned again to pro-independence parties a majority of seats, but failed once again to give them a majority of votes. After Puigdemont' escape, the formation of a new government has been particularly complex. A sort of normalization of the political situation has been achieved with the election of Joaquim Torra as the new President of Catalonia. Currently, the region finds itself in a sort of limbo: the goal of independence is reiterated, more strongly than ever, by the parties governing Catalonia; but at the same time the new government has not pursued unilateral actions since it was sworn in. As the political figures who had the most prominent role in the (failed) referendum (Puigdemont, Junqueras, Romeva, Forn, Rovira, Forcadell) are either in prison or abroad, the tension remains high. While it is unlikely that we will observe an escalation like the one of 2017 any time soon, any solution for this conflict will require the gradual emergence of new political equilibria, at regional and national level.

References

Alesina, A. and Spolaore, E. (1997) 'On the number and size of nations', *The Quarterly Journal of Economics* 112(4): 1027–1056.

Bélanger, L., Duchesne, É. and Paquin, J. (2005) 'Foreign interventions and secessionist movements: the democratic factor', *Canadian Journal of Political Science/Revue canadienne de science politique* 38(2): 435–462.

Casella, A. and Feinstein, J. S. (2002) 'Public goods in trade: on the formation of markets and jurisdictions', *International Economic Review* 43(2): 437–462.

Closa, C. (2016) 'Secession from a member state and EU membership: the view from the union', *European Constitutional Law Review* 12(2): 240–264.

Closa, C. (ed.) (2017) *Secession from a Member State and Withdrawal from the European Union: Troubled Membership*. Cambridge, UK: Cambridge University Press.

Coggins, B. L. (2017) 'How do states respond to secession? The dynamics of state recognition', in D. Muro and E. Woertz (eds.). *Secession and Counter-Secession: An International Relations Perspective*. Barcelona, Spain: Barcelona Centre for International Affairs, pp. 27–30.

Coppieters, B. (2017) 'The EU's policies towards contested states', in D. Muro and E. Woertz (eds.). *Secession and Counter-Secession: An International Relations Perspective*. Barcelona, Spain: Barcelona Centre for International Affairs, pp. 37–44.

Crawford, B. (1996) 'Explaining defection from international cooperation: Germany's unilateral recognition of Croatia', *World Politics* 48(4): 482–521.

Cuadras-Morató, X. (2016) 'Introduction: Catalonia, a new state in Europe?', in X. Cuadras-Morató (ed.). *Catalonia: A New Independent State in Europe? A Debate on Secession within the European Union*. London; New York: Routledge, pp. 1–19.

Griffiths, R. D. (2017) 'Who counts? Why do governments deny secession in some cases but not others?', in D. Muro and E. Woertz (eds.). *Secession and Counter-Secession: An International Relations Perspective*. Barcelona, Spain: Barcelona Centre for International Affairs, pp. 79–84.

Guibernau, M. (2006) 'National identity, devolution and secession in Canada, Britain and Spain', *Nations and Nationalism* 12(1): 51–76.

Guinjoan, M. and Rodon, T. (2016) 'Catalonia at the crossroads: analysis of the increasing support for secession', in X. Cuadras-Morató (ed.). *Catalonia: A New Independent State in Europe? A Debate on Secession within the European Union*. London; New York: Routledge, pp. 20–61.

Hannum, H. (1998) 'The specter of secession: responding to claims for ethnic self-determination', *Foreign Affairs* 77(2): 13–18.

Heraclides, A. (1990) 'Secessionist minorities and external involvement', *International Organization* 44(3): 341–378.

Maynard Smith, J. (1974) 'The theory of games and the evolution of animal conflicts', *Journal of Theoretical Biology* 47(1): 209–221.

Mendelsohn, M. (2003) 'Rational choice and socio-psychological explanation for opinion on quebec sovereignty', *Canadian Journal of Political Science/Revue canadienne de science politique* 36(3): 511–537.

Moe, T. M. and Caldwell, M. (1994) 'The institutional foundations of democratic government: a comparison of presidential and parliamentary systems', *Journal of Institutional and Theoretical Economics (JITE)/Zeitschrift für die gesamte Staatswissenschaft* 150(1): 171–195.

Muñoz, J. and Tormos, R. (2015) 'Economic expectations and support for secession in Catalonia: between causality and rationalization', *European Political Science Review* 7(2): 315–341.

Pattie, C. and Johnston, R. (2017) 'Sticking to the Union? Nationalism, inequality and political disaffection and the geography of Scotland's 2014 independence referendum', *Regional & Federal Studies* 27(1): 83–96.

Prodi, R. (2004) Answer given on behalf of the Commission to written question P-0524/04 by Eluned Morgan (PSE), *Official Journal of the European Union* 2004/C 84 E/0492 of 3.4.2004, available at: https://eur-lex.europa.eu/legal-content/EN/ALL/?uri=uriserv:OJ.CE.2004.084.01.0421.02.ENG (accessed on 12 January 2019).

Riker, W. H. (1957) 'Events and situations', *The Journal of Philosophy* 54(3): 57–70.

Samuelson, W. and Zeckhauser, R. (1988) 'Status quo bias in decision making', *Journal of Risk and Uncertainty* 1(1): 7–59.

Woertz, E. (2017) 'Economic aspects of counter-secession strategies', in D. Muro and E. Woertz (eds.). *Secession and Counter-Secession: An International Relations Perspective*. Barcelona, Spain: Barcelona Centre for International Affairs, pp. 99–106.

Young, R. A. (1994) 'How do peaceful secessions happen?', *Canadian Journal of Political Science/Revue canadienne de science politique* 27(4): 773–792.

Part IV

Case studies

11 On Brexit and secession(s)

Nikos Skoutaris[1]

1. Introduction

Unlike breach, withdrawal from an international treaty is in principle a lawful act. Article 54 of the Vienna Convention on the Law of the Treaties allows a state to withdraw from a treaty either in conformity with the relevant provisions or by consent of all parties.[2] In that sense, Article 50 TEU that allows a Member State "to withdraw from the Union in accordance with its own constitutional requirements" could be seen as a *lex specialis* to the general international law rule. In fact, Helfer has convincingly shown that clauses authorizing denunciation and withdrawal from international conventions are far from uncommon (Helfer, 2005).

Having said that, the EU is also a "community of unlimited duration, having its own institutions, its own personality, its own legal capacity [and] real powers stemming from a limitation of sovereignty or transfer of powers from the [Member] States."[3] To the extent that Brexit marks the withdrawal of the UK from that community of law and the abrupt end to the symbiotic relationship of its legal order with the EU one, it is also a process that bears significant resemblance with secession.

At the same time, Brexit might become the catalyst for the secession of the two UK constituent nations that voted to remain: Scotland and Northern Ireland. With regard to the former, we should note that the Scottish parliament does not have the competence to organize an independence referendum without the consent of Westminster. Notwithstanding, the process that led to the 2014 referendum shows that a secession of Scotland from the rest of the UK could possibly happen in a consensual and democratic fashion.

On the other hand, the right of Northern Ireland to democratically secede from the UK is constitutionally guaranteed.[4] However, any discussion on signifi-

1 Associate Professor in EU law, UEA Law School. I would like to thank the editors of the volume and all the participants of the workshop on 'Discussing Secession: An Interdisciplinary Debate' (EUI, 12 March 2018) for the very constructive comments and suggestions. The usual disclaimer applies.

2 Vienna Convention on the Law of the Treaties, 23 May 1969, 1155 UNTS 331.

3 Case 6/64 Costa v ENEL [1964] ECR 585.

4 The people of the Irish Republic should also agree to this in a separate referendum.

cant changes to its constitutional position and the status of its land border with the Republic of Ireland and its sea boundary with the rest of the UK is destined to be fraught with animosity due to the turbulent past of the region. This is one of the reasons that the Northern Irish conundrum has become the equivalent of the Schleswig-Holstein question of the Brexit negotiations.

Despite the intractability of the problem, the EU and the UK government managed to provisionally agree on a solution to that Gordian knot in November 2018. The famous "backstop option" provided by the Protocol of Ireland/Northern Ireland of the draft UK Withdrawal Agreement, however, has been portrayed as a threat to the UK constitutional and territorial integrity. The leader of the DUP has gone as far as saying that it would lead to the de facto secession of the region from its metropolitan state and its annexation by the EU.[5]

All the aforementioned point to the fact that the relationship between the withdrawal of the UK from the EU and the phenomenon of secession does not limit itself to the similarities between the Article 50 TEU process and secessionist processes around the world. Because of the composite (Besselink, 2007; Claes, 2005) nature of the European constitution and the multi-level character of the European political landscape there is a possibility that Brexit will have a spillover effect on the constitutional status of the UK constituent nations that voted to remain and their relationship with the EU.

The present chapter aims at understanding the complex relationship between Brexit and secession by focusing on three aspects. First, it compares Article 50 TEU with constitutional provisions that allow for secession. Second, it explains the constitutional framework concerning the possible independence of Scotland and reunification of Ireland. Third, it discusses why a solution to the "Irish border" conundrum that would entail a much closer relationship of this region with the EU than the rest of the UK should be seen as a pragmatic solution that protects the fragile balance struck by the Good Friday Agreement rather than as an annexation of Northern Ireland to the EU. As such, the chapter is a testament to the intertwined nature of the European constitutional landscape[6] and the compound EU polity (Fabbrini, 2007) even in an area such as the one that deals with the withdrawal of a state from an international organization; an area where states are supposed to possess almost unfettered autonomy.

2. Brexit as a secession

UK's withdrawal from the EU will mark the first time that a Member State decides to put an abrupt end to the federalist "Sonderweg" of "an ever closer union." In a way, and although the EU is "under international law, precluded by its very nature from being considered a State"[7] Brexit and especially the Article 50 TEU

5 Available at https://www.rte.ie/news/2018/1013/1002900-brexit/.

6 See generally Ziller, 2005, at 452.

7 Opinion 2/13 On the EU's Accession to the ECHR ECLI:EU:C:2014:2454, para. 156.

procedure bear some resemblance to secessionist processes around the globe. In fact, Article 50 TEU is similar to constitutional clauses that regulate secession while the European Union (Withdrawal) Act 2018 secures the smooth transitioning between the old and the new legal regime as "continuance clauses" often do.

Article 50 TEU as a secession clause

As it is evident from other chapters of this volume, secession should not be understood as an absolute constitutional taboo. There are some constitutional orders that allow for a consensual and democratic process of partition. Take, for example, Article 39 of the Ethiopian constitution that provides "every nation, nationality or people in Ethiopia" with "the unrestricted right to self-determination up to secession."[8] Even the miniscule State of Liechtenstein allows individual municipalities to secede from the union according to Article 4 of its constitution.[9] Similarly, as we will see in the following section, the UK constitutional order allows the secession of one of its regions. Westminster has formally conceded that Northern Ireland can secede from the UK to join a united Ireland, if its people, and the people of the Irish Republic, voting separately, agree to this. *Mutatis mutandis* Article 50 TEU allows a Member State to break away from this 'community of unlimited duration' (Case 6/64 Costa v ENEL [1964] ECR 585).

Having said that, there are significant differences when one compares Article 50 TEU with those constitutional clauses that allow for secession. First of all, the right contained in the EU treaty is characterized by unilateralism in that it 'is totally independent of the will of the EU [and] the remaining Member States' (Closa, 2017b, at 193–194). In contrast, the Canadian Supreme Court, in its famous *Reference re Secession of Quebec*,[10] held that "a referendum unambiguously demonstrating the desire of a clear majority of Quebeckers to secede from Canada, would give rise to a reciprocal obligation of all parties of the Confederation to negotiate secession" (Mancini, 2012, at 497).

More importantly, it is unconditional in that "the exercise of the right to withdrawal is not subjected to any preliminary verification of conditions nor is it even conditional on the conclusion of the agreement foreseen in the provision" (Closa, 2017b, at 195). Article 50(1) TEU allows a Member State "to withdraw from the Union in accordance with its own constitutional requirements." Article 50(3) TEU foresees that the withdrawal can take place two years after the Member State has notified the EU of its intention to leave if no withdrawal agreement has been achieved by then.

This is in marked contrast with the majority of constitutional provisions that regulate secessions. They provide for conditions with regard to the organization of a referendum that could potentially lead to secession and/or foresee an *inter*

8 Available at http://www.africa.upenn.edu/Hornet/Ethiopian_Constitution.html.
9 Available at http://hrlibrary.umn.edu/research/liechtenstein-constitution.pdf.
10 *Reference re Secession of Quebec* [1998] 2 SCR 217.

parties agreement as an important step to finalize the process. For instance, a referendum for the reunification of Ireland can only be organized if "it appears likely to [the UK Secretary of State] that a majority of those voting would express a wish that Northern Ireland should cease to be part of the United Kingdom and form part of a united Ireland."[11] Equally, Article 113 of the Constitution of Saint Kitts and Nevis allows for the secession of Nevis Island following a process that is prescribed in a detailed manner in paragraph 2. In the case of Liechtenstein, secession can only be regulated by law or by treaty while the Ethiopian constitution[12] allows for it "when the division of assets is effected in a manner prescribed by law."[13]

The European Union (Withdrawal) Act 2018 as a "continuance clause"

Secessions mark the rupture with the old constitutional order and the creation of a new one. However, in order to achieve a smooth transition between the old order that is "dying" to the new one that is "born," certain constitutions opt for "continuance clauses" that allowed them to deal with the legal vacuums that could be created by the abrupt end of the old legal regime. For instance, Articles 4(1) of the Constitution of Jamaica and 188(1) of the Constitution of Cyprus provide for the continuation of the colonial laws until they were replaced by new laws adopted by the parliaments of the newly independent States. Douglas-Scott has noted the similarity of those clauses provided in constitutions of former colonies with the European Union (Withdrawal) Act 2018 (Douglas-Scott, 2016).

This legislative act received its royal assent on 26 June 2018. Its constitutional significance of that piece of legislation cannot be overstated. Section 1 repeals the European Communities Act 1972 which is considered one of the "constitutional statutes" of the UK.[14] Crucially, however, its purpose is to preserve and carry over into UK law the full body of EU law even after Brexit takes place as provided in sections 2, 3 and 4 of the Act.

The reason why a legislative act that was initially called "the Great Repeal Act" "copies and pastes" huge swathes of EU law in the legal order of a future third country is the following. Given the symbiotic relationship of the two legal orders for more than 40 years, there are thousands of directly applicable and directly effective pieces of EU law that would cease to apply to the UK after Brexit takes place. This would mean that legal vacuums would be created in a number of areas such as environmental law, consumer protection, workers' rights etc. In order to avoid such a situation, it was of utmost importance that the UK administration

11 Northern Ireland Act 1998, schedule 1.

12 Constitution of Liechtenstein, Art 4(2).

13 Constitution of Ethiopia, Art 39(4)(e).

14 In *Thoburn v Sunderland City Council* [2003] QB 151, Sir John Laws introduced the idea that the UK legal order recognizes a hierarchy of statutes by accepting the distinction between "ordinary statutes" and "constitutional statutes." The latter are immune from implied repeal.

and Westminster would find a way to bridge those gaps without clogging up the parliamentary timetable for years to come.

3. Brexit triggering secession(s)

What we saw in the previous section, are the similarities between Brexit and secession processes around the globe. However, Brexit marks a seismic change in the constitutional and territorial politics of the UK as well. For one, although 52% of voters who participated in the Brexit referendum voted to leave the EU, Scotland and Northern Ireland, two out of the four UK constituent nations, voted to remain.[15]

As a result, the following morning, the First Minister of Scotland, Nicola Sturgeon, made clear that she intended to "take all possible steps and explore all options to give effect to how people in Scotland voted – in other words, to secure [their] continuing place in the EU and in the single market in particular."[16] The reason being that "Scotland faces the prospect of being taken out of the EU against [its] will."[17] At the same time, Sinn Féin called for a referendum for the unification of Ireland and thus for Northern Ireland to remain in the EU.[18]

Unsurprisingly, the UK government has not been amenable to the idea of consenting to the organization of such referendums at least in the current political climate. Notwithstanding the politics, one has to ask whether those two regions possess the constitutional right to secede. This is an important question that could allow us to assess the EU prospects of those nations that voted to remain. In any case, the effect of the UK's withdrawal from the EU on the secessionist tendencies of those two constituent nations points to the intertwined nature of the European constitutional landscape and the EU polity.

The constitutional right of Scotland and Northern Ireland to become independent

The Scottish Parliament has had the power to enact primary legislation from the very beginning. Its powers are defined negatively. This means that, according to section 29 of Scotland Act 1998, it may legislate in areas that are not considered as "reserved" competences of Westminster. The latter are enlisted in Schedule 5 of Scotland Act 1998, which provides for a list of those "reserved matters" over which the Scottish Parliament does not have legislative authority. They include the constitution of which "the Union of the Kingdoms of Scotland and England"

15 In Scotland, 62% voted to remain in the EU, while 56% in Northern Ireland. In England, 53% voted to leave while 52.5% in Wales.

16 N Sturgeon's speech after the referendum result. Available at <stv.tv/news/politics/1358534-nicola-sturgeon-speech-in-full-after-eu-referendum-result/>.

17 *Ibid.*

18 Available at www.businesspost.ie/sinn-fein-seeks-irish-reunification-vote-as-britain-votes-for-brexit/.

is part. This means that "[a]s a matter of UK law, the Scottish Parliament cannot pass a declaration of independence" (Smith and Young, 2017). However, referendums are not listed as a reserved matter in Schedule 5. Therefore, there is a question to be made whether Holyrood can lawfully "hold a referendum about whether another constitutional institution should do so" (Smith and Young, 2017). To put it differently, it is rather unclear whether the Scottish Parliament can exercise the unreserved power to hold an advisory referendum for a reserved matter such as "the Union of the Kingdoms of Scotland and England."

This was precisely the topic of the constitutional debate that took place between academics and political elites in the aftermath of the landslide win of the Scottish National Party in the 2011 Scottish Parliament elections.[19] Central to that debate was the question whether an Act of the Scottish Parliament allowing the organization of an independence referendum would relate directly to the reserved matter of the constitution and thus it would be deemed *ultra vires.*

Notwithstanding the legal arguments,[20] the "two governments of Scotland" decided to resolve this important constitutional question with a political agreement.[21] The *Edinburgh Agreement*[22] underscores the flexible nature of the UK idiosyncratic constitution. According to it, David Cameron and Alex Salmond agreed to amend the text of Scotland Act 1998. In accordance with section 30 of the Act, an Order[23] was issued that introduced new section 29A. This new section explicitly conferred the power on Holyrood to organize an independence referendum by no later than 31 December 2014.

More importantly, for the purposes of the present chapter, on 28 March 2017, Holyrood passed a motion according to which there should be another independence referendum. Following that, Nicola Sturgeon asked Theresa May "to begin early discussions between our governments to agree an Order under section 30 of the Scotland Act 1998 that would enable a referendum to be legislated for by the Scottish Parliament."[24] By asking Whitehall to allow the organization of the referendum, the Scottish First Minister has implicitly accepted that a convention at a minimum or a legal obligation at a maximum has been created whereby Holyrood needs to seek the permission of the UK government. Therefore, it seems that the constitutional right of the Scottish legislature to organize another independence referendum is at least disputed. This is why the Scottish government tries to achieve a similar political arrangement to the one that led to the *Edinburgh Agreement.*

19 For an analysis of the debate, see McHarg et al., 2016; Armstrong, 2017, at 106).

20 For a view in favour of Holyrood's powers to organize such a referendum see Barber, 2012). *Contra* see for example Tomkins, 2012.

21 For an analysis of the legal nature of the *Edinburgh Agreement*, see Bell, 2012.

22 Available at http://www.number10.gov.uk/wp-content/uploads/2012/10/Agreement-final-for-signing.pdf.

23 The Scotland Act 1998 (Modification of Schedule 5) Order 2013.

24 Available at https://www.snp.org/nicola_sturgeon_s_section_30_letter_to_theresa_may.

Unlike the case of Scotland, "Westminster has formally conceded that Northern Ireland can secede from the United Kingdom to join a united Ireland, if its people, and the people of the Irish Republic, voting separately." Section 1 of the Northern Ireland Act 1998 is a rare example of a provision of a constitutional statute explicitly recognizing the right of secession of a region. In that sense, the organization of such a referendum faces less constitutional hurdles – at least from a UK constitutional law point of view. This does not mean that it is politically more feasible. In fact, according to Schedule 1 of the Northern Ireland Act, a referendum for the reunification of Ireland can only be organized if "it appears likely to [the UK Secretary of State] that a majority of those voting would express a wish that Northern Ireland should cease to be part of the United Kingdom and form part of a united Ireland." Recently, the Prime Minister's official spokesman told reporters in Westminster that "[i]t remains the Northern Ireland Secretary's view that the majority of the people of Northern Ireland continue to support the current political settlement and that the circumstances requiring a border poll are not satisfied" (Black, 2019). To this effect, one has to bear in mind that there does not seem to be an agreement among the Northern Irish political elites concerning the need to organize such a referendum and that the ethno-religious segment that would be more willing to support the reunification of Ireland i.e. the Republican one, is in the minority.

The EU law perspective

Now let us assume, for the purposes of the present chapter, that Whitehall and Holyrood reach a similar agreement to the one that led to the 2014 referendum and that the Scottish electorate votes in favour of independence in that second referendum. The next question we should address is what is the appropriate legal basis in order for Scotland to become an EU Member State.[25]

The official position of the Commission has been that Article 49 TEU is the appropriate legal route for the accession of an independent Scottish State:

> If part of the territory of a Member State would cease to be part of that State because it were to become a new independent state, the Treaties would no longer apply to that territory. In other words, a new independent state would, by the fact of its independence, become a third country with respect to the EU and the Treaties would no longer apply on its territory. [26]

Admittedly, the procedure under Article 49 TEU can be arduous and cumbersome. However, this has not been the only concern that made the Scottish government and a number of experts to argue in 2014 that a different legal basis was

25 For an analysis of that debate, see Closa, 2016; Closa, 2017a.

26 President JM Barroso's letter of 10.12.2012 to the House of Lords Economic Affairs Committee regarding the status of EU membership for Scotland in the event of independence.

applicable.[27] It was mainly the fact that, if Scotland followed that procedure, it would have found itself outside the EU between the time of its independence and the time of its accession to the EU. This could have been a significant time period during which "Scotland's laws, policies and regulatory structures could diverge sharply from the EU's" (Hughes, 2017).

Therefore, the Scottish government argued that the Scottish situation is *sui generis.*[28] It would have been the first time that a region would secede from an EU Member State by a consensual and lawful constitutional process. According to the Scottish position, Article 49 only regulates "conventional enlargement where the candidate country is seeking membership from outside the EU."[29] But Scotland is part of the EU since 1973. Therefore, the appropriate legal basis that could facilitate Scotland's transition to Union membership is Article 48 TEU, the generic provision on the amendment of the EU Treaties. In other words, the Scottish position was that the amendment of Article 52 TEU, which provides for the states to which the treaties apply and the relevant articles concerning the composition of the EU institutions would be, by and large, sufficient in order for Scotland to become an EU Member State after its independence.

Of course, it has been reported recently that an "indyref2" may not take place until after the next Holyrood election in 2021 (Macnab, 2018). This makes the use of Article 48 TEU for securing Scotland's continuing EU membership virtually impossible. Be that as it may, I would still argue that, in the current legal framework, Article 49 TEU is the appropriate legal basis to regulate the accession of a region that has seceded from a Member State.

"The choice of the legal basis for a [certain measure and/or action] may not depend simply on an institution's [or Member States'] conviction as to the objective pursued but must be based on objective factors... Those factors include in particular the aim and content of the" action.[30] So, as long as the objective pursued by this treaty amendment will be the accession of a new Member State, the EU Treaties provide for a *lex specialis* rule, i.e. Article 49 TEU. In other words, if the Treaty on European Union is interpreted in accordance with the ordinary meaning to be given to its terms, following the well-established rule of Article 31(1) of the Vienna Convention on the Law of the Treaties, it would be difficult to justify the use of the generic provision on the amendment of the Treaties (Article 48 TEU) when there is a special provision regulating the accession of new Member States (Article 49 TEU).

The counterargument is that it would not be the accession of a new Member State but rather a change in status of an entity that is already part of the EU. From a public international law perspective, this is a rather unconvincing argument. If

27 For the different views on this debate, http://verfassungsblog.de/category/focus/scotlands-eu-membership/.

28 See Scottish Government's blueprint on Scotland's Future, at 216-224. Available at www.gov.scot/resource/0043/00439021.pdf.

29 *Ibid*, 21.

30 *Commission v Council*, C-300/89, EU:C:1991:244.

Scotland secedes from the UK, it would be considered to be a newly independent country under public international law. It would have to apply to be admitted as the 194th member of the United Nations. In that sense, it would be a new European State that would also have to apply for EU membership under Article 49 TEU.

It is important to note that the EU Treaties, including Articles 48 and 49 TEU, do not make any distinction based on the process of the formation of the states with regard to their EU accession. If the EU and the Member States opted for Article 48 in order to regulate Scotland's EU accession, they would *de facto* distinguish between European States that have become independent from old Member States through a consensual procedure and the rest. Consequently, they would create a special procedure for the EU accession of the former, although this is not envisaged in the Treaties. Of course, the Member States as Masters of the Treaties could always amend the text in order to provide for such a distinction. But until that happens, Article 49 TEU seems like the more appropriate procedure, also because it allows for the same level of pre-accession scrutiny that all the candidate states have to be subjected to.

Concerning Northern Ireland, the situation again seems to be simpler from an EU law point of view. The secession of Northern Ireland will not mean the creation of a new (Member-)State. Instead, it will trigger the territorial expansion of an EU Member State – the Republic of Ireland – to which EU law already applies in accordance with Article 52 TEU. In a way, the reunification of Ireland could follow the precedent of the German reunification where the application of the *acquis* was extended to East Germany without an amendment of the primary legislation, as agreed in a special meeting of the European Council in Dublin on 28 April 1990.[31] The difference is that, in the case of Germany, the *acquis* did not apply at all in the East before the reunification, something that is very different from the situation in Northern Ireland.

However, former Taoiseach Enda Kenny has asked for a special provision in any Brexit deal to allow Northern Ireland to rejoin the EU should it be united with the Republic.[32] He did so, notwithstanding the fact that a special deal for Northern Ireland is the declared goal of the UK government.[33] So, the question is what would such a provision look like.

31 For an analysis of the community law implications of the German reunification see generally Tomuschat, 1990; Timmermans, 1990.

32 Available at https://www.theguardian.com/politics/2017/feb/23/irish-leader-enda-kenny-calls-for-united-ireland-provision-in-brexit-deal.

33 The European Council agreed the following statement in the minutes to the agreement on the Brexit negotiating guidelines on 29 April 2017: "The European Council acknowledges that the Good Friday Agreement expressly provides for an agreed mechanism whereby a united Ireland may be brought about through peaceful and democratic means; and, in this regard, the European Council acknowledges that, in accordance with international law, the entire territory of such a united Ireland would thus be part of the European Union." European Council, *Minutes of Special Meeting of the European Council (Art.50) Held on 29 April 2017* (23 June 2017). Available at http://data.consilium.europa.eu/doc/document/xT-20010–2017-INIT/en/pdf.

There are few EU law provisions that regulate the (re)unification of (Member-) States. The closest example is Article 4 of Protocol No 10 on Cyprus of the Act of Accession 2003. Protocol No 10 provides the terms for the application of EU law in Cyprus given that the island had not been unified at the moment it joined the EU. In particular, it provides for the suspension of the application of the *acquis* in Northern Cyprus, a suspension which shall be lifted in the event of a solution.[34] If such a solution occurs in the future, Article 4 provides for a simplified procedure that enables the union to accommodate the terms of the reunification plan. In particular, Article 4 allows the EU, by a unanimous Council Decision at a future date and in the event of reunification, to alter the terms of Cyprus' EU accession that are contained in the Act of Accession 2003. In other words, it allows the council to amend primary law (i.e. Act of Accession 2003) with a unanimous decision.

To the extent that the "Brexit" Agreement will be part of primary law, a similar provision regulating the reunification of Ireland could have been included to assist the smooth transitioning of Northern Ireland back to the EU should the people in both sides of the Irish border so decide in simultaneous democratic referendums. Given the fraught with tension negotiating environment around Northern Ireland, it is rather unsurprising that such provision was not included in the final draft of the Withdrawal Agreement.

Still, a number of UK politicians have expressed their concerns over the effect of backstop on the constitutional integrity of the UK and few have gone as far as saying that that arrangement would trigger the annexation of the region to the EU. Statements like those highlight the third and final aspect of the complex relationship between Brexit and the concept of secession. Could a differentiated and more integrated relationship of Northern Ireland with the EU mean its de facto secession from its metropolitan state? The paper argues that such positions are grossly misrepresenting the effect of backstop. Having said that, that debate underlines the composite nature of the European constitution where the decision of a state to withdraw from the EU has a spillover effect on its territorial politics.

4. Brexit leading to annexation

Brexit as a threat to the Good Friday Agreement

Twenty years ago, the Good Friday/Belfast Agreement (GFA hereafter)[35] put an end to the sectarian violence that had plagued Northern Ireland for decades. The GFA highlighted that Northern Ireland is an integral part of the UK but established its constitutionally recognized right to secede as already mentioned. Such unique constitutional status was "accompanied by unusual multi-level governance: regional, north/south and British/Irish" (Hayward, 2017).

34 Art 1 of Protocol No 10 on Cyprus of the Act of Accession 2003 [2003] OJ L 236/955.
35 Available at https://www.gov.uk/government/publications/the-belfast-agreement.

Although the text of the GFA does not include many references to the EU,[36] Elizabeth Meehan has explained that EU membership has facilitated the design of the GFA (Meehan, 2000): "The sharing of sovereignty within the EU has spilled over into some sharing of sovereignty over Northern Ireland" (Douglas-Scott, 2015, at 9). In a way, the GFA "was premised on the assumption of common policies and interests across a wide range of policy areas" (Phinnemore and Hayward, 2017, at 7), which the EU membership of both the UK and the Republic of Ireland had secured. In that sense, Brexit puts all three strands of the GFA at risk of deep fissures.[37] It challenges "the narrative of a shared and interdependent Northern Ireland" (Farry and Eastwood, 2017) and impedes the sharing of sovereignty across the region, since the UK and (by extension) Northern Ireland will no longer be part of the EU. By definition, this situation will change the balance of powers between the two guarantors: the UK and the Republic of Ireland. At the same time, the EU framework will no longer be providing its much-needed paradigm of power-sharing between the two main communities. One particular danger is that at least part of the segmented post-conflict society of Northern Ireland will not welcome the strengthening of more UK-centric notions of sovereignty that Brexit might lead to.

Finally, the creation of a customs border – at a minimum – will pose a significant threat to the island of Ireland as a single economic area. In particular, such a development would not only require a massive investment by Ireland, as the EU Member State required to enforce the EU external customs border with the UK at this point, but also bring back painful memories of the times of conflict on the island, when the trade border was not only (ab)used for intimidation through its harsh enforcement, but also had a real impact on livelihoods (Schiek, 2018, at 6).

John Doyle and Eileen Connolly have summed up the threat that Brexit poses to the GFA. According to the authors, the withdrawal process from the EU "has the potential to destabilise the idea of incremental progress embodied in the Good Friday Agreement. The potential also exists for increased instability to be deepened by the worsening economic situation for Northern Ireland in a post-Brexit world" (Doyle & Connolly, 2017).

36 The text of the GFA has three sets of references to the EU. The first aims to ensure "effective coordination and input by Ministers [from the Northern Ireland Executive] to national [UK] policy-making, including on EU issues" (Strand One, para. 32). A second set relates to the work of the North South Ministerial Council (Strand Two, para. 17; Strand Three, paras 5 and 31). The third set underlines the need for the Irish and UK governments "to develop still further the unique relationship between their peoples and the close co-operation between their countries as friendly neighbours and as partners in the European Union" (British-Irish Agreement, Preamble).

37 The Joint Report recognizes that "the United Kingdom's withdrawal from the European Union presents a significant and unique challenge in relation to the island of Ireland." Joint Report from the negotiators of the EU and the UK government on progress during phase 1 of negotiations under Article 50 TEU on the United Kingdom's orderly withdrawal from the EU (hereafter Joint Report), at para. 42. Available at https://ec.europa.eu/commission/sites/beta-political/files/joint_report.pdf.

This is why the EU has recognized that "the unique circumstances and challenges on the island of Ireland will require flexible and imaginative solutions."[38]

Politicians on both sides of the Irish Sea have repeatedly underlined the importance of the "Northern Irish question" in the context of the Brexit negotiations.[39] In her letter to President of the European Council Donald Tusk with which she triggered Article 50 TEU, the then UK Prime Minister Theresa May expressed her intention "to avoid a return to a hard border" as well.[40] This position was broadly in line with the post-referendum letter she received from the then First Minister and the Deputy First Minister of Northern Ireland in which the two figures highlighted the need to ensure that the Irish border does not become an impediment to the movement of goods, services and capital.[41]

If the UK had decided to remain in the single market and the EU customs union after Brexit, then the vast majority of the challenges Brexit raises with regard to Northern Ireland would have been effectively dealt with. In her Lancaster House speech, however, former Prime Minister May clarified that the UK's aim is to leave both the single market and the EU customs union.[42] She repeated this message in her Florence speech[43] and her Mansion House speech.[44] The proposal regarding the Irish border that the UK government released reaffirms this position vis-à-vis Northern Ireland. It clarifies that the region will fall outside the single market and the EU customs union.[45] This means that – at a minimum – a customs border will need to be established on the territory of the island.

The Backstop(s)

The decision of the UK government to leave the single market and the customs union raises unique and complex legal and practical issues with regard to the Irish border, many of which are linked to the GFA. These issues include the question of the territorial border; the threat to the island of Ireland as a single economic area; the rights of the Irish passport holders in the North; practical questions

38 See EU Negotiating Directives, 22 May 2017, at para. 14. Available at http://www.consilium.europa.eu/en/press/press-releases/2017/05/22-brexit-negotiating-directives/.

39 See for instance 'L. Varadkar Warns "Clock Is Ticking" on Brexit Talks,' BBC News. Available at http://www.bbc.co.uk/news/uk-northern-ireland-40819687; Kenny, 2016.

40 Available at http://www.independent.co.uk/news/uk/politics/article-50-letter-read-full-brexit-theresa-may-takes-uk-out-of-eu-statement-a7655566.html .

41 Available at https://www.executiveoffice-ni.gov.uk/sites/default/files/publications/execoffice/Letter%20to%20PM%20from%20FM%20%26%20dFM.pdf.

42 Available at http://www.telegraph.co.uk/news/2017/01/17/theresa-mays-brexit-speech-full/.

43 Available at https://www.gov.uk/government/speeches/pms-florence-speech-a-new-era-of-cooperation-and-partnership-between-the-uk-and-the-eu,.

44 Available at https://www.gov.uk/government/speeches/pm-speech-on-our-future-economic-partnership-with-the-european-union.

45 UK Government Position Paper, 'Northern Ireland and Ireland'. Available at https://www.gov.uk/government/uploads/system/uploads/attachment_data/file/638135/6.3703_DEXEU_Northern_Ireland_and_Ireland_INTERACTIVE.pdf.

that are directly related to the thousands of people who cross the border every day to work and have access to childcare and healthcare, among other activities. Therefore, in a way, the UK and the EU have been trying to find the balance between two seemingly irreconcilable goals: leaving the single market and the customs union without returning to a hard border on the island of Ireland.

The December 2017 Joint Report has provided for a pathway that could lift that gridlock. According to the report, the UK remains committed to protecting North–South cooperation and to its guarantee of avoiding a hard border. Any future arrangements must be compatible with these overarching requirements. The United Kingdom's intention is to achieve these objectives through the overall EU–UK relationship. Should this not be possible, the UK will propose specific solutions to address the unique circumstances of the island of Ireland. In the absence of agreed solutions, UK will maintain full alignment with those rules of the internal market and the customs union which, now or in the future, support North–South cooperation, the all-island economy and the protection of the 1998 Agreement.[46]

In other words, the overall aim of the negotiations would be to address the challenge of the Irish border through the overall EU–UK relationship. If that proves impossible, then there is the possibility for specific solutions being applied to Northern Ireland. Should there not be an agreement on those specific technological solutions, then Northern Ireland at a minimum (or the UK as a whole) should remain aligned to the single market and the EU customs union.

Indeed, that third backstop option was legally codified in a Protocol on Ireland/Northern Ireland contained in the final version of the Withdrawal Agreement.[47] Barring a deal on free trade that secures a frictionless border, the UK as a whole will remain in a "bare bones" customs union with the EU; while Northern Ireland will additionally remain aligned to the single market rules necessary to maintain free movement of goods across the Irish border.

This final draft marks a significant amendment to the initial proposal of the EU published on 28 February 2018.[48] According to it, a common regulatory area comprising the EU and Northern Ireland would have been established and the region would remain as part of the EU customs territory.[49] Theresa May vehemently rejected the plan[50] noting that "no UK prime minister could agree to it" (Staunton, 2018).

46 Joint Report, at para. 49.

47 Available at https://ec.europa.eu/commission/sites/beta-political/files/draft_withdrawal_agreement_0.pdf.

48 "Draft Agreement on the Withdrawal of the United Kingdom of Great Britain and Northern Ireland from the European Union and the European Atomic Energy Community" (hereafter Draft UK Withdrawal Agreement), Protocol on Ireland/Northern Ireland. Available at https://ec.europa.eu/commission/sites/beta-political/files/draft_agreement_coloured.pdf.

49 *Ibid.*, Arts 3 and 4.

50 Available at http://www.bbc.co.uk/news/uk-politics-43224785.

In fact, the latest amended version of the Protocol on Ireland/Northern Ireland accepted the basic UK demand for a UK-wide backstop solution. Such request was officially revealed in June 2018 when the UK government published their counterproposal for a backstop arrangement to avoid a hard border on the island of Ireland.[51] The biggest difference between the two backstop proposals was that the UK one would apply to the whole country and not just to Northern Ireland. According to it, the entire territory of the UK and the Channel Islands would remain part of the customs territory of the EU even after the end of the transition period in December 2020. Such arrangement respected the promise of the UK government "to ensure that no new regulatory barriers [will] develop between Northern Ireland" and the rest of the UK.[52] More importantly, it eased the concerns of DUP whose leader had said that she would withdraw her support to Theresa May's government "if Northern Ireland was treated differently from the rest of the UK" after Brexit (Carswell, 2018).

Despite the significant amendments to the backstop that were introduced following the UK demands, the Prime Minister and the DUP continued expressing their concerns over the effect of the backstop on the "constitutional integrity" of the UK.[53] Some UK politicians have gone as far as stating that the backstop is an "outrageous attempt to revert to the annexation of Northern Ireland" (Boffey and Elgot, 2018). However, as we will see in the following section, to argue for Northern Ireland that maintaining regulatory equivalence with the EU would threaten the UK's constitutional integrity is a gross and needless overstatement.

A threat to constitutional integrity?

Notwithstanding whether the backstop is politically acceptable to the UK government, it should be noted that from a legal point of view such a solution would not be unprecedented. Within the EU legal order, there are a number of cases where different parts of a Member State have different relationships with the EU.

Indeed, in many Member States, there are special territories such as the overseas territories and the outmost regions[54] which for either historical, geographical or political reasons have differing relationships with their national governments – and consequently also the EU – than the rest of the Member State's territory. The sovereignty of the respective metropolitan state over a given area that enjoys such a differentiated arrangement has never been challenged. To put it simply, the fact that EU law does not apply in the same way to the French Overseas Territories as it does to the French mainland, does not in any way question France's sovereignty

51 Available at https://www.gov.uk/government/publications/technical-note-on-temporary-customs-arrangement.

52 Joint Report, para. 50.

53 See for instance https://hansard.parliament.uk/commons/2019-01-29/debates/BB8A5769-12B4-4D0E-9B4E-158F89F9FCDE/EuropeanUnion(Withdrawal)Act2018.

54 Art 355 TFEU.

over those territories. Instead, those arrangements aim at accommodating specific historical and political conditions present in those regions.

The UK itself has made extensive use of the flexibility that territorial differentiation within the union legal order allows. Gibraltar, the Channel Islands and a number of other overseas territories have a differentiated relationship with the EU. If such differentiated membership to the EU has not undermined the constitutional relationship of those territories with the UK, why would a differentiated Brexit threaten the UK's constitutional integrity?

The status that the protocol on Northern Ireland provides for that region should not be understood as undermining the UK constitutional integrity. Because of the Belfast/Good Friday Agreement, Northern Ireland already enjoys a unique constitutional status. A differentiated Brexit should be viewed as a site-specific arrangement that respects and protects a system of internal constitutional differentiation that already exists. It is a pragmatic solution to the specific circumstances of Northern Ireland rather than a staging post towards a united Ireland or an annexation of the region to the EU.

Contrary to conventional wisdom, such status would not even be unique. The UK has accepted the principle of differentiated Brexit in the case of the UK Sovereign Base Areas in Cyprus.[55] In order to honour their international legal obligations under the Treaty of Establishment, the UK in a Special Protocol to the Withdrawal Agreement has accepted that those areas will remain within the EU customs territory even after Brexit takes place.[56] This is not to suggest that the historical and political contexts of the UK Sovereign Base Areas bear any similarity to those of Northern Ireland. However, a similar argument could be constructed *mutatis mutandis* with regard to a differentiated arrangement for Northern Ireland as a protection to the Good Friday Agreement in order to "detoxify" the backstop.

Arguably, all the aforementioned cases are small territorial exceptions because of certain historical and political circumstances or even insularity. In addition, in all these cases, the metropolitan state fully participates in the political and constitutional life of the EU – something that would not apply to the case of the UK in the future. More importantly, in all those cases, the relevant regions have opted out from areas of EU law, while Northern Ireland would opt in to the EU legal order in case it wants to remain within the EU without seceding from the UK. Still, it is important to highlight the fact that territorial differentiation is an important characteristic of the EU legal order that respects and accommodates rather than challenges the constitutional relationships of the respective regions with their metropolitan states. In fact, those differentiated arrangements respond to specific needs that the constitutional status of these areas has created and do not in any way question the sovereignty of the metropolitan state. In that sense, the backstop as proposed by the EU should be understood as a pragmatic solution to the specific circumstances of Northern Ireland rather than as a staging post towards a united Ireland.

55 For an analysis see Hadjigeorgiou, Skoutaris, 2019.

56 UK's EU Withdrawal Agreement, Protocol on Sovereign Base Areas, Art 2.

5. Conclusion

The chapter has highlighted the complex relationship between Brexit and secession. The Article 50 TEU process bears some similarity to secessionist constitutional processes around the globe, while the European Union (Withdrawal) Act 2018 aims at effectively dealing with similar problems that the continuance clauses try to solve. At the same time, the UK's withdrawal from the EU could have a domino effect on its territorial constitution. It may trigger the secession of two UK constituent nations and lead to their "re-Europeanisation." But even if the reunification of Ireland does not take place, the solution that the Withdrawal Agreement has adopted to deal with the Irish border conundrum has been accused of leading to the "annexation" of Northern Ireland to the EU. All the aforementioned could be seen as a testament to the intertwined character of the European constitutional and political landscape where the decision of a sovereign state to leave an international organization has ripple effects on its internal constitutional architecture.

At the time that this chapter was authored, the UK government was engaging in a massive effort to convince the EU-27 to accept legally binding amendments to the backstop. Across the Hadrian's Wall, there was uncertainty over the constitutional future of Scotland in the UK while in the other side of the Irish Sea, the discussions on a possible border poll were intensifying. At this precise moment, it seems that it will take a number of years for us to be able to fully appreciate Brexit's relationship with secession and more importantly its seismic effect on the UK constitutional order.

References

Kenneth A. Armstrong, 'The reach and resources of European law in the Scottish independence referendum' in Closa Carlos (ed.), *Secession from a Member State and Withdrawal from the European Union*, CUP, Cambridge, 2017, 106–133.

Nick Barber, 'Scottish independence and the role of the United Kingdom', *UK Constitutional Law Blog*, 11 January 2012. Available at: https://ukconstitutionallaw.org/2012/01/11/nick-barber-scottish-independence-and-the-role-of-the-united-kingdom/.

Christine Bell, 'The legal status of the Edinburgh agreement', *Scottish Constitutional Futures Forum*, 5 November 2012. Available at: www.scottishconstitutionalfutures.org/OpinionandAnalysis/ViewBlogPost/tabid/1767/articleType/ArticleView/articleId/431/Christine-Bell-The-Legal-Status-of-the-Edinburgh-Agreement.aspx.

Leonard Besselink, *A Composite European Constitution/Een Samengestelde Europese Constitutie*, Europa Law Publishing, Groningen, 2007.

Rebecca Black, 'Sinn Fein's border poll call rejected out of hand by London', *Belfast Telegraph*, 7 February 2019. Available at: https://www.belfasttelegraph.co.uk/news/northern-ireland/sinn-feins-border-poll-call-rejected-out-of-hand-by-london-37791141.html.

Daniel Boffey, Jessica Elgot, 'Barnier criticises May's UK-wide Brexit backstop plan', *The Guardian*, 8 June 2018.

Simon Carswell, 'DUP would not back May if NI treated differently post-Brexit', *The Irish Times*, 4 June 2018.

Monica Claes, *The National Courts' Mandate in the European Constitution*, Hart Publishing, Oxford & Portland, 2005.

Carlos Closa, 'Secession from a member state and EU membership: the view from the union', *European Constitutional Law Review*, 12(2): 2016, 240–264.

Carlos Closa, 'Changing EU internal borders through democratic means', *Journal of European Integration*, 39(5): 2017a, 515–528.

Carlos Closa, 'Interpreting article 50: exit, voice and… what about loyalty?', in Closa Carlos (ed.), *Secession from a Member State and Withdrawal from the European Union*, CUP, Cambridge, 2017b, 187–214.

Sionaidh Douglas-Scott, 'A UK exit from the EU: the end of the United Kingdom or a new constitutional dawn?', *Cambridge Journal of International and Comparative Law*, 2015, Available at: http://papers.ssrn.com/sol3/papers.cfm?abstract_id=2574405.

Sionnaidh Douglas-Scott, 'The 'Great Repeal Bill': constitutional chaos and constitutional crisis?', *UK Constitutional Law Blog*, 10 October 2016. Available at: https://ukconstitutionallaw.org/2016/10/10/sionaidh-douglas-scott-the-great-repeal-bill-constitutional-chaos-and-constitutional-crisis/.

John Doyle, Eileen Connolly, 'Brexit and the future of Northern Ireland', DCU Brexit Research & Policy Institute Working Paper 1/2017.

Sergio Fabbrini, *Compound Democracies: Why the United States and Europe Are Becoming Similar*, OUP, Oxford, 2007.

Stephen Farry, Sorcha Eastwood, 'How to underpin a special deal for Northern Ireland', *UK in a Changing Europe*, 31 October 2017. Available at: http://ukandeu.ac.uk/how-to-underpin-a-special-deal-for-northern-ireland/.

Nasia Hadjigeorgiou, Nikos Skoutaris, 'The Status of the SBAs following Brexit', PRIO Cyprus Centre Occasional Paper, 2019.

Katy Hayward, 'Specific solutions' & 'distinct arrangements': more of the same for post-Brexit NI?', *Slugger O' Toole*, 12 December 2017. Available at: https://sluggerotoole.com/2017/12/11/specific-solutions-distinct-arrangements-more-of-the-same-for-post-brexit-ni/.

Laurence R Helfer, 'Exiting treaties', *Virginia Law Review*, 91: 2005, 1579–1648.

Kirsty Hughes, 'Brexit transition, Scotland and independence: has a new route opened up?', *SCER Blog*, 28 July 2017. Available at: https://www.scer.scot/database/ident-3193.

Enda Kenny, 'Irish Times Brexit Summit keynote address', Merrionstreet.ie, 7 November 2016. Available at: https://merrionstreet.ie/MerrionStreet/en/News-Room/Speeches/Irish_Times_Brexit_Summit_-_Keynote_address_by_the_Taoiseach.html.

Scott Macnab, 'Nicola Sturgeon says independence referendum could come after Holyrood election', *The Scotsman*, 20 November 2018.

Susanna Mancini, 'Secession and self-determination' in Rosenfeld Michel & Sajó Andras (eds.), *The Oxford Handbook of Comparative Constitutional Law*, OUP, Oxford, UK, 2012, 481–500.

Aileen McHarg, Tom Mullen, Alan Page, Neil Walker (eds.), *The Scottish Independence Referendum: Constitutional and Political Implications*, OUP, Oxford, UK, 2016.

Elizabeth Meehan, 'Britain's Irish question: Britain's European question? British-Irish relations in the context of European Union and the Belfast agreement', *Review of International Studies*, 26(1): 2000, 83–97.

David Phinnemore, Katy Hayward, 'UK withdrawal ("Brexit") and the good friday agreement', *Study for the AFCO Committee*, 2017. Available at: http://www.europarl.europa.eu/RegData/etudes/STUD/2017/596826/IPOL_STU(2017)596826_EN.pdf.

Dagmar Schiek, 'The Island of Ireland and "Brexit" – A legal-political critique of the draft withdrawal agreement', TREUP Occasional Paper, 22 March 2018. Available at: http://qpol.qub.ac.uk/island-of-ireland-brexit-draft-withdrawal-agreement/.

Ewan Smith, Alison Young, 'That's how it worked in 2014, and how it would have to work again', *UK Constitutional Law Blog*, 15 March 2017. Available at: https://ukconstitutionallaw.org/2017/03/15/ewan-smith-and-alison-young-thats-how-it-worked-in-2014-and-how-it-would-have-to-work-again/.

Denis Staunton, 'Theresa May rejects draft Brexit withdrawal agreement', *The Irish Times*, 28 February 2018.

Christiaan WA Timmermans, 'German unification and community law', *Common Market Law Review*, 27(3): 1990, 437–449.

Adam Tomkins, 'The Scottish parliament and the independence referendum', *UK Constitutional Law Association*, 12 January 2012. Available at: https://ukconstitutionallaw.org/2012/01/12/adam-tomkins-the-scottish-parliament-and-the-independence-referendum/.

Christian Tomuschat, 'A United Germany within the European community', *Common Market Law Review*, 27(3): 1990, 415–436.

Jacques Ziller, 'National constitutional concepts in the new constitution for Europe', *European Constitutional Law Review*, 1(247): 2005, 452–480.

12 An attempt to disentangle the Crimean impasse

Luigi Crema[1]

1. Introduction: history does matter

When the disruptive wave of the Golden Horde captained by Genghis Khan withdrew, back from the borders of Europe towards the belly of Asia, many Tatar principalities emerged on the drying sands. Among these was the Khanate of Crimea, which occupied an area more or less covering the Crimean Peninsula and the lands surrounding the Azov Sea, corresponding to what today are the territory of Southern Ukraine and the Russian region along the Black Sea.

Two centuries later, in 1475, the Khanate was militarily defeated by the Ottomans, and became a vassal of the Sublime Porte (Kizilov, 2016, at 53).[2] Three centuries later, in 1783, when the tide of the Ottoman Empire receded, as well, bringing to light the "Eastern Question" (Lyon Macfie, 1996), Crimea was annexed (for the first time) by the Czarist Empire, in the early days of what Arthur Conolly called "the Great Game" (Hopkirk, 1992). The roots of multicultural Crimea can be found in this age, when layers of different ethnicities, cultures and rulers overlapped in the region and continued to do so until now, notwithstanding the adverse forces of repression.

In 1853, this small, jagged and often-troubled peninsula reluctantly stepped into the centre of European history. For three years, Ottoman, French, Savoy and UK troops, driven by a dispute over who held the rights to manage sites in the Holy Land, fought against Russia, and obtained a victory which would have many historical consequences.[3] It was an extremely bloody war, the same that was witnessed and narrated by a young Lev Tolstoy (1855),[4] and it fuelled strong anti-Russian sentiment in Europe.

1 Senior Researcher (Rtd-B) at the Università degli Studi, Milan.

2 Further historical references can be found in Kent (2016).

3 For the first time since the Napoleonic conflicts, Russia lost a war; and for the first time, Savoy was admitted to a peace conference, where arguments in support of unifying the Italian peninsula could be exposed; (Figes, 2011).

4 Polomochnykh (2014) describes the enthusiasm of a young person for the war, and then his dismay before the extremely violent conflict, which he witnessed, eventually developing into the pacifism that permeates his masterpiece *War and Peace*.

Once again, in the last years, history knocked at Crimea's door, and, like in the nineteenth century, put a strain on the relationship between Europe and Russia. The confrontation between Russia and Ukraine, and between the two souls of Ukraine, brings to mind one of the opening pages of Samuel Hungtington's *The Clash of Civilizations*. The book became well known and widely celebrated in the wake of the 2001 attack on the World Trade Center in New York, because of the "fault lines" between Islam and the rest (Hungtington, 1996, at 28),[5] but the example he chose to illustrate his international relations theory in the first pages of the book had to do with Ukraine.

> A statist paradigm, for instance, leads John Mearsheimer to predict that "the situation between Ukraine and Russia is ripe for the outbreak of security competition between them." A civilizational approach, on the other hand, emphasizes the close cultural, personal, and historical links between Russia and Ukraine and the intermingling of Russians and Ukrainians in both countries… […] While a statist approach highlights the possibility of a Russian-Ukrainian war, a civilizational approach minimizes that and instead highlights the possibility of Ukraine splitting in half… (Hungtington, 1996, at 28 and 37)

This was both prophetic and wrong, given that Ukraine faces both internal strife and a conflict with Russia, which has already occupied and annexed a piece of Ukraine and is still involved in its civil war. We can say today that Huntington had a point – and Mearsheimer did too.

However, law usually tries to step back from history and concepts such as "civilization" in order to affirm principles and legality. Especially when historical facts are complicated and tend to heat up the emotional intensity of a situation, law tends to step in as a cooling factor, detached from the tensions in play. History cannot be entirely ignored – at least, it cannot be ignored by those who live in the territories touched by it – and in the case of Crimea, it is central for those who study it, as well.

This chapter will focus on the Crimean issue between Ukraine and Russia and, in particular, on the contradictory elements it entails. On the one hand, it played out in violation of one of the most important – if not, *the* most important – rules of international law, the prohibition of the use of force for conquering a territory. It is clear that Russia interfered in Crimean affairs, and that this interference involved the use of force, prohibited under international law, albeit without bloodshed. On the other hand, Crimea became Russian without a single shot being fired, and following several democratic, if opaque, steps.

The purpose of this chapter is to ask what we can make of manifestations of political will in a context where the use of force is in play. In order to do so,

5 "In this new world the most pervasive, important, and dangerous conflicts will [be] between peoples belonging to different cultural entities."

this chapter will first go through some recent events that are often invoked in the narrative in favour of the Russian annexation (Section 2). Then Section 3 will highlight the events surrounding the 2014 occupation and annexation (or reunification, depending on the narrative) of Crimea. Section 4 will highlight the importance of the prohibition of annexation in contemporary international law. Finally, Sections 5 and 6 will reflect on the reactions of the international community and whether it is possible to separate the democratic processes from Russian occupation.

2. 1954: an authoritative, and not democratic, transfer

A century after the bloody Crimean war, in 1954, the histories of Russia and Crimea diverged. The Soviet Union Supreme Soviet, under the leadership of Nikita Khrushchev, decided to transfer Crimea from the Russian Soviet Federative Socialist Republic to the Ukrainian Soviet Socialist Republic on 19 February 1954. This operation was far from democratic: Gwendolyn Sasse, in particular, stresses both the lack of legal legitimacy of this transfer and the poor (totally absent) democratic process it involved (Sasse, 2007, at 107–126; also Kramer, 2014).

Concerning the first point, she observes that "[t]he formality of the transfer is underscored by a lack of details on the motives," and that there were "slight inconsistencies" between legal decisions regarding that relocation (Sasse, 2007, at 107). The process of transferring Crimea from Russia to Ukraine in 1954 was, therefore, opaque, and seems to have been enacted by following the rule of authority, rather than the rule of law.

Not only was the legal framework of the transfer weak, but there was also a notable lack of democratic involvement. Sasse points out that the Supreme Soviet implemented its decision "from above," while making it seem to happen "from below":

> representatives of both the Crimean oblast and its city councils (including the head of the Sevastopol city council) did not speak to the motion. Even if they had spoken, it is unlikely that they would have diverged from the official line. Their presence may be seen as part of the stage managing of a demand "from below" for the transfer. [...] The ultimate decision to transfer Crimea was made in Moscow and formally approved in Kyiv.
>
> (Sasse, 2007, at 110)

In the new course of the Ukrainian history of Crimea, issues about its special status emerged before the collapse of the Soviet Union and during the negotiations on the separation between Ukraine and Russia, and saw the emergence of the Crimean autonomy movement (Sasse, 2007, at 135). In January 1991, a referendum on the creation of an autonomous Soviet of Crimea obtained an overwhelming majority, making it the last born Soviet before the collapse of the Soviet Union in late 1991, and the only one that was established through a democratic process (Sasse, 2007, at 135–140). Then, during years in which the border between Russia and Ukraine was drawn with difficulty, and the constitutional legal order of Ukraine was designed, Crimea became an autonomous province of the Ukrainian State (Sasse, 2007, at 142–173).

One read of this complicated 60-year history is what former president of the Soviet Union, Mikhail Gorbachev, was referring to in his statement reacting to the 2014 annexation of Crimea: "the people decided to correct a mistake."[6]

The importance of the 1954 transfer, together with the subsequent, fraught relationship between Russia and Ukraine in the aftermath of the Soviet Union over the status of Crimea, show, at the very least, that Crimea cannot be taken for granted as a solely Ukrainian entity, and suggest that the people living there may have varied views on the matter.

3. The 2014 events

The facts surrounding the 2014 occupation and annexation are recent, well known and subject to extensive speculation,[7] but repeating them briefly here is useful for understanding the positions of the key players today and their legal grounds.

After a decade of political movement towards the European Union, NATO, and the West, marked by internal cyclical political struggles, on 21 November 2013, the Ukrainian government, under the leadership of President Viktor Janukovyč, suspended the process of concluding the Deep and Comprehensive Free Trade Area with the EU, which should have been signed in Vilnius, instead of proposing a closer relationship with Russia.[8] Several protests brought hundreds of thousands of people to Maidan Square in Kiev, which became the physical and symbolic centre of protest. After 3 months of protests, with the western part of Ukraine protesting in favour of a closer partnership with the European Union, the Ukrainian Parliament voted, on 14 February 2014, to remove President Janukovyč.

6 *Gorbaciov: Crimea ha corretto errore*, ANSA (17 March 2014), at http://www.ansa.it/web/notizie/rubriche/mondo/2014/03/17/Gorbaciov-Crimea-ha-corretto-errore_10244937.html

7 The bibliography is extended. The online *Map Debate* on Crimea published by Oxford and updated at 3 August 2014 has 98 blog posts and articles, "Debate Map: Ukraine Use of Force," at http://opil.ouplaw.com/page/ukraine-use-of-force-debate-map. After this first wave of opinions, many articles and books have been published: the online catalogue of the Peace Palace in The Hague counts 95 journal articles, monographic studies and chapters in books, between 2015 and 2018. Among the many publications, a full spectrum of legal and political analysis can be read in the special issue "Crisis in Crimea" of the *German Law Journal*, 2015, at 351 (in particular Korhonen, 2015, at 451 gives a fresh look to the motives and the forces behind the conflict between Ukraine and Russia), and in the book Czapliński, Dębski, Tarnogórski, Wierczyńska, 2017.

8 In 2014, the EU and Ukraine started a broad Association Agreement (Brussels on 21 March 2014, at http://trade.ec.europa.eu/doclib/docs/2016/november/tradoc_155103.pdf), and on the 1 January 2016, they started the provisional application of Deep and Comprehensive Free Trade Area (at http://ec.europa.eu/trade/policy/countries-and-regions/countries/ukraine/).

Two weeks later, Russian military forces without insignia began entering Crimea: at first, about 2,000 soldiers parachuted in,[9] and then the Russian military presence in the peninsula and in the waters along the Crimean coast was increased, in an intimidating display of power. Irregular militias, including Crimean people and officers, spread through the cities and seized the local parliament. The Russian presence was real, as the Russian president explicitly acknowledged, but Crimean involvement was also a real factor, and the tension did not result in bloodshed.[10] Eventually the Crimean Parliament, on 6 March 2014, declared the removal of the Ukrainian president in Kiev unconstitutional, and asserted its independence from Ukraine, together with its decision to accede to Russia. A referendum on this decision was scheduled for March 16 in Crimea. On March 15, the Security Council drafted a resolution to proclaim the referendum invalid,[11] but it could not be passed with 13 votes in favour, the abstention of China, and Russia's veto.[12]

In the meantime, the Crimean Parliament also passed a law establishing that, in case of independence, Crimea would be annexed to Russia (Bering, 2017, at 757–776). As a result, the referendum was not on the independence of Crimea, but rather on its belonging to Ukraine or Russia. The two options on the ballot, written in the three official languages of Crimea (Crimean Tatar, Russian and Ukrainian) did not mention independence, but asked:

'Do you support reunifying Crimea with Russia as a subject of the Russian Federation?

Do you support the restoration of the 1992 Crimean constitution and the status of Crimea as a part of Ukraine?'

The ballot concluded with a warning in all three languages that choosing both options would render the vote invalid.[13] The final result of the referendum was

9 https://www.repubblica.it/esteri/2014/02/28/news/ucraina_crimea_uomini_armati_prendono_il_controllo_dell_ aeroporto_di_simferopol-79832862/

10 In an interview on April 16, Russian President Vladimir Putin admitted to the presence of Russian forces in Crimea, "Putin Admits Russian Forces Were Deployed to Crimea," Reuters (17 April 2014), at http://uk.reuters.com/article/russia-putin-crimea-idUKL6N0N921H20140417

11 S.C. Draft Res. 2014/189 (15 March 2014).

12 "Security Council Fails to Adopt Text Urging Member States not to Recognize Planned 16 March Referendum in Ukraine's Crimea Region," U.N. Press Release SC/11319 (15 March 2014); Fabry, 2015, at 418.

13 For a picture of the ballot and for its translation see https://www.bbc.com/news/world-europe-26514797. On the Crimean referendum and the need for "clarity" in a democratic process of secession see the chapter of Stéphane Beaulac, Chapter 7, this volume. The Venice Commission contested the transparency of the referendum held in Crimea, and objected to the lack of clarity of the question on the ballot, see European Commission for Democracy through Law (Venice Commission), Opinion No. 762/2014, Whether the Decision Taken by the Supreme Council of the Autonomous Republic of Crimea in Ukraine to Organise a Referendum on Becoming a Constituent Territory of the Russian Federation or Restoring Crimea's 1992 Constitution Is Compatible with Constitutional Principles [2014] at https://www.venice.coe.int/webforms/documents/default.aspx?pdffile=CDL-AD(2014)002-e. On the rhetorical, political use of referendums in contemporary struggles for secession see (Tierney, 2015).

an overwhelming majority for Crimean secession from Ukraine and transfer to Russia: with 83% voter turnout, 95% voted for the reunification with Russia.[14] If we follow the call for clarity in referendums on the mutation of a territory, which Stéphane Beaulac makes (Chapter 7, this volume), in the wake of the Supreme Court of Canada's *reference re Quebec* of 1998 (requiring clarity of the question of the referendum, clear participation and a clear majority) the intention of the Crimean people to secede from Ukraine was manifest.

It was right after this chain of events, on 18 March 2014, that Russia proclaimed the *incorporation* of the Crimean territory, as the result of an agreement between the nascent independent Crimean State and Russia (Bering, 2017, at 756). As Juergen Bering observed, "From a Russian perspective, this means that Crimea first seceded from Ukraine to form its own independent state. This State then concluded a treaty with Russia that led to the incorporation into Russian territory" (Bering, 2017, at 756; Pronin, 2015, 133).

The issue was eventually brought up at the UN General Assembly, which adopted Resolution 262, on 27 March 2014, proclaiming the legal invalidity of the Referendum,[15] and triggering a series of General Assembly initiatives on the Crimean situation (most recently in December 2018), all characterized by more abstentions than votes in favour.[16]

4. History returns, and the forgotten challenge of annexation makes a comeback

Of all the problematic factors in this complex political and factual landscape, each of them contested by one side or the other, perhaps *the most problematic of all is the outcome.* In the end, Crimea did not become an independent territory (a solution that was, more or less, able to be swallowed in the cases of South Sudan and Kosovo, for example) but as a territory occupied and annexed by a powerful neighbouring state following that state's military involvement in the process.

This is not to say that conducting a legal analysis of the 2014 facts is a pointless effort. On the contrary, all these events have been described with careful references to international law, Western countries alleging violations and Russia justifying them on legal grounds. Studies attempting to analyze the Crimean Parliament's decision to reject the Ukrainian change of government, the decision to ask for help

14 The figures are taken from Vidmar (2015 at 365), with further references.

15 UN GA Res 262, 27 March 2014, calling all states "to desist and refrain from actions aimed at the partial or total disruption of the national unity and territorial integrity of Ukraine, including any attempts to modify Ukraine's borders through the threat or use of force or other unlawful means." For a complete analysis of the UN debates in 2014, both at the Security Council and at the General Assembly, see Fabry (2015 at 418–422).

16 UN GA Res 205, 19 December 2016, 70 in favour, 26 contraries, 77 abstentions; UN GA Res 190, 19 December 2017, 70 in favour, 26 contraries, 76 abstentions; UN GA Res 194, 17 December 2018, 66 in favour, 19 contraries, 72 abstentions; UN GA Res 263, 22 December 2018, in favour 65, 27 contraries, and 70 abstentions.

from the powerful close neighbour,[17] the decision to proclaim Crimean independence, the decision to hold a referendum and the purity of the referendum itself[18] are all important. Even Russia's President, Vladimir Putin, used the language of remedial secession to justify Russia's intervention in Crimea,[19] although his claims can be easily dismissed as hypocritical (there was no Ukrainian oppression of Crimean populations).[20] But every legal analysis is effectively derailed by two facts: i) the infiltration of the Crimean territory by Russian operatives without insignia, amounting to the beginning of an illegal occupation of Crimea, one of the most heinous violations of international law; and ii) the final annexation itself. The latter, in particular, is a move that harkens back to the nineteenth century and violates one of the fundamental principles underlying international relations, the prohibition to disrupt the national unity of another state (Korman, 1996, at 199–218).

These two things (illegal occupation and final annexation) tend to override any possible speculation on the legal and political implications of the events. Let us take the problem of occupation and the display of force alone. This problem generally causes some issues to fade away in the legal analysis, for example: the overwhelming majority vote against the Ukrainian change of government, and the overwhelming turnout for and majority vote on the referendum (one may well wonder why the turnout was so high – it would be difficult to argue that

17 The possibility to frame Russia's intervention as legitimized by the Crimean authorities and by the "ousted" Ukrainian President Yanukovych, is convincingly rejected by Tancredi, 2014 at 13–18.

18 See above (XI).

19 *Address by President of the Russian Federation* (18 March 2014), at http://eng.kremlin.ru/news/6889: "I understand those who came out on Maidan… […] However, those who stood behind the latest events in Ukraine had a different agenda: they were preparing yet another government takeover; they wanted to seize power and would stop short of nothing. […] The new so-called authorities began by introducing a draft law to revise the language policy, which was a direct infringement on the rights of ethnic minorities. […] Nevertheless, we can all clearly see the intentions of these ideological heirs of Bandera, Hitler's accomplice during World War II. […] Naturally, we could not leave this plea unheeded; we could not abandon Crimea and its residents in distress. This would have been betrayal on our part. First, we had to help create conditions so that the residents of Crimea for the first time in history were able to peacefully express their free will regarding their own future."

20 It is interesting to note that they are claims intended to legitimize Russian intervention in Crimea. They do not go to the question of whether Crimea was entitled to legally secede from Ukraine and then to decide to be reincorporated into another, neighbouring state, through an act that international law *neither authorizes nor encourages*. In Accordance with International Law of the Unilateral Declaration of Independence in Respect of Kosovo, Advisory Opinion [2010] ICJ Reports, 403, at 438–439, para. 84; Tancredi, 2008; Vidmar, 2015, at 367–374. The dangerous indifference proclaimed by the ICJ in its Advisory Opinion on Kosovo becomes central in the narrative of the above-mentioned speech (31): "[T]he Crimean authorities referred to the well-known Kosovo precedent… […] Pursuant to Article 2, Chapter 1 of the United Nations Charter, the UN International Court agreed with this approach and made the following comment in its ruling of July 22, 2010, and I quote: 'No general prohibition may be inferred from the practice of the Security Council with regard to declarations of independence', and 'General international law contains no prohibition on declarations of independence.'."

these numbers could result purely from Russian intimidation in the absence of violence). However, if we compare Crimea with similar scenarios elsewhere, we can see that, elsewhere, occupation has not been an ultimately determinative factor dictating our reservations concerning the authenticity of the process on the whole. Surely external involvement in local dynamics was a factor in Kosovo, where independence would have been unthinkable without the intervention of a coalition of western states.[21] It must also be at play in the acts of the Iraqi government after the American invasion (e.g. its repeated requests for the Americans to maintain a presence in Iraq). Despite this, today the recognition of independent Kosovo is not universal, but at least is not as fraught as the recognition of Crimea as a part of Russia.[22] And no one questions the independence of Iraq as a state with regard to the choices it has made in recent years. What makes Crimea different? Because of the second problematic factor in Crimea: annexation.

This whole affair is teaching us that the *prohibition of annexation* is one of the last absolute rules that we have in the international landscape. While the prohibition of the use force has emerged in international law more recently, after the Second World War (Gray, 2018, at 30–33), the prohibition of wars of conquest and annexations can be traced back to the end of the First World War and the *moral turning point* of international law towards self-determination (Korman, 1996, at 135–178). It is also proclaimed by the *magna carta* of the law governing contemporary international relations, the *Declaration on Principles of International Law concerning Friendly Relations and Co-operation among States* adopted by the United Nations General Assembly.[23] The whole decolonization phase is the latest development of this turn, and a step backward towards annexation is simply unconceivable, in contemporary international law.

21 De Sena, Gradoni, 2014 at 11: "The Supreme council of Crimea, composed of 100 representatives, expressed a favourable vote of 78 members out of the 81 present; the Assembly of Kosovo unanimously approved the unilateral declaration of independence, with only 11 representatives missing out of the 120, among them the 10 representatives of the Serbian minority. […] It is often stressed that the genuine Crimean hope for independence, contrary to that of Kosovo, was undermined by the presence of the armed forces of a foreign Country. Here, too, however, there are more similarities than differences. Kosovo proclaimed its independence when (and, certainly, thanks to) foreign forces granted internal and external security to the former Serbian province (NATO), the presence of which was authorized by the Security Council, and after that, several States belonging to that very same international organization [NATO] conducted a series of illegal (according to many) bombings. If, moreover, Russian interference is at the origin of the Crimean Assembly's initiative, then the intervention of the Western Countries in the constitutive process of contemporary Kosovo, in particular that of the United States, is intrusive as well." Translation mine.

22 On non-recognition in theory and in practice in the Crimean affair see (Milano, 2017, at 203–215).

23 UN GA Res 2625 of 24 October 1970, *Declaration on Principles of International Law Concerning Friendly Relations and Co-operation among States in Accordance with the Charter of the United Nations*, in particular Principle 5, *Principle of equal rights and self-determination of peoples* where it says: "Every State shall refrain from any action aimed at the partial or total disruption of the national unity and territorial integrity of any other State or country."

Indeed, recent violations of other rules, even fundamental rules, of international law, have proven to be less problematic. For example, the use of force to regulate international disputes is prohibited, but diplomacy has proven capable of brushing off the consequences of many such violations more successfully than Russia has been able to do with the sanctions imposed by many states after the annexation of Crimea (the comparatively soft reactions of the international community to the recent wars in Iraq, Libya and Yemen are striking) (Ferro and Ruys, 2018, at 899).

However, the Crimean transfer was not *just* a military annexation, but was also characterized by several procedures involving the people of Crimea and their representatives. International law proclaims the unity of the state, but then it exhibits a certain degree of tolerance towards independence movements, as the 2010 Advisory Opinion on Kosovo clarified, even outside the decolonization context.[24]

The problem with this move towards independence is not just Russia's military intervention prior to Crimea's proclamation of independence, but also Russia's later move to incorporate Crimea. A shady process of Crimean independence could potentially be tolerated by the international community; the existence of a small new state might be acceptable. But it becomes unacceptable when independence becomes unification. Kosovo can be acknowledged, at least for many states, as long as it does not become a part of Albania. What the Crimean events make clear is that it is the narrative of expansion, conquest and seizing new territory that, more than anything else, clashes with the grammar of contemporary international coexistence.

Without entering into the debate on the legitimacy of sanctions against Russia concerning Crimea, or considering whether their effectiveness or ineffectiveness renders them illegitimate (Arcari, 2017, at 223; Milano, 2017, at 201), we may certainly say that the exceptional circumstance of annexing a territory following a murky process full of entanglements generates a broad reaction of condemnation.

5. Annexation is prohibited – but are the reactions of the international community a defence of the law or a containment strategy?

Given that the process regarding Crimea's secession was contaminated, that the imposition of UN sanctions is not possible because of the Russian veto at the Security Council, and that the unilateral measures adopted by EU members and the US are very strong but so far unable to mobilize any change in Crimean territorial status, we are left with two unanswered questions. The first is whether it is possible that Crimea really did wish to secede from Ukraine and become a part of Russia. The second is whether the international reaction can be entirely explained by the heinousness of annexation, or if it also has to do with a political strategy of containment of Russia.

24 "Security Council Fails to Adopt Text Urging Member States not to Recognize Planned 16 March Referendum in Ukraine's Crimea Region," U.N. Press Release SC/11319 (15 March 2014). Fabry, 2015, at 418.

Customary international law prescribes that, "No State shall recognize as lawful a situation created by a serious breach [of a peremptory norm of general international law], nor render aid or assistance in maintaining that situation."[25] The non-recognition of the Crimean shift, therefore, is absolutely legitimate, and keeps on being repeated when new events occur that mark the Russification of Crimea. For example, after the recent construction of the so-called Crimean Bridge connecting Crimea and Russia through the Strait of Kerch (a bridge blatantly built too low to allow free naval traffic towards the important Ukrainian harbour of Mariupol), Canada issued a very clear statement condemning the move and reaffirming the immovable, adamantine, constant position of western states.[26]

However, international law also prescribes that countermeasures (and, therefore, all the more so, unilateral measures) should aim to restore the legality of a given situation, and should not become a retorsion.[27] Such continuous and strong opposition to the violating state, Russia, does have a strong legal basis, but also begs the question of whether this attitude to some degree reflects a political strategy.

The current evolution of the Crimean issue seems to suggest that, for the West, the points about Crimean purported secession and occupation are not relevant, because they pale in comparison to the containment of Vladimir Putin. This is a political decision (and an understandable one – many voices have asked which Baltic Republics will be next, and have evoked the spectres of the Sudeten and of Munich), and not one that derives entirely from the facts of the Crimean case. In a different context, the above-mentioned facts could perhaps fit into a scenario of accepting the unilateral desire to secede and become annexed to another state. If Northern Ireland, in the absence of bloodshed, were to assert its independence through its elected parliament, and then, through a referendum in which the vast majority of voters both turned out and voted for unification with Ireland rather than the UK, would the analysis stop with the non-violent, but intimidating infiltration (imagine this scenario) of republican Irish forces on the

25 Article 41.2 of the ILC Draft Articles on International State Responsibility for Wrongful Acts.

26 *Annexation of Crimea Breaches International Law*, Global Affairs Canada, Statement of 28 July 2018, at https://www.canada.ca/en/global-affairs/news/2018/07/annexation-of-crimea-breaches-international-law.html: "Through its illegal invasion and annexation of Crimea, Russia has violated the international rules-based order and the vital international norm that no country can change another country's borders by force. Canada reaffirms its enduring commitment to the territorial integrity of Ukraine and condemns actions taken by Russia towards the forcible integration of the Crimean peninsula into Russia, including through the opening of the Kerch Strait Bridge in May 2018." The issue has also come up in international arbitration: *Dispute Concerning Coastal State Rights in the Black Sea, Sea of Azov, and Kerch Strait* (Ukraine v. the Russian Federation), PCA Case 2017–2006, application filed on 16 September 2016.

27 Article 22 and 49 of the ILC Draft Articles on International State Responsibility for Wrongful Acts.

ground? It is possible that the contaminating factor of Irish meddling would be considered less troubling and, ultimately, less determinative of the legal status of Northern Ireland than the meddling of Putin's Russian in Crimea has been.

This is a paradoxical example used just to push the argument that the Crimean issue deals with two problems: one is the powerful presence and influence of Russia in the region, which has already, in Georgia and other parts of Ukraine, proven to resort quickly to acts of military intimidation. The other is the legitimacy of a secession affected by the infiltration of foreign forces and the possibility for voters to express themselves notwithstanding anti-democratic factors. The issue we are addressing here is the second: a process that had democratic steps, but was also contaminated and opaque.

6. Doubts on a democratic process

The process which led Crimea to become part of Russia was marked by both intolerable interference by a powerful neighbouring state and overwhelming numbers of democratic consultations. Any reasoning based completely on only one of these two elements is incomplete. To accept the 2014 Crimean Assembly vote and referendum as fully legitimizing the incorporation of Crimea into Russia seems shallow, prone to the reasons of power; but, to reject them completely on the basis of the Russian interference seems unrealistic. After five years of the current status quo, are we content to throw up our hands and stop at the impasse created by the contamination and complexity of the independence process?

Four factors can be useful for clarifying whether something is a blatant situation of annexation with rhetorical manipulation of the annexed persons, or whether, instead, the final outcome is not opposed by the annexed territory, making for a more workable scenario. These factors are the will of the people, the presence or absence of bloodshed or violent conflict, the effectiveness of the new governance and the historical context.

In terms of the will of the Crimean people, in the last election under the Ukrainian government, in 2012, Crimeans had the lowest voter turnout in Ukraine (under 50%), and the pro-Russia parties took the vast majority of the local parliament.[28] Then, in 2014, the local parliament openly challenged the legitimacy of the government in Kiev, prior to any known issues of infiltration and the Russian push to take over the peninsula. After that, the local parliament, with extremely high participation by its members, and an overwhelming majority vote (78 favourable votes out of a total of 100), proclaimed separation from Kiev and established the referendum. This happened after Russian intimidation began, but in the absence of violence and with no apparent resistance among the members of the local parliament. Then, the referendum itself had a very high turnout

28 *CEC: Turnout in Ukraine's Parliamentary Elections 57.99%*, Kyiv Post, 29 October 2012, at https://www.kyivpost.com/article/content/oct-28-parliamentary-election/cec-turnout-in-ukraines-parliamentary-elections-5799-315149.html

among Crimeans, and resulted in a striking majority vote for unification with Russia. The Russian presidential elections followed in 2016, and also provide telling information. Here, Crimean turnout was very similar to the 2012 Ukrainian Presidential elections, but the outcome dramatically favoured Vladimir Putin's Party (United Russia, 72.80% of the Crimean votes). All these figures clash with a narrative that sees Crimean as opposed to Russia and manipulated into serving Russian goals.

It is, of course, debatable whether the more recent votes were authentic (Kalinin and Mebane Jr., 2017), but the figures are impressive, and the lack of any kind of visible resistance by the Crimeans against the new Russian ruler makes it very different from other contested regions in Russia.

Third, the new Russian government has very effective control over the Crimean territory, and shows no sign of any intent to relinquish it. Thus, not only is it unforeseeable at this time that Crimea would return to the Ukraine, but Russia is also acting in a way typical of statehood in Crimea, and treating it as an integrated part of its territory. Compared with the situations in Afghanistan and Iraq, where state control is absent in many regions, and resistance to governing forces erupt in the form of daily bombings and violence, and yet the political status is considered legitimate, Crimea stands out for the absence of conflict. Stability in the Crimean Peninsula is a value to be preserved: compared to other areas (including some in Ukraine) that are divided by open conflict between factions, Crimea is marked by the absence of any para-military group attempting to oppose the new status quo.

Fourth, as for the historical context, the unclear and undemocratic way in which Crimea was transferred from the Russian Soviet to the Ukrainian Soviet not long ago (1954) raises legitimate questions about whether the 2014 decisions of the Crimean Assembly to secede from Ukraine and the results of the referendum can really be brushed off as the result of Russian manipulation, or whether some strong ties remain between Crimea and its Russian neighbour.

The situation between Russia and Ukraine, and between Russia and the West, is far from settled. The four factors suggested here are not intended to accommodate an illegitimate status quo and encourage blindness towards Russian moves in East Europe: international law is very clear in condemning the occupation and annexation of territories, and political strategies to contain Russian expansion are a legitimate political move. The point of this chapter is to ask whether, even when military forces are in play, it is possible to determine that there has been a genuine expression of political will by voters. After five years in which Crimea has made no move to challenge the new status quo, it is an important question to ask.

References

Maurizio Arcari, 'International reactions to the Crimea annexation under the law of state responsibility: "collective countermeasures" and beyond?', in Czapliński Władysław, Dębski Władysław, Tarnogórski Rafał & Wierczyńska Karolina (eds.),

The Case of Crimea's Annexation under International Law, Scholar Publishing, Warszawa, Poland, 2017.

Juergen Bering, 'The prohibition on annexation: lessons from Crimea', *NYU Journal of International Law & Politics* 49: 2017, 747–832.

Władysław Czapliński, Władysław Dębski, Rafał Tarnogórski & Karolina Wierczyńska (eds.), *The Case of Crimea's Annexation under International Law*, Scholar Publishing, Warszawa, Poland, 2017.

Pasquale De Sena & Lorenzo Gradoni, 'Crimea: le ragioni del torto (russo) e il torto delle ragioni (occidentali)', *I quaderni di SIDI Blog* 1: 2014, 5–21.

Mikulas Fabry, 'How to uphold the territorial integrity of Ukraine', *German Law Journal* 16: 2015, 416–433.

Luca Ferro & Tom Ruys, 'The Saudi-led military intervention in Yemen's civil war', in Tom Ruys & Olivier Corten (eds.), *The Use of Force in International Law: A Case-Based Approach*, OUP, Oxford, UK, 2018.

Orlando Figes, *Crimea: The Last Crusade*, Penguin, London, UK, 2011.

Christine Gray, *International Law and the Use of Force*, 4th ed., OUP, Oxford, UK, 2018.

Peter Hopkirk, *The Great Game: On Secret Service in High Asia*, John Murray, London, UK, 1992.

Samuel P. Hungtington, *The Clash of Civilization and the Remaking of World Order*, Simon & Schuster, New York, 1996.

Kirill Kalinin & Walter R. Mebane Jr., 'When the Russians fake their election results, they may be giving us the statistical finger', *The Washington Post*, 11 January 2017.

Neil Kent, *Crimea: A History*, Hurst/OUP, Oxford, UK, 2016.

Mikhail Kizilov, 'Administrative structure of the Crimea before and after the Russian Annexation of 1783', *Vostok (Oriens)* 5: 2016, 53–63.

Outi Korhonen, 'Decontructing the conflict in Ukraine: the relevance of international law to hybrid states and war', *German Law Journal* 16: 2015, 452.

Sharon Korman, *The Right of Conquest: The Acquisition of Territory by Force in International Law and Practice*, Clarendon, Oxford & New York, 1996.

Mark Kramer, 'Why did Russia give away Crimea sixty years ago?', *Wilsoncenter*, 19 March 2014. Available at: https://www.wilsoncenter.org/publication/why-did-russia-give-away-crimea-sixty-years-ago

Alexander Lyon Macfie, *The Eastern Question, 1774–1923*, Revised ed., Routledge, London & New York, 1996.

Enrico Milano, 'Reactions to Russia's annexation of Crimea and the legal consequences deriving from grave breaches of peremptory norms', in Czapliński Władysław, Dębski Władysław, Tarnogórski Rafał & Wierczyńska Karolina (eds.), *The Case of Crimea's Annexation under International Law*, Scholar Publishing, Warszawa, Poland, 2017, 201.

Tatiana Polomochnykh, 'La Crimea di Tolsoj', *Limes Online*, 20 November 2014. Available at: http://www.limesonline.com/la-crimea-di-tolstoj/67500

Anatoly Pronin, 'Republic of Crimea: a two-day state', *Russian Law Journal* 3: 2015, 133.

Gwendolyn Sasse, *The Crimea Question: Identity, Transition, and Conflict*, HURI Harvard, Cambridge, UK, 2007.

Antonello Tancredi, 'Neither authorized nor prohibited? Secession and international law after Kosovo, South Ossetia and Abkhazia', *Italian Yearbook of International Law* 18(1): 2008, 37–62.

Antonello Tancredi, 'The Russian annexation of the Crimea: questions relating to the use of force', *Questions of International Law* 1: 2014, 5–34.

Leo Tolstoy, *The Sebastopol Sketches*, Penguin, London, UK, 1855, 1986.

Jure Vidmar, 'The annexation of Crimea and the boundaries of the will of the people', *German Law Journal* 16: 2015, 365–383.

This volume is part of the JEAN MONNET MODULE EUROPEAN PUBLIC LAW-IUS (EUR.PUBL.IUS) coordinate by Prof. Giuseppe Martinico and held at the Scuola Superiore Sant'Anna, Pisa

Funded by the European Union

Index

www.ingramcontent.com/pod-product-compliance
Lightning Source LLC
LaVergne TN
LVHW011126300926
849160LV00008B/528
9780367726720